THE LOCH NESS MYSTERY SOLVED

Ronald Binns was born in Yorkshire in 1948 and first went to look for the monster when he was sixteen. He has since taken part in many expeditions to the 'monster' lochs of the Highlands. He now lives in London and his writings on modern novelists have appeared in a wide range of literary magazines and anthologies.

D1340664

Acknowledgements

We would particularly like to thank Ian Johnson B. Sc., Ph.D., and J. W. Binns B.A., M.A., Ph.D., for their encouragement and assistance in the writing of this book.

The author and publisher would like to thank the following for permission to reproduce copyright material:-

Academy of Applied Science (Plates 9 and 10; Copyright © Academy of Applied Science, Boston, Massachusetts).

Trevor Aldous (Map, Drawings 2, 3, 4).

Associated Newspapers Group Ltd (Plates 1 and 2).

R. J. Bell (Plates 15 (f), 17, 18).

Camera Press Ltd (Plates 7 and 8).

Alex Campbell (Figure 6(ii)).

The Daily Record and Mail (Plate 4).

Express Newspapers (Plate 5).

Hamish Hamilton Ltd (Figure 5(i)).

Ian Johnson (Plates 15(a), (d) and (e).

David Kent (Plate 16(a) and (b)).

Professor W. H. Lehn (Plate 12).

Nature (Plate 12). (*Nature*, Vol. 289, January 1981, pp 362–6. Copyright © 1981 Macmillan Journals Ltd).

Wiggins Teape (U.K.) Ltd., (Drawing 6(i)).

All other photographs by the author.

THE LOCH NESS
MYSTERY SOLVED

Ronald Binns
with R. J. Bell

A STAR BOOK

published by
the Paperback Division of
W. H. ALLEN & Co. PLC

A Star Book

Published in 1984
by the Paperback Division of
W. H. Allen & Co. PLC
44 Hill Street, London W1X 8LB

First published in Great Britain by
Open Books Publishing Ltd, 1983

Copyright © Ronald Binns, 1983, 1984

Printed in Great Britain by
Cox & Wyman Ltd, Reading

ISBN 0 352 31487 7

For Lizzie

Contents

Preface

The mystery of Loch Ness and its monsters has continued now for more than half a century.

It was in May 1933 that a small Scottish local paper first carried a report of a gigantic unknown animal being sighted in Loch Ness. A couple driving along the main road that runs along the north shore of the loch reported seeing an enormous creature rolling and plunging in its dark waters. Further sightings followed and by the end of that year the mystery animal was nationally famous.

Loch Ness has never looked back. There have been hundreds of sightings and numerous photographs, but firm indisputable scientific proof of the monster's existence remains teasingly absent. When the Smirnoff vodka company recently ran an advert showing a girl in a swimming costume on waterskis being towed by the monster, set against their familiar caption, 'Well, they said anything could happen', they summed up the Loch Ness story more aptly than they perhaps realised. There are times when it seems that almost everything *has* happened at Loch Ness.

Pop star Adam Faith appeared in *What a Whopper!*, an early sixties comedy film about the monster. A decade later Billy Wilder used Loch Ness as a location for his film *The Private Life of Sherlock Holmes*, bringing an expensive fifty-foot mechanical monster which promptly sank and lies on the loch floor to this day. A yellow submarine, its colour presumably determined by the Lennon and McCartney song, was brought to the loch in a fruitless attempt to hunt the monster down. A gyrocopter used in a James Bond film was hired to maintain an aerial observation of the loch's mysterious waters. Year after year the gadgets and stunts have continued to keep the monster in the public eye. But all the time the original enigma has remained, and it is one which is in many ways unique.

There have been other great riddles of our century, such as flying-saucers or the abominable snowman, but there is one important feature which situates these enigmas in a different category from the Loch Ness mystery. This is their geographical remoteness. Few people have the resources to investigate the slopes of the Himalayas. Flying-saucer sightings are universal, and the UFO enthusiast might equally as well watch the skies of Arizona, Dorset or New Zealand. Mysteries like these may endure for decades, perhaps centuries.

What makes the Loch Ness monster such a puzzle is the very restricted location involved in the mystery. It surely ought to be possible to solve the question of a huge unknown animal or animals living in such a small habitat. Loch Ness has captured the imagination of the world, yet by global standards it is a tiny lake. Even in Britain there are other lakes wider and deeper than Ness.

Although its length is about the same distance as the stretch of Channel between Dover and Calais, Loch Ness is only a mile and a half wide at its widest point. Its surface area is smaller than that of Loch Lomond, and it is easily accessible to the public. A major trunk road runs in an elevated position along the northern shore of the loch, and there are numerous points around its shores from which the surface can be viewed. Loch Ness is overlooked by hotels, campsites and houses. It forms part of the Caledonian Canal system, and throughout the year trawlers and other vessels pass through. But still the mystery persists.

Why, after half a century, is the monster still shrouded in ambiguity? Why have all the expeditions in search of the monster failed? Examination of the sightings record reveals a curious paradox. The more people go to Loch Ness to look for monsters the less the creatures are seen. The great surge of sightings from the period 1933–34 has never been repeated. Anyone who has talked, as we have, to eye-witnesses, has to

admit that fraud can in most cases be ruled out. The majority
of persons who claim to have seen something inexplicable in
the loch are undoubtedly sincere.

The quest for the monster has often been seen in terms of a
band of dedicated amateurs challenging the hidebound
assumptions of a sceptical, indifferent scientific establishment. But the solution of the Loch Ness mystery involves
another kind of quest – a quest in which we invite the reader
to share. It takes in not just the history and natural history of
Loch Ness – matters which have previously received
astonishingly little investigation – but also requires a fresh
look at the sources of the mystery. It involves peeling back
fifty years of received wisdom, legend and anecdote about
the monster. It involves a new look at the riddles posed by the
photographic evidence, and a re-examination of the results
produced by sonar and other underwater devices. We regard
the Loch Ness mystery as a mystery which can be solved. Our
solution will probably be controversial but it is, we believe,
unanswerable.

Each of us has been actively involved with both the Loch
Ness Investigation Bureau and the Loch Morar Survey. We
have both made numerous visits to Loch Ness since the 1960s.
It is from this basis of close personal knowledge of the loch
and of the continuing quest that we believe we can offer a
solution to the fifty-year-long mystery.

Ronald Binns
R. J. Bell

1 The Setting

We met a charming couple in an Inn, who were in touch,
through friends, with the Monster. They had seen him. He
is like several broken telegraph posts and swims at
immense speed. He has no head. He is constantly seen.

Virginia Woolf (in a letter to her sister, April 1938)

Loch Ness, the most famous stretch of water in the British
Isles, is a strange and compelling place. It occupies the
eastern end of the Great Glen, running in a straight line for
twenty-two miles from Fort Augustus almost as far as
Inverness. For most of its length it is only one mile wide. Its
dark waters are shadowed by mountains, its shores craggy
and inhospitable. Loch Ness provides a gloomy, romantic
setting for what has come to be known as the greatest riddle
of modern natural history. It is a riddle which remains as
perplexing today as it was fifty years ago when reports of the
now legendary monster first came to the attention of the
nation.

The mystery began in 1933 when a local newspaper carried
a report telling how two local people had seen an amazing
disturbance in Loch Ness, apparently caused by a huge
unknown animal as big as a whale. Before long other reports
were published of this extraordinary humped 'monster'.
Witnesses spoke of seeing a huge black back breaking the
surface, and of sometimes as many as twelve humps cutting
through the water, creating a great splashing and commotion. Others reported seeing a long snake-like head and
neck raised upright like a telegraph pole.

The monster was seen at the surface on numerous
occasions that year, and by Christmas the mystery animal

was receiving widespread coverage in the national press. In December the first photograph of the monster was published. It showed a serpentine body hidden in a blur of spray. The following April a London surgeon took what is probably the most famous monster photograph of them all (*Plate* 1). It shows a giraffe-like head and neck rearing gracefully out of the water near the shore at Invermoriston. At this time there were even reports of the monster being sighted on land. A girl in a house at Fort Augustus watched through binoculars a weird animal which had dragged its bulk out of the water and was lying on the shore at Borlum Bay.

By the end of 1934 public interest in the monster had waned. In the years that followed people still reported seeing unusual objects and disturbances in the loch, but the press treated the whole affair as a joke. New evidence appeared in 1951 when a local man, Lachlan Stuart, took an astonishing photograph of three huge black humps which, he said, had swum past his lochside house early one morning (*Plate* 5).

In 1960 the mystery came dramatically alive again when a young aeronautical engineer named Tim Dinsdale filmed a mysterious object churning its way across the loch. The film was shown on television and attracted world-wide interest. Dinsdale afterwards dedicated his life to solving the mystery, and has made many expeditions to Loch Ness. His book *Loch Ness Monster* (1961) is by far the most important study of the subject, and has inspired twenty-five years of investigation at the loch by numerous individuals and organisations. The most famous of these was the Loch Ness Phenomena Investigation Bureau, which was formed in 1962. The well-known naturalist Sir Peter Scott was one of its directors. From 1962 onwards the Bureau mounted an increasingly ambitious series of annual expeditions to the loch, keeping more and more of its surface under surveillance through the summer months, using ever more powerful cameras. Success came in 1967 when a Bureau volunteer filmed a mystery object breaking surface off Dores.

In the late sixties the Bureau deployed an increasingly sophisticated range of equipment at the loch, including hydrophones, submarines and a gyrocopter. Its most dramatic success came in 1972, at the very moment the Bureau closed down. A Bureau team working with members of the American Academy of Applied Science obtained a sequence of astonishing underwater photographs, showing what appeared to be diamond-shaped flippers belonging to a huge unknown animal (*Plate* 9).

After this sensational success the Academy continued its work at the loch, and more amazing underwater photographs were taken in 1975. These were widely publicised in the national press, though scientists remained sceptical about whether or not they provided evidence of monsters. One photograph appeared to be a close-up of the monster's head, showing a hideous gargoyle-like face with snarling mouth and horns (*Plate* 10).

In the 1980s research at the loch has continued. Tim Dinsdale still makes annual visits to the loch, pursuing his twenty-year-old ambition of shooting the monster's head and neck in close-up on movie film. The Academy of Applied Science continues its work at the loch with underwater cameras and sonar, and so do other large bodies like the Ness and Morar Project. At the same time the shores of Loch Ness are dotted with other, unpublicised individuals, pursuing their own private surveillance of its mysterious waters, each dreaming of being the one who finally obtains that conclusive piece of film which has eluded monster-watchers for half a century.

The most dramatic approach to Loch Ness is along the A 862 out of Inverness. The road passes through the outskirts of the town and then enters an area of gloomy woodland. After a few miles the road passes over a slight incline and suddenly Loch Ness is directly ahead.

At first sight it seems overwhelming, a vast black expanse of water stretching as far as the eye can see, overshadowed by barren, sombre hillsides. Seeing the loch you begin to realise

Figure 1

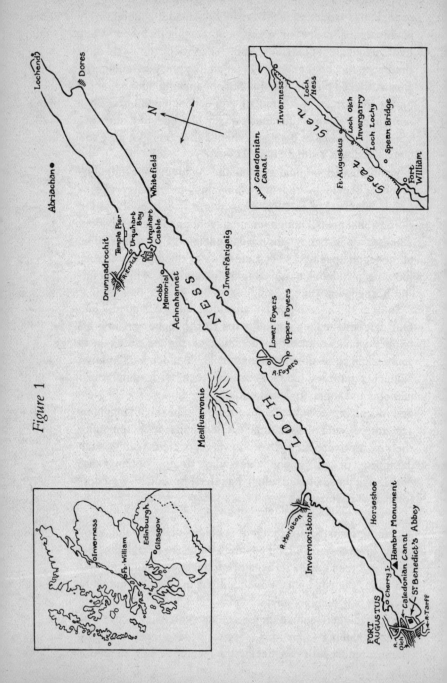

just how easy it is to believe that monsters lurk in that vast, sinister-looking body of water.

A little way further and you arrive at the village of Dores. Here, opposite the village pub (once an old coaching inn used by the military), the road forks off along the lochside. It was built by General Wade for use by English troops in putting down rebellious Jacobites in the early eighteenth century. Now over two centuries old there have been a few improvements made to the road, but not many. It is still a winding, narrow highway, much of it single-track. At first the loch is hidden from view behind bushes, alders and hazel trees, but then you come to a farmhouse and catch glimpses of its grey-blue waters.

Revisiting the loch in the summer of 1981 we encountered a small sign at the roadside here: 'Ness and Morar Project.' Through an open gateway could be seen a field crammed with parked cars, khaki-coloured marquees, and rows of tents.

It is only a short scramble down to the shoreline at this point. The beach here consists of a grey band of rocks and pebbles only a few yards deep. Forty yards out in the loch, filled with sonar scanners and underwater photographic equipment, the Project's main boat floated at anchor – a weird, top-heavy vessel, mounted securely on two long inflatable runners, like a huge floating sledge. On the shore Sea Scouts, Venture Scouts and other volunteers were preparing for another night of investigation at the loch. Figures in wetsuits splashed in the shallows, and a dinghy ferried equipment across the choppy waters under the watchful gaze of Adrian Shine, field commander of the Project.

Shine is a tall, thin, bushy-bearded man, passionate about solving the mystery. 'Photographic surveillance of the loch went out in the sixties,' he argued. 'It's a waste of time. I ban all cameras from the site.' He looked in the direction of the Project launch, lurching roughly among the waves. 'You see,' he added quietly, 'We don't spot monsters. We *hunt* them.'

'We'll be out tonight,' Shine added enthusiastically, 'hunting in *six hundred feet of water*.'

We took some photographs and waved farewell. The Project's aim is to discover more about the monster's environment and behaviour and eventually, with the aid of sonar, come close enough for definitive underwater photography. It has been at Loch Ness since 1973, besides making expeditions to Loch Morar, another loch reputed to hold monsters.

Driving on in the direction of Foyers you begin to see more of the loch. Between Dores and Foyers there are a score of lay-bys, all with stunning panoramic views. The road curls round below a huge outcrop of rock, then dips down almost level with the water. Then it rises towards Inverfarigaig, passes the old ruined church of Boleskine and arrives at the Foyers Hotel. A cul-de-sac leads downhill to Lower Foyers, following the direction of a sign at the roadside which reads THE FRANK SEARLE LOCH NESS INVESTIGATION and points towards the loch.

We passed the tall stone walls of the old aluminium factory and arrived at a large car park, which occupies a flattened area of waste ground on the site of the old pier. The first thing we saw was a hut joined to a blue caravan, decorated with red and blue plastic flags. A sign said OPEN.

Inside, tacked to the walls, were numerous newspaper clippings about Frank Searle, together with others about the loch's retired water-bailiff, Alex Campbell. These two men claim to have seen the monster more often than any other person. On one wall a magazine article was displayed, which made the sensational suggestion that John Cobb, the speedboat ace who was killed on Loch Ness in 1952, died when his boat disintegrated after hitting the monster!

In the early nineteen-seventies Frank Searle was a minor celebrity at the loch, but since then the credibility of his numerous monster photographs has been widely called into question. Former Loch Ness monster-hunter Nicholas Witchell (now a BBC TV news reporter) identified Searle as one of 'the fakers' in his history of the monster-watchers, *The Loch Ness Story* (1975).

Back up the hill in Upper Foyers the road swings away out

of sight of the loch and twists in among the foothills for a dozen miles. You drive across bleak moorland, following a sequence of black marker posts which guide the snowploughs in winter. The road runs down, crosses a river, then rises up sharply to a point where the western end of the loch comes suddenly into view beyond the trees. From here the road descends steeply down to Fort Augustus and the distant towers of the abbey. The monastery there is built around the remains of the old military fort after which the town is named.

Most traffic along the Great Glen avoids the winding road along the south of the loch and takes instead the fast A 82 trunk road out of Fort Augustus. Half a mile outside the town Cherry Island comes into view on the right. It's an ancient man-made construction once joined by a rocky causeway to the mainland, and largely submerged when the Caledonian Canal was built, a feat of engineering which raised the surface of Loch Ness by nine feet.

For much of the way Loch Ness is hidden from the road by trees. The loch does not come properly into view until you are opposite Foyers, its collection of little white-painted houses distinctive, scattered among the dark pines. Further on, at Achnahannet, you pass an empty field, with a breathtaking view of the loch. This was once the bustling headquarters site of the Loch Ness Investigation Bureau.

Above Strone Point a new car park has recently been built below the road, allowing tourists to pull in and visit the most prominent landmark at Loch Ness, ancient ruined Urquhart Castle. The view here is spectacular, and the loch is at its deepest and widest. The loch runs away toward the north-east, a massive belt of water spread out for twelve miles, Inverness buried away amid the far horizon.

The easiest access to the loch at this point is through the ruined castle, which has three beaches hidden away beyond its towering ramparts. Urquhart Castle is hundreds of years old and built on the site of a much older vitrified fort. Today it is just a romantic ruin, but once it was an important fortress, a pawn in the perpetual conflict between English authority and rebellious Scotland. The castle features in two famous photographs of the monster, taken by Lachlan Stuart and Peter MacNab. Urquhart Castle is widely held to be one of the best places for 'a sighting'.

From Strone Point the road curves inland to the villages of Lewiston and Drumnadrochit, and the loch dips out of view behind the dense scrubland which covers the delta of the River Enrick. After crossing the river the road swings back to the loch and hugs the shoreline all the way to Lochend. On this stretch of road there are numerous lay-bys affording excellent views of the loch. At Lochend the loch narrows, and the Caledonian Canal runs on to Inverness and the Beauly Firth.

For those interested in the monster a visit to the newly-opened 'Loch Ness Monster Exhibition' at Drumnadrochit is essential. The Exhibition occupies a specially-built annexe of the Drumnadrochit Hotel. There are buttons to press, moving displays, model monsters and displays of sonar and camera equipment. A copper plaque on the wall solemnly records the opening of the Exhibition by Robert Rines. Rines is the man who produced the first underwater photographs of the monster.

It's perhaps an appropriate historical irony that the Exhibition is located at the Drumnadrochit Hotel. The monster has, after a fashion, returned home. It was the proprietors of this hotel who first saw the monster back in 1933, and who helped turn an obscure piece of Highland folklore into a living myth. And it is back to 1933 that anyone who wants to solve the Loch Ness mystery must first turn, in order to understand the circumstances of the incredible story which came out of Scotland in that year and which has continued to the present day.

2 The Early Sightings and Theories

'Just the place for a Snark! I have said
   it twice:
That alone should encourage the crew.
Just the place for a Snark! I have said
   it thrice:
What I tell you three times is true.'

Lewis Carroll, *The Hunting of the Snark* (1876)

On 2 May 1933 there appeared a major news item in the *Inverness Courier* headlined STRANGE SPECTACLE ON LOCH NESS. This news report has since become famous as the spark which ignited the eventual explosion of interest in Loch Ness during the latter months of 1933. Many monster-hunters have paid tribute to the item's historical significance. But no-one has ever examined the strange circumstances which lay behind the report, and no-one has ever bothered to go back and look at the *Courier*'s files to see what sort of response the report drew from local people who knew Loch Ness well. To submit this original news report to critical examination is to uncover some curious and surprising facts.

STRANGE SPECTACLE ON LOCH NESS

———

What was it?

———

(FROM A CORRESPONDENT)

Loch Ness has for generations been credited with being the home of a fearsome-looking monster, but, somehow or other, the 'water-kelpie', as this legendary creature is called, has always been regarded as a myth, if not a joke. Now, however, comes the news that the beast has been seen once more, for, on Friday of last week, a well-known business man, who lives near Inverness, and his wife (a University graduate), when motoring along the north shore of the loch, not far from Abriachan Pier, were startled to see a tremendous upheaval on the loch, which, previously, had been as calm as the proverbial mill-pond. The lady was the first to notice the disturbance, which occurred fully three-quarters of a mile from the shore, and it was her sudden cries to stop that drew her husband's attention to the water.

There, the creature disported itself, rolling and plunging for fully a minute, its body resembling that of a whale, and the water cascading and churning like a simmering cauldron. Soon, however, it disappeared in a boiling mass of foam. Both onlookers confessed that there was something uncanny about the whole thing, for they realised that here was no ordinary denizen of the depths, because, apart from its enormous size, the beast, in taking the final plunge, sent out waves that were big enough to have been caused by a passing steamer. The watchers waited for almost half-an-hour in the hope that the monster (if such it was) would come to the surface again: but they had seen the last of it. Questioned as to the length of the beast, the lady stated that, judging by the state of the water in the affected area, it seemed to be many feet long.

It will be remembered that a few years ago, a party of Inverness anglers reported that when crossing the loch in a rowing-boat, they encountered an unknown creature, whose bulk, movements, and the amount of water it displaced at once suggested that it was either a very large seal, a porpoise, or, indeed, the monster itself!

But the story, which duly appeared in the press, received scant attention and less credence. In fact, most of those people who aired their views on the matter did so in a manner that bespoke feelings of the utmost scepticism.

It should be mentioned that, so far as is known, neither seals or porpoises have ever been known to enter Loch Ness. Indeed, in the case of the latter, it would be utterly impossible for them to do so, and, as to the seals, it is a fact that though they have on rare occasions been seen in the River Ness, their presence in Loch Ness has never once been definitely established.

We now know that the un-named couple were John and Donaldina Mackay, who ran the Drumnadrochit Hotel, and that the anonymous author of this news item was Alex Campbell. The *Courier* report was inaccurate in a number of ways. For a start, the Mackays' strange experience had taken place not in April but several weeks earlier, in March. Their story eventually came to the ears of 31 year-old Alex Campbell, the loch's water bailiff, who earned money on the side by working as the Fort Augustus correspondent for the *Inverness Courier* and its sister paper, the *Northern Chronicle*, which duly published his monster report on 2 and 3 May respectively.

Now, for the first time, the word 'monster' had appeared prominently in print in relation to Loch Ness. Significantly the word had not been used by the Mackays but was superimposed on their eye-witness account by the newspaper. It remains unclear whether Alex Campbell or the editor was responsible for introducing the term. According to tradition the editor of the *Courier* responded to Campbell's report with the words, 'Well, if it's as big as Campbell says it is we can't just call it a creature: it must be a real monster.' But forty years later Campbell boasted to a journalist, 'I've seen it eighteen times, I'm the man who first coined the word "monster" for the creature.'[1]

There is strong evidence that Alex Campbell, even before

1 *The Sun*, 27 November 1975.

he heard about the Mackays' experience, was himself deeply committed to the belief that Loch Ness was the home of monsters. Some of this evidence will be considered in the next chapter; the most immediate evidence is contained in the news item itself. Looked at carefully it becomes clear that Campbell's report was by no means a neutral, detached account of two people having sighted something unusual in the loch. Campbell was writing as a passionate believer, interested in establishing a dramatic context for the Mackays' experience. Months later it turned out that Campbell's version of the 'sighting' was wildly exaggerated. Mrs Mackay revealed that her husband had seen nothing, since he had been concentrating on driving. She herself had first seen at a range of only one-hundred yards, a violent commotion in the water which seemed to be caused 'by two ducks fighting.'[1] It also afterwards emerged that Mr Mackay's brother Kenneth was the source of a story of the monster being seen *before* 1933.[2]

The last three paragraphs of Campbell's report are very revealing since they draw attention to reports of strange happenings in Loch Ness published in the local press three years earlier, in 1930. On 27 August 1930 an anonymous correspondent in the *Northern Chronicle* reported how three unidentified anglers had recently seen something very odd while fishing in Loch Ness one evening:

> We heard a terrible noise on the water, and looking round we saw, about 600 yards distant, a great commotion with spray flying everywhere. Then the fish – or whatever it was – started coming towards us ... we could see a wriggling motion but that was all.

The reporter went on to say that he had made further enquiries and uncovered another witness, an anonymous

1 Rupert Gould, *The Loch Ness Monster and Others* (1934), p. 39.
2 *Ibid.*, p. 31.

keeper 'who dwells on the shores of the loch, and who is a man of unimpeachable veracity and a first-rate observer':

> some years ago [he] saw a similar phenomenon on the loch. He saw the fish – or whatever it was – coming along the centre of the loch, and afterwards stated it was dark in colour and like an upturned angling boat and quite as big.
>
> What was it? We shall be greatly obliged if any of our readers can enlighten us on the subject, and if any of them have had a similar experience.

This request did not fall on deaf ears, and the next issue of the paper saw the publication of three anonymous letters. Someone signing himself 'CAMPER' wrote in to say that once, when camping by the River Ness, he had heard 'a tremendous splashing and snorting in the river':

> looking out of my tent I saw what I took to be a huge seal disporting on the surface with a fish in its mouth. It had a flat head and was a great size. I turned to get my boots on so as to get closer to the river to have a better look, but when I turned round again the monster had disappeared.

This was the first time anyone had used the term 'monster' in print in connection with the mystery. But the animal had been sighted in the River Ness, not in Loch Ness.

There was not much enlightenment, either, to be gained from 'INVERNESSIAN', who wrote:

> About forty years ago the skipper and crew of a steamer on the canal saw in Loch Ness a monster animal or fish. It was swimming on its back and had legs and a furry body. I give the story as it was told me.

There seemed to be little real connection between the 'wriggling' object reported by the anglers, the upturned boat seen by the keeper, the camper's flat-headed snorting beast with a fish in its mouth, or the furry monster with legs seen swimming on its back. The appeal for further information seemed only to have trawled responses from the kind of eccentrics who regularly fill the letters columns of small provincial newspapers.

Some readers nevertheless felt obliged to supply a rational explanation for the anglers' mysterious experience. 'NOT AN ANGLER' wrote in to suggest that what the fishermen had seen was 'either a seal, a porpoise or a monster conger-eel' – but then added, somewhat paradoxically, 'The only objection to that theory is that a seal or a porpoise moves quietly through the water, and that a conger-eel has too slender a body to create a heavy disturbance of the water.'

On 10 September 1930 the *Northern Chronicle* published two more letters on what by then it was calling 'the Loch Ness mystery'. One 'R.A.M.' (the *Chronicle*'s readers seem to have been extraordinarily reticent about ever identifying themselves) wrote:

> Referring to the appearance of a strange animal or fish in Loch Ness. I think it is more than possible that what the three gentlemen saw was a seal. A friend tells me that he once observed a large seal disporting himself in the Little Isle Pool on the River Ness, and as its appearance there is a fact, it is highly probable that the seal might find its way up the river and into Loch Ness.

On the other hand 'ANOTHER ANGLER' commented:

> I suggest that the young anglers saw an otter which was racing along the surface of the water with a salmon in its mouth; hence the wave it was raising.

And that was the end of the matter. The Loch Ness mystery fizzled out through lack of public support, and nothing more was published on the matter. A monster in Loch Ness seemed to be something which no-one in the neighbourhood either knew about or cared to substantiate.

The end of Campbell's historic 1933 news report is

interesting because its tone suggests a certain irritability on his part that no-one previously was interested in a monster. It now seems quite possible that Campbell was also responsible for the earlier 1930 news reports, and their style is very similar to his 1933 item. In 1930 various rational explanations were put forward to explain the phenomenon reported by the *Northern Chronicle*'s anonymous correspondent. This time Campbell seemed to be going out of his way to pre-empt common-sense explanations for his 'monster'. He concluded by firmly ruling out porpoises or seals.[1]

According to the conventional account of the 'Loch Ness story' what happened next is simple. The Mackay sighting was followed by a flood of other sightings, and before long the monster was nationally famous.

The files of the *Northern Chronicle* and *Inverness Courier* actually reveal a rather different version of events. Although no-one has ever admitted it before, Alex Campbell's historic report was in fact squashed flat by a lengthy critique which appeared in the very next week's issue of the *Courier*. On 12 May 1933, under the headline LOCH NESS 'MONSTER' the newspaper introduced its readers to Captain John Macdonald, supervisor of the various MacBrayne's steamers which had plied Loch Ness regularly for fifty years. 'No-one is more fitted than Captain Macdonald to express a sound opinion on the subject, as he has been a close observer of Loch Ness and intimately acquainted with its vagaries during his long life.'

Captain Macdonald made it clear that he was not very impressed by Alex Campell's dramatic report of the Mackays' sighting:

While I have no doubt that the parties, when motoring along Loch Ness, saw something that to them was unusual

1 In his book *In Search of Lake Monsters* (London: Panther, 1975) Peter Costello mistakenly assumes that Alex Campbell disbelieved in the monster when he wrote his *Courier* news item, and comments, 'His suggestion that the pair [i.e. the Mackays] might well have seen a seal seemed plausible to many people at the time' (p. 24). Actually Campbell suggested nothing of the sort. On the contrary, he went out of his way to deny that a seal could be responsible.

and perhaps uncanny in the great disturbance of the water, I am afraid that it was their imagination that was stirred, and that the spectacle is not an extraordinary one. I say that from a close and intimate experience of the loch for well-nigh seventy years.

In the first place, it is news to me to learn, as your correspondent states, that 'for generations the Loch has been credited with being the home of a fearsome monster.' I have sailed on Loch Ness for fifty years, and during that time I have made no fewer than 20,000 trips up and down Loch Ness. During that half century of almost daily intercourse with Loch Ness I have never seen such a 'monster' as described by your correspondent.

I have, however, seen what at first might be described as a 'tremendous upheaval in the Loch' but which to myself became a very ordinary occurrence as the years rolled on. On a day when the Loch was as calm as a mill pond, reports reached me of what was described as an 'awful commotion in the Loch' perhaps ¾ of a mile or so distant. As the steamer drew nearer to the place it was plainly seen that it was sporting salmon in lively mood who, by their leaping out of the water, and racing about, created a great commotion in the calm waters, and certainly looked strange and perhaps fearsome when viewed some distance from the scene. While I do not desire to question the credulity of those who witnessed the spectacle, might I suggest that what they saw was nothing more or less than salmon at play, and that the occurrence was merely what I have seen many hundred times in voyaging up and down Loch Ness?

Sir John Murray of the Survey Department, and his able staff, made a thorough survey of the entire Loch some years ago, and made a minute chart of its surroundings. The survey was carried on for three years. Every part of the Loch was carefully sounded. Nothing in the way of abnormal fish or beasts were seen. I have no desire to kill a good yarn that adds to the romance of a beautiful Loch, but as I have been asked or rather twitted by many of my friends about the great monster I felt it my duty to tell in as plain a way as possible my own experiences of unusual experiences in Loch Ness.

Alex Campbell made no reply. A fortnight later the *Inverness Courier* carried a short item which in effect dismissed the mystery:

THE ELUSIVE 'MONSTER'

We have received many suggestions and explanations in regard to the alleged 'monster' which has been seen disporting himself in Loch Ness. Some think it is a big otter, others a huge eel, and others have ventured the opinion that the disturbance in the water is of a seismoscopic nature. Many, too, are of the opinion that Captain John Macdonald's views are correct.

This new suggestion that commotions in Loch Ness might be of a seismoscopic nature was not as outlandish as it might at first have seemed. Loch Ness is situated directly above one of the major fault-lines in the British isles, that which follows the line of the Great Glen in a direction approximately N.35⁰E. and S.35⁰W. Analysing the shock-waves which resulted from the Inverness earthquake of November 1890, a seismologist commented that earthquakes and shocks were 'of frequent occurrence along the line of this fault' – especially at Inverness, 'along the course of the Ness Valley' and at Dores (a village overlooking the north-eastern end of the loch).[1] In September 1901 another severe earthquake shook the Inverness and Loch Ness region. Fore-shocks were felt in the vicinity of the loch as early as June of that year, and when the earthquake finally occurred at half-past one on the morning of 18 September it caused a long crack in the northern bank of the Caledonian Canal near Dochgarroch

1 See Charles Davison, 'On the Inverness earthquakes of November 15 to December 14, 1890,' *Quarterly Journal of the Geological Society*, vol. 47 (1891), pp. 618–32.

Locks. The after-shocks rumbled on for weeks around Loch Ness. On 28 September shocks were felt twice: once in Glen Urquhart, and later on Loch Ness itself. 'The observer was in a boat on Loch Ness at 1.40 p.m. The boat moved distinctly, and a slight tremor was felt.' On 22 October there were more disturbances in the region; it was later concluded that 'the focus lay probably beneath Loch Ness.' The seismologist who studied both earthquakes concluded:

> The region which lies between Loch Ness and the sea appears to be in a stage of more rapid development than any other in the British Islands. In all probability, the earthquakes of 1816, 1888, and 1890 originated within it, as well as many of the minor shocks which followed them. It is worthy of notice that, so far as we can judge from the scanty materials that have come down to us, the foci of some of these after-shocks lay beneath the north-eastern end of Loch Ness. After the earthquake of 15 November, 1890, the foci of the minor shocks showed a tendency, though with some oscillations, to recede in a south-westerly direction towards Loch Ness; while in 1901 this tendency was revealed in a very striking manner. There can be little doubt that Loch Ness is still growing; but, without instrumental observations continued for many years, it can hardly be decided whether the lake is now contracting in area, or whether it is gradually, though very slowly, pushing its way outward to the sea.[1]

Whether or not disturbances seen in the waters of Loch Ness were caused by underground earth-movements, otters, or simply fish, few seemed to take the 'monster' very seriously.

1 See Charles Davison, 'The Inverness earthquake of September 18, 1901, and its accessory shocks,' *Quarterly Journal of the Geological Society*, Vol. 58 (1902), pp. 377–98.

In recent years the Great Glen has continued to experience minor earth tremors, with the result that the newly-opened Kessock Bridge outside Inverness contains a device to defend against possible earthquakes. It is the only bridge in Britain to have two immense hydraulic shock absorbers to absorb horizontal shock waves.

Nor did Campbell's report of the Mackay sighting produce a flood of reports of sightings by other people. For a period of three months there was only one other published report. On 2 June 1933 the *Courier* ran a small item stating that a squad of road workers at Abriachan had seen a monster 'in the centre of the loch immediately behind a passing drifter'. This was coupled with a vague claim that some passengers in a bus were said to have seen a monster the previous Wednesday.

If Campbell was hoping to revive the legend with this new item then he failed miserably. No-one else reported seeing the monster, and no new theories were put forward, either for or against the legendary beast. It looked as if the situation which had occurred in 1930 was about to repeat itself, and the mystery dwindle away into obscurity through sheer lack of public interest.

Then, eight weeks later, on 4 August 1933, the *Courier* published a sensational new sighting which was destined to put the Loch Ness monster firmly on the map, though not in a way that anyone could possibly have anticipated.

The dramatic new development came in the form of a letter from a London man which arrived at the newspaper's Inverness office. IS THIS THE LOCH NESS 'MONSTER'? blared the *Courier*, publishing the man's letter in full. The correspondent, a Mr Spicer, described how some weeks earlier, holidaying in Scotland, he had been driving along the road between Dores and Foyers, on the south shore of Loch Ness, when, suddenly,

I saw the nearest approach to a dragon or pre-historic animal that I have ever seen in my life. It crossed my road about fifty yards ahead and appeared to be carrying a small lamb or animal of some kind.

It seemed to have a long neck which moved up and down in the manner of a scenic railway, and the body was fairly big, with a high back; but if there were any feet they must have been of the web kind, and as for a tail I cannot say, as it moved so rapidly, and when we got to the spot it had probably disappeared into the loch. Length from six feet to eight feet and very ugly.

I am wondering if you can give me any information about it, and am enclosing a stamped addressed envelope anticipating your kind reply.

Whatever it is, and it may be a land and water animal, I think it should be destroyed, as I am not sure whether had I been quite close to it I should have cared to tackle it. It is difficult to give you a better description, as it moved so swiftly, and the whole thing was so sudden. There is no doubt it exists.

Perhaps understandably books about the monster never quote this original letter in full, preferring later versions of the episode where Spicer made his story rather less melodramatic (if no more convincing). Although Spicer claimed that his motive in writing the letter was to enquire what this remarkable animal was, it is clear from the letter itself that he already knew all about the 'monster' legend. Months afterwards it emerged that he had even discussed the 'monster' with a local man *before* he had written the letter.

Nevertheless someone at the *Inverness Courier* was sufficiently impressed (or sufficiently desperate for copy) to make the letter a major news item. Perhaps recalling Captain Macdonald's lengthy rebuke to their previous 'monster' item the paper felt obliged to put Spicer's dramatic 'sighting' into proper perspective, prefacing it with a few sober comments:

From Mr Spicer's description of the animal, one who knows the habits of otters, says he has no doubt but that the animal was a large otter and that it was carrying a young otter in its mouth. An otter, which is a land as well as water animal, if disturbed would scramble rapidly across the road, giving the appearance of having no feet. It will be remembered that some persons who saw the mysterious Loch Ness 'monster' gave it as their opinion that the animal which was making so much commotion in the loch was probably an otter with its young.

Whatever it was Mr Spicer had seen, the publicity surrounding his letter immediately gave the monster a new lease of life. *The very next day* Miss Nellie Smith, a girl who worked at the Abbey in Fort Augustus, announced that she had seen the monster for ten minutes, moving about in large circles. 'It seemed to have huge legs, which could be seen working quite distinctly,' she said. It had barely gone before her friend Miss Prudence Keyes, a maid at the Abbey, reported that she, too, had seen the monster in the same locality only half-an-hour afterwards. It was, she said, 'careering round and round in great circles.' News of this event reached Alex Campbell's neighbours, Commander and Mrs Meiklem who, though an hour and a half had elapsed since Miss Keyes had seen the beast, had the remarkable good fortune to find it still in the same place.

Commander Meiklem, who is in the Royal Navy, told the *Courier* representative at Fort Augustus that the monster was about half a mile away and was at rest on the surface of the water. At that point the water is quite shallow, the depth being about six feet. As far as Commander Meiklem could make out the creature looked just like a horse, a black horse, resting on the surface, and it had a very rough sort of knobby back.

Next day in the *Northern Chronicle* Alex Campbell waxed ecstatic. 'Many people in the district now think that the "monster" is certainly a prehistoric creature, and that there may be a great deal more truth in the "water-kelpie" legend than the great majority of the public realise.' Or: I told you so. Certainly there could be no quarrelling with the writer's first statement – if 'district' is taken to mean Fort Augustus. 'It is sure to be seen again,' the *Courier* excitedly commented, and sure enough it was – mostly by the good folk of Fort Augustus, including the esteemed water-bailiff and part-time newspaper correspondent himself.

After the publicity given to Mr Spicer, Commander Meiklem and the Misses Prudence Keyes and Nellie Smith the monster never looked back. New sightings came in thick and fast. On 11 August the *Courier* reported that another English visitor, a Mrs Cheshire of Stafford, had seen 'a big black object in the water, which she thought was a piece of shining rock.' After due reflection and a chat with somebody in a shop in Fort Augustus Mrs Cheshire realised she must have seen the monster!

A month passed. Had the monster become exhausted by its recent exhausting schedule and returned to the depths? No. On 15 and 26 September another flurry of minor sightings were reported by the *Courier*'s redoubtable Fort Augustus correspondent. Soon afterwards October arrived, and with it a letter from a Mr A. Russell Smith of Sussex who felt that the *Courier* ought to know that he had just heard 'from two residents on Loch Ness whose veracity it is impossible to doubt, who have both seen the monster at different times, and who are convinced that it bears a striking resemblance to the supposedly-extinct plesiosaurs.'

By this time someone on the *Courier* obviously felt that a poor joke was in danger of getting completely out of control, and there appeared in the paper a lengthy parody of Alex Campbell and his monster reports, under the headline,

THE LOCH NESS 'MONSTER'
True Story of His Life
TOLD TO A MERE WOMAN

Unfortunately previous writers on the monster have never had the space to mention this long-lost item, but since Nessie so rarely gives interviews it would be a pity if it remained neglected. The lady journalist herself was most impressed by the beast:

He was cultured, I saw at once, and had the Gaelic. 'I am a *Courier* representative,' said I, in what I hope was a firm voice.

'Pleased to meet you,' said Mr Otterserpentdragonplesiosaurus, waving one of his flail-like flippers.[1] 'I have a soft side to the *Courier*, as it was the gentleman who writes to you from Fort Augustus who brought me out of my cavernous depths, and planted me right in the public eye. I see they know all about me in London now, so my fortune's made ...

I asked Mr O— very politely if he would give me some particulars about his life for the Press. 'Certainly,' said Mr O— with alacrity, for like all the truly great he loves to bask in the sunshine of publicity.[2]

The monster, it transpired, liked browsing at the bottom of the loch reading P. G. Wodehouse and listening to Stravinsky on the gramophone.

Others, too, counselled caution. A week later Captain D. E. Munro, R. N., wrote in the *Courier*:

It may be dismissed at once that any large animal of a new species has appeared in Loch Ness. The animal in question is probably a large otter or seal.

Otters frequenting the sea coast attain a much greater size than those found in inland waters, and one may have found its way into the loch from the sea, or a pair of them. Otters are great travellers, and think nothing of a twenty-mile jaunt during a wet night.

Lately in a loch in New Galloway a motor driver saw what he thought was a large animal playing in the middle of the loch. A closer view proved this to be a male and female otter, with three half-grown ones, gambolling and playing.

Captain Munro, however, had not reckoned on the interest and influence of the newspaper industry.

In October 1933 a man arrived at Loch Ness who was to

1 The previous week Alex Campbell had described the monster's 'flail-like' flippers.
2 *Inverness Courier*, 11 August 1933.

galvanise the national press into taking an interest in the half-born myth which was beginning to take shape there. This man was Philip Stalker, later described by *The Listener* as 'a sober matter-of-fact Scots journalist'.

At this time the Loch Ness mystery did not really amount to very much. There was Alex Campbell's initial news report, which had been shot to pieces by Captain Macdonald and others; there was the weird letter from Mr Spicer; and there were a scattered handful of vague sightings. The publicity surrounding these events had come to the attention of the editor of the national daily, *The Scotsman*. He promptly ordered Philip Stalker to make an investigation on behalf of the paper.

Stalker arrived at Loch Ness in the second week of October and spent two days at the loch, interviewing a handful of witnesses. Two witnesses in particular made a deep impression on Stalker. One was Alex Campbell; the other was his neighbour, Commander Meiklem. Campbell told Stalker that he hadn't believed in the monster until a thirty-foot specimen had surfaced in front of his very eyes only weeks earlier. This was, to put it mildly, disingenuous of Campbell, since he was the one who had first reported and then enthusiastically promoted the monster's existence. Unknown to Stalker Campbell subsequently retracted his dramatic sighting, explaining that he had actually seen a line of cormorants distorted by heat-haze.

Stalker, who happened to be a naval reservist, was equally impressed by Commander Meiklem, who was, after all, 'a retired officer holding high rank in the Engineering Branch of the Royal Navy.'[1] Meiklem also just happened to be a believer in the survival of plesiosaurs – a popular belief which can be traced back to the Victorian amateur naturalist, Sir Philip Gosse.

After his two-day 'investigation' Stalker filed a series of articles about the monster which appeared in *The Scotsman*

1 Philip Stalker, 'The Monster of Loch Ness,' *The Listener*, 8 November 1933, pp. 690–1.

during mid-October 1933. Ironically most of Stalker's material consisted of recycled *Courier* reports which had of course been written anonymously by Alex Campbell. There was also Campbell's own dramatic sighting. The appearance of these *Scotsman* reports was instrumental in alerting the English daily newspapers to the existence of a Loch Ness 'monster'. The *Daily Mail* and *Daily Express* were quickly on the scene, and soon 'Nessie' was national, then international news.

In October Stalker broadcast a talk to the nation on BBC radio. He stressed the respectability of the witnesses, and dismissed the much-canvassed theory that otters were the cause of monster sightings. He rounded off his talk with the suggestion that a living plesiosaur had found its way into Loch Ness:

> Of course, you say, it's impossible. But nothing is impossible until experience has proved it to be so, and no scientist on earth would say that the sea cannot contain the legendary sea serpent, however remote the possibility, or that such a creature if in existence could not possibly find its way, perhaps before full growth, up the River Ness, which is separate from the Caledonian Canal, and into the loch. Let me finish with a quotation from *The Case for the Sea-Serpent*, a book published three years ago by Commander R. T. Gould, who collected a strong body of evidence in favour of a much-ridiculed creature. 'To my mind', says Commander Gould, 'the evidence available at present goes all the way to demonstrate the real existence of a creature much resembling in outline and structure the plesiosaurus of Mesozoic times.'[1]

Stalker was not the first person to suggest that the Loch Ness monster was a living plesiosaur. The idea had earlier been canvassed in the *Northern Chronicle* of 9 August 1933, which commented that sea-serpents undoubtedly existed. 'It is

1 Philip A. Stalker, 'The Monster of Loch Ness', p. 691.

strange indeed,' the paper commented, 'how the best authenticated narratives of unimpeachable eye-witnesses have been laughed at. Have any of these marine monsters any bearing on the Loch Ness monster? Granted their existence – and the evidence for sea-serpents is overwhelming – there can be little doubt that it is a surviving variant of the Plesiosaurus.' Fifty years later this explanation for the Loch Ness phenomenon remains a popular one.

Stalker's broadcast had a dramatic result. It attracted the attention of the great sea-serpent scholar himself. And without Rupert Gould the monster would, one suspects, have died a quiet death in the summer of 1934 and never been heard of again.

Lieutenant Commander Rupert Gould, R. N. (Retd.) was a six foot tall seventeen-stone Falstaffian eccentric whose name will be forever associated with the Loch Ness mystery. Born at Portsmouth in 1890 Gould entered the Royal Navy in 1906 and sailed around the globe. In 1915 he was invalided, and for the next twelve years he worked in the Hydrographic Department of the Admiralty. Gould was a colourful figure, a wild mixture of the scholar and the romantic. He was the author of *The Marine Chronometer* (1923) and *The Story of the Typewriter* (1949) – but the public knew him better as a broadcaster and as the author of *Oddities* (1928), *Enigmas* (1929) and *The Case for the Sea-Serpent* (1930). By the late nineteen-thirties he was something of a celebrity, appearing regularly on the popular BBC 'Brains Trust' programme.

Though Gould was to become the monster's keenest admirer he later claimed that he had not at first believed in the beast's existence. It seemed to him, he said afterwards, that the first witnesses 'had probably seen, but failed to recognise, some well-known sea-creature which in some unexplained manner had made its way into Loch Ness.' But when a wealthy friend offered to pay Gould's expenses if he cared to investigate the mystery, he jumped at the chance. He hurried north as soon as possible, stopping at Edinburgh to confer with none other than Philip Stalker. Later, in

Inverness, Gould bought a small motorbike, which he whimsically christened 'Cynthia'. Heaving his vast frame on to the little machine Gould sputtered off in the direction of Loch Ness on 14th November 1933. It was to prove an historic mission.

Nine days later, after two complete circuits of the loch and numerous interviews, he returned to civilisation and drafted a dramatic communiqué for the Press Association:

> Lieut.-Commdr. R. T. Gould, R. N. (ret.), left Inverness on Saturday after making an independent personal investigation, on the spot, of the evidence in connection with the so-called 'Loch Ness monster.' In the course of his enquiry he made two complete circuits of the Loch shores, and obtained first-hand information from some fifty eye-witnesses.
>
> He considers that the evidence which he has collected indicates clearly that the 'monster' is a large living creature of anomalous type, agreeing closely and in detail with the majority of the reports collected in his book *The Case for the Sea-Serpent*. In his opinion, no other theory can be advanced which covers the whole of the facts. He hopes to publish his results in book form at an early date.

The communiqué duly appeared in Stalker's *Scotsman* and Campbell's *Courier*, but was ignored by English newspapers. When Gould impatiently telephoned the Press Association to find out why such a major piece of news was being, incomprehensibly, ignored, he was told, crushingly, that the monster was no longer news.

The Press Association could not have been more wrong. Almost immediately afterwards the Loch Ness saga lurched towards an exciting new chapter with the publication, on 6 December 1933, of the first photograph of the monster in all the popular papers.

At this juncture the quality press decided to get in on the act, and three days later the *Times* ran the results of Gould's investigation as a leading article. Gould told *Times* readers, in a voice of quiet authority, that 'The monster has a length of at least 50′ or so, with a maximum diameter of some 5′.'[1] This produced a flood of letters, and the second half of December was marked by a fresh outburst of journalistic investigation of the Loch Ness mystery, culminating in the much-publicised and anticlimactic *Daily Mail* expedition.

In December the *Mail* announced that it had engaged a big-game hunter and his assistant to track the beast down. Within days of their arrival the pair managed to discover evidence of the monster's footprints on the shore (this was just after the Spicer sighting had been resurrected from the files of the *Courier* by the national press). 'MONSTER OF LOCH NESS IS NOT A LEGEND BUT A FACT' blared the *Mail* on 21 December 1933.

The following month experts at the British Museum announced that the footprints were those of the rear left leg of a hippopotamus. It was, they thought, probably a stuffed one. It was at this point that the Loch Ness monster lost its respectability and became a national joke. In *Scotland's Loch Ness Monster* William Owen portrays the *Mail* investigators as innocent victims of a disgraceful prank. Peter Fleming (brother of the James Bond novelist) remembered it rather differently:

Wetherall described himself as a big-game hunter, was a Fellow of the Royal Geographical Society and had something to do with films; Pauli was a less colourful but quicker-witted character with a Glasgow accent. They induced the *Daily Mail* to engage them as investigators. In no time at all Wetherall and Pauli found and photo-graphed the Monster's tracks on the shore of the loch, and for a few days round about Christmas, 1933, the intrepid *shikaris* bathed in the limelight.

1 *The Times*, 9 December 1933. In his book Gould preferred to confine the monster's dimensions 'within quite reasonable limits' – which turned out to be a slightly more conservative 'probable length of 45 feet or so' with a maximum diameter of 4–5 feet (*Op. Cit.*, pp. 154–5).

For some strange reason I was then doing a short tour of duty at the BBC, and it fell to my lot to 'produce' this pair of (as even I could see) transparent rogues on what must have been an early version of 'Radio Newsreel'. Wetherall was a dense, fruity, pachydermatous man in pepper-and-salt tweeds; Pauli was the brains of the enterprise. Their account of their discoveries carried little conviction and was weakened by their inability to decide whether the word 'spoor' could properly be applied to a single footprint.[1]

After the hippo hoax the monster once again dropped from view, until interest was renewed in April 1934 by the *Daily Mail*'s publication of the famous 'surgeon's photograph', showing what purported to be the monster's head and neck.

Unperturbed by the ups and downs of the beast's reputation Gould continued at his task of writing up his researches in book form. His *Times* article meanwhile brought a swift rebuke from zoologists. An anonymous critic in *Nature* magazine remarked:

Experience of alleged wonders and the results of investigation – where investigation was possible – lead to deep scepticism concerning reports by inexpert observers describing phenomena with which they are unfamiliar, and in the present case the variations in the descriptions suggest either fertile (if unconscious) imagination, or the observation of different phenomena.

The writer was unimpressed by the evidence which Gould had marshalled from witnesses like Commander Meiklem and others at Fort Augustus:

To a zoologist, Commander Gould's acceptance and

1 'Strix' (psd. Peter Fleming), 'Monster in Aspic', *The Spectator*, 5 April 1957, p. 440.

analysis of at any rate some of the evidence appears to be uncritical and even credulous, and his conclusion unjustified.[1]

Upset by his critic's anonymity Gould later commented (somewhat feebly), 'although I had all the cards in my hand I did not reply.'

The Spectator published a much more substantial critique of Gould's findings, which the Commander only brusquely acknowledged. Dr W. T. Calman, the Keeper of Zoology at the Natural History Museum, wrote scathingly of sea-serpents and monsters:

The man in the street is sometimes apt to be a little impatient or even slightly irritated by the scientific man's attitude in such cases. The evidence is abundant and the witnesses (or some of them) unimpeachable; what more do you want before giving a verdict? And yet the only scientific reply to the question is 'I do not know.'

Perhaps only those who have worked in a great museum, where collections are constantly being received from the remotest corners of the earth and the depths of the seven seas, can realise just how seldom the unexpected comes to hand. That new and strange forms of animal life remain to be discovered we cannot doubt, and some of them may even be of great size. We know very little of the inhabitants of the deeper abysses of the ocean. Dr Oudemans and, more recently, Commander Gould have laboriously collated all the better-attested stories of the so-called 'sea serpent' and believe that they can discern in them some shadowy animal of monstrous size, of which not a bone, not a tooth, not a shred of skin, has ever come into the hands of a zoologist. It is possible that they are right, but it is only just possible.

To suppose that anything of the sort is to be found in a freshwater lake in the British Islands is to pile

1 Anon., 'The Loch Ness "Monster"', *Nature*, 16 December 1933, p. 921.

improbability upon improbability. The freshwater fauna of Europe has been exhaustively studied, and it is as certain as anything of the sort can be that no species of much more than microscopic size remains to be added to the list.

As to the evidence, Commander Gould has collected and proposes to publish the testimony of fifty-one witnesses. There is no need to doubt the good faith of any of these; there is no need to question that all of them saw something unusual in the familiar surroundings of the loch; but there is a possibility that neither they nor Commander Gould fully realise how easily and inevitably recollections of things seen become tinged and distorted by previous or even by subsequent impressions. The subject had been discussed in the popular Press for many months; picture postcards, in which drawings of the monster (apparently studied from *Punch*) are superimposed on photographs of the loch, have been widely sold; and the recurrent and meaningless adjective 'prehistoric' throws light on the nature and sources of some of the witnesses' preconceptions.

Nevertheless, if someone can find a scrap of concrete evidence, or even a convincing photograph, no one will be more pleased than the zoologists.[1]

Monster enthusiasts regularly portray scientists as narrow-minded stick-in-the-muds, blindly refusing to acknowledge the existence of an unknown species in the face of an avalanche of evidence. Calman's article (abbreviated in the above extracts) remains one of the most powerful and considered statements to come out of 1933 on the subject of the Loch Ness monster. Gould made no reply.

In the last week of June, 1934, *The Loch Ness Monster and Others* duly appeared. It received a sceptical but kindly review from E. G. Boulenger in the *Observer*. Boulenger,

1 W. T. Calman, 'The Evidence for Monsters', *The Spectator*, 22 December 1933, pp. 925–6.

Director of the Aquarium at London Zoo, was sympathetic to sea-serpents, but found the idea of a Loch Ness monster altogether too much to swallow. His rather mild reservations about Gould's book provoked a lengthy and passionate letter (22 July 1934) from none other than Philip Stalker, the sober matter-of-fact Scots journalist, who was as anxious as anyone to defend the beast's existence.

The Loch Ness Monster and Others does not seem to have been a great success. The public had begun to lose interest in the enigma, and interest soon switched to other curiosities of the thirties such as the ghosts of Borley Rectory. Gould died in obscurity in 1948, as forgotten as his cherished monster. And that, it seemed, was that.

Only with the beast's revival in the late nineteen-fifties did Gould's study of the monster begin to take on an importance which previously it had lacked. It was, after all, a book, and books linger on, unlike newspapers, which are read then thrown away. In the long run Gould's book gave the monster credibility.

The trickle of sightings which continued through the thirties and forties seemed to prove the case which Gould had set out to argue. Among the monster fraternity his book is today treated with the reverence owed to a classic. It has achieved an eminence its author can scarcely have dreamed of. Although never reprinted in Britain, and unread by the general public, Gould's book has exercised an immense influence over all the other Loch Ness monster books. Later writers have shamelessly plundered Gould for their materials. It was Gould who first produced an inventory of classic sightings, Gould who first mused over what the beast might *be*. Later writers have done little but bring the sightings record up to date and indulge in alternative speculations as to the monster's identity.

Gould is usually represented in monster books as an unbiased investigator who brought a cool objectivity to bear upon the mystery. This image is difficult to substantiate. Certainly Gould was diligent in recording as much information as possible about witnesses and their sightings.

In this sense *The Loch Ness Monster and Others* is, if not a very readable work, invaluable as a source book. Ironically it is Gould we must thank for first exposing Alex Campbell's phoney 'monsters' of 1933. But Gould was scarcely a neutral, detached investigator of the mystery. As a list of his publications shows he was a man deeply fascinated by the marvellous and the enigmatic. Moreover he had written a full-length study of another, equally-hypothetical beast, the great sea-serpent, only three years earlier. Significantly many sightings of sea-serpents had occurred around the coast of Scotland.

It was also rather disingenuous of Gould to claim that he approached the subject with an open mind, since he was clearly influenced by Stalker's verdict on the mystery given on BBC radio. Gould also met Philip Stalker on his way to Loch Ness. *The Loch Ness Monster and Others* simply endorses Stalker's own conclusion that a sea-serpent must have swam up the River Ness and lodged itself in the loch.

Gould's mind seems to have been made up before he even arrived at Loch Ness. He made no attempt to go through the files of the *Inverness Courier* and discover how the monster first came to public attention. Had he done so he might have uncovered the curious circumstances of Alex Campbell's keen promotion of the mystery. Instead Gould busied himself with discovering whether Stalker was right in believing that a large marine animal might have sneaked up the river (which runs through Inverness) and into Loch Ness. He decided that it was indeed just possible, if the river was in flood, and the creature was a powerful swimmer drawing not more than five feet of water. Gould also realised that the creature would have to perform this remarkable feat at night. Big 'ifs', perhaps, but nevertheless 'quite possible'. Having established this possibility to his own satisfaction Gould went on to state, 'From my point of view it was exceedingly likely that one *had* done so. In order to identify this creature the evidence of eye-witnesses had next to be obtained.'[1] In other words Gould had made up his mind

1 *The Loch Ness Monster and Others*, p. 11.

before meeting a single eye-witness. He conceived his task as *identifying* the creature rather than seriously questioning whether or not it actually existed.

Gould then proceeded on his way around the loch. In all he personally interviewed some 30 eye-witnesses, and corresponded with several others. He finally collected details of 42 separate sightings of unidentified objects in Loch Ness. The majority of these sightings had occurred in 1933.

Gould's star witness was none other than Alex Campbell's neighbour, Commander Meiklem. In disposing of the more rational explanations of the monster Gould turned time and time again to the evidence kindly supplied by Meiklem.[1]

Commander Gould had an easy task in demolishing the extravagant explanations put forward by zoologists who ought to have known better (Sunfish, Ray, Catfish, Salamander, Turtle, Whale, Squid, Crocodile and Seal). Squids, whales, and marine fish simply could not survive for more than a few hours in the loch's fresh water. Seals were a more reasonable alternative but there had never been an authenticated sighting of a seal in Loch Ness. Besides, seals are inquisitive creatures and could not remain unrecognized for long. A few people had suggested that the monster might simply be a rather large sturgeon. Gould found this idea 'rather attractive' since a sturgeon at the surface could conceivably present the appearance of a humped animal with a slender head and neck. In the end he ruled it out because 'it postulates a sturgeon of quite enormous size; one, say, 60 feet long – or nearly three times as large as the biggest yet known.'

That left only the mis-perception of inanimate objects, boats' wakes, or known animals. Gould believed that the great commotion and tremendous speed which the monster showed in the water clearly ruled out anything so banal as logs, birds, fish, or otters. There was only one possible conclusion: 'On the evidence there can, I suggest, be little

1 The references to Meiklem in the index of *The Loch Ness Monster and Others* provide a very inadequate listing of the number of occasions on which his name actually features in the book.

question that Loch Ness contains a specimen of the rarest and least-known of all living creatures.' In other words – a sea-serpent. But what *were* sea-serpents? Philip Stalker, quoting Gould's own *Case for the Sea-Serpent*, had little doubt that they were a surviving form of plesiosaurus. What Stalker did not know was that *The Case for the Sea-Serpent* had earned Gould a bloody nose from the eminent palaeontologist Dr F. A. Bather. Bather wrote to the *Times Literary Supplement* to point out that Gould's theory of living plesiosaurs was highly improbable since fossil remains had never been found later than the Mesozoic era. A lively correspondence then ensued (15 January – 26 February, 1931) at the end of which Gould sheepishly confessed his ignorance of advances in modern palaeontology and conceded that he was wrong.

As numerous surveys have discovered, the bed of Loch Ness is, in most places, as flat as a billiard table. If the loch contains an unknown species of giant animal with a bone-structure then evidence of skeletal remains ought not to be hard to find. Acknowledging these facts Gould ended up attacking the plesiosaur theory, remarking:

> to suppose that plesiosaurs could survive in Loch Ness alone (and, therefore, breed in fairly considerable numbers) for millions of years entails some rather startling consequences. What, on this assumption, has become of the bones which should, by now, have carpeted the entire floor of the loch? No trawl net – and many have been put down for biological purposes – has ever brought up any fragment of this kind. This objection, alone, appears fatal to the theory.[1]

It is an objection which most modern commentators appear to have overlooked, since the plesiosaur theory is now one of

1 *The Loch Ness Monster and Others*, p. 120.

In his pamphlet *The Loch Ness Animal* (1934) A. C. Oudemans also attacked the plesiosaur theory on the grounds that 'though it is true that such an animal may have been able to bend its long neck in all directions, like a swan, the structure of its trunk must have been so firm that it was practically inflexible; certainly not vertically flexible.'

the most popular monster theories of them all.

What, then, *was* the Loch Ness monster? Gould's conclusion was casual, almost evasive. 'A vastly-enlarged, long-necked marine form of the newt is the hypothesis which, however improbable it may appear, I should personally be inclined to favour.' Unfortunately Gould failed to explain why a newt was any more likely than a squid or a turtle. Calman had previously responded in caustic fashion to the theory when Gould had tentatively put it forward in his *Times* article: 'The suggestion that the monster is a giant form of newt is singularly unhappy in view of the marked intolerance of the Amphibia for salt water; but it would explain the creature's anxiety to get into fresh water at all costs.'[1] To this rather fundamental objection Gould had no answer.

Gould seems never to have revisited Loch Ness or pursued the mystery any further. At the end of *The Loch Ness Monster and Others* he suggested that an airship be kept at the lochside, with a pilot and photographer ready to take off at a moment's notice in pursuit of the beast. 'An ordinary photograph, unless taken when the head and neck was raised would probably reveal little – but one taken from vertically above, or almost so, would reveal, at one exposure, all its characteristic features.' All that would be required would be 'a single fine day'. The idea, Gould cannily concluded, was 'not, perhaps, altogether devoid of commercial value.'

The imagination of British entrepreneurs remained unstirred.[2] One businessman was nevertheless sufficiently impressed by the enigma to finance further investigation. This was Sir Edward Mountain, Bart., Chairman of the Eagle Star Insurance Company. He had read Gould's book and been greatly impressed:

1 'The Evidence for Monsters,' *The Spectator*, 22 December 1933, p. 925.
2 The idea was finally taken up 48 years later, when 'the Great Glen Airship Expedition' arrived at Loch Ness. In the event Gould's commercial instincts proved correct. After this 'scientific survey' was over, a 'unique offer' was advertised in the *Daily Telegraph* (9 August 1982) – commemorative covers signed by the expedition leader Lt. Col. John Blashford-Snell at £5 each.

It occurred to my mind that it was a curious thing that while these rumours about a strange creature in the loch have been current for many months, no search organised on adequate lines and with proper equipment has ever been undertaken. It seemed to me that if 20 men equipped with cameras and field glasses were to be stationed around the loch at strategic points for a month or so it ought to be possible definitely to establish whether there is anything there or not.[1]

Sir Edward employed twenty local men, 'familiar with all parts of the loch, used to outdoor life, and with family responsibilities which assured that they would attend strictly to business.' Each watcher was armed with binoculars and a still camera, and observation points were established around the circumference of the loch. Duty hours were from 9 a.m. to 6 p.m. To ensure that they did attend strictly to business the monster-watchers were themselves kept under observation by an army officer on a motorbike, Captain James Fraser. The search began on 13 July 1934, while Sir Edward relaxed at nearby Beaufort Castle, chewing his nails, impatiently awaiting 'the vital photograph – a really good picture – which would crown his venture with the success it deserved.'[2]

Though it failed to come up with the conclusive proof which everyone was seeking the Mountain expedition proved to be among the most successful of any of the ventures which have taken place at Loch Ness. During the first two weeks alone a staggering total of 21 photographs were taken, and there were numerous sightings. Unfortunately there was a flaw in Mountain's great idea. His watchers were all unemployed men, drawn from Inverness labour exchange. In the hungry thirties to be paid £2 a week just to sit at the side of Loch Ness on a summer's day must have been an attractive

1 Sir Edward Mountain, 'Solving the Mystery of Loch Ness,' *The Field*, 22 September 1934, p. 668.
2 *More Than a Legend*, p. 110.

proposition. To be offered a bonus of ten guineas each time any-one photographed Nessie must have provided a great incentive to pander to the noble baronet's whimsy that there was a monster in the loch. Perhaps the reason for the expedition's great success occurred to Captain Fraser and he had a quiet word with his men; at any rate the photography abruptly ceased and during the next three weeks no additional snaps were obtained. The men were then laid off and Sir Edward retired to write an article for *The Field* in which he proudly announced:

> It has been generally admitted that the photographs my men obtained definitely prove that there is something in the loch. I am of the opinion that the creature probably went up the River Ness when in spate, after salmon; having got into the loch it would have difficulty in finding its way out again, as the entrance to the river is narrow.

Although reluctant to speculate about the beast's identity, Mountain hinted that the monster was probably a grey seal:

> This grows to a much larger size than the seals often seen around the coasts of the British Isles, and in a body of water as comparatively calm as Loch Ness would be capable of making a disturbance which would lead people to believe it much larger than it probably is in actuality.

Unfortunately the two photographs which Mountain used to illustrate his article show all too clearly that the photographers had been pulling his leg. The humped 'monster' and 'the heavy wash created by the monster after it had passed with amazing speed across the surface of the water' are all too obviously boats' wakes, as the photographers themselves must have been well aware.

Mountain's *Field* article ended (just as many other articles and books about the monster would over the next fifty years) with the dramatic announcement that new evidence had just been obtained which might end the enigma once and for all:

Since writing the above, one of my watchers, Captain Fraser, has obtained several feet of film of the creature on the telephoto ciné camera. It will be of great interest to examine this as soon as developed and it may prove a definite solution of the mystery.

After the unemployed men had returned to the dole, Captain Fraser had stayed on at the loch, camping out inside a bell tent on the hillside above Urquhart Castle. At about 7.15 a.m. on 15 September the Captain's vigil was blessed with success.

There was that morning a thick haze hanging over the loch, it afterwards turned out to be a very hot day. I carried out my usual procedure, that was to scan the loch westwards then turn to scan the loch eastwards; then to my surprise I observed what I thought was a rock about 100 yards from the shore East of the Urquhart Bay. This object which appeared inanimate I had under observation for over a minute then I remembered that there was no rock that far out from the shore. I then took up my camera and trained it on this object and started to film it, when to my surprise the object raised out of the water either its head and neck or a flipper then lowered it, raising quite a volume of water, then it disappeared.

Fraser shot about ten feet of film on a Kodak ciné camera with a 6″ telephoto lens at a range of about ¾ mile. The film, which has since been lost, was shown to members of the Linnaean Society. Two members believed the animal to be a seal, another that its movements resembled those of a whale. Another believed Kodak's estimate of size (eight feet long) to be too great. Rupert Gould, who attended the film-show, afterwards wrote to Fraser, remarking that one member 'was absolutely satisfied, on the evidence of the film, that the "monster" was a large otter!'

And that was that.

The Loch Ness mystery had, it seemed, come to an end – more through exhaustion than the achievement of any very satisfactory conclusion. A book had been written, an investigation mounted. The results, though negligible, remained tantalisingly inconclusive. Investigators and journalists went away perplexed, perhaps even bored. The story had well and truly dried up, and although there were three more minor contributions to the subject they were somewhat comical ones and did nothing to revive interest in the mystery.

The first of these was a short pamphlet by A. C. Oudemans, a Dutchman, and author of *The Great Sea-Serpent: An Historical and Critical Treatise* (1892). Oudemans is nowadays treated with reverence by the monster fraternity, who hail his study of the sea-serpent as 'definitive'. In fact *The Great Sea-Serpent* is a nightmare of a book, vast, meandering, humourless, and peppered with exclamation marks. It was published at the author's expense by a vanity press. As Rupert Gould observed, 'its style has a peculiar sharpness – approaching petulance. Occasionally, too, there are amusing *laches*, as when we are informed that the whale is encased in a thick layer of "bacon" – for blubber.'[1]

Oudemans's pamphlet *The Loch Ness Animal* (1934) was no better. Written in a similarly prickly style, the pamphlet dramatically announced that the monster had swum up the River Ness 'most probably on the 13th or 27th March, 1933.' Oudemans was convinced that the creature was 'hairy' and gave a sombre warning of the dangers it posed to residents:

> The Loch is comparatively void of fish. So it is not at all improbable that it has been seen with a lamb in its mouth ... A hairy animal, of course, may rest, may make a little trip, on land; so the reports, stating that the Loch Ness Animal has been seen on land more than ten times, are certainly not untrustworthy.

In *The Great Sea-Serpent* Oudemans had looked forward with bloodthirsty relish to the assassination of one of the

1 R. T. Gould, *The Case for the Sea-Serpent* (1930), p. 7.

creatures by a reader, and gave precise instructions on how
the cadaver should be measured. Similarly Oudemans's
monster monograph concludes by urging that Nessie be
slaughtered as soon as humanly possible:

> We had better not be too tender-hearted, for, if the Loch
> Ness Animal should die in its element, it will be lost to
> Science for ever. So let us take this rare chance to possess
> our selves of it.

An even more bizarre contribution to the subject was R. L.
Cassie's two volume study, *The Monsters of Achanalt*
(1935–36). Volume One described monsters which inhabited a loch near the author's home; Volume Two dealt with
land sightings 'especially on the tops, ridges and slopes of the
mountains.' Cassie had read Gould and Oudemans, and
praised the 'incontrovertible testimony' of witnesses like the
Spicers and Arthur Grant. 'Is the Loch Ness monster forever
to monopolize the stage?' Cassie complained, drawing
attention to his local monsters:

> On the 25th I betook myself to the points of vantage
> commanding Loch Achanalt. Both sections of the loch
> always show signs of agitation here and there, and several
> reptiles – or portions of bodies – can often be seen at a
> single glance. The Colossus of nine hundred feet is often
> visible, extending over the open loch in a straight line
> from near the north-eastern end to within fifty or eighty
> yards from the western bay. About thirty or forty feet of
> the middle region of the back are often depressed below
> water. Cavillers will affirm, without an atom of
> knowledge or experience, that it must be a case of two or
> more animals in line. But I back my eyesight and
> knowledge against their armchair conjectures.

The Monsters of Achanalt is so self-evidently absurd that it is
difficult to know what to make of it. Cassie's style is
curiously ironical, and his occasional remarks to the effect

that 'it should always be remembered that I am handicapped by distance and want of glasses' suggest that the book was conceived as a colossal leg-pull.

An appropriate finishing touch to thirties Nessie-mania was provided by Ealing Studios, which released *The Secret of the Loch* (1934), a romantic melodrama starring Seymour Hicks. Disappointingly this film was entirely a studio production, except for one brief panning shot from Foyers. The monster turned out to be a solitary man-eater, hatched from a dinosaur egg but much resembling Gould's giant newt. The film's dramatic climax involves some trick photography with an iguana.

After 1934 an hiatus occurs in the Loch Ness story. For almost a quarter of a century nothing happened. In 1953 the *Scottish Anthropological and Folklore Society Proceedings* referred dismissively to 'The case of the Loch Ness monster ... a few years ago ... which attracted a number of believers.' The Society was almost right. The Loch Ness monster did seem to have died a quiet death in obscurity.

Then, out of the blue, there appeared Constance Whyte's *More Than a Legend: The Story of the Loch Ness Monster* (1957). As her title indicated, Mrs Whyte, though she had never seen the monster herself, was a passionate believer. Gould had gestured in the direction of what he regarded as scientific rigour; Mrs Whyte adopted a much chattier, anecdotal approach. She felt it was pointless trying to convert sceptics, and so where sightings were concerned was 'inclined to omit details such as [the identity of the observer] and location.' By failing to identify many of her witnesses (except by their initials), and by her economical attitude to the context of their experiences, Mrs Whyte rendered her 'evidence' largely worthless. Like Campbell, Stalker and Gould she had her own star witnesses. Mrs Whyte's great discovery was Count Bentinck of Holland, the only witness on record to see steam coming from the monster's mouth. The Count wrote to Mrs Whyte telling her that he had visited Loch Ness on three separate occasions lasting a fortnight each, and been privileged to see the beast 'seven times altogether'.

Mrs Whyte was aware that the alert reader might notice 'certain discrepancies' in the way the monster was described by witnesses. Engagingly she explained that all this meant was that witnesses were describing *different* monsters – 'males, females, old and young' (and, presumably, steaming and non-steaming). Here Mrs Whyte was boldly putting forward a radically different interpretation from Gould's. Gould was acutely aware of the force which lay behind the argument that if monsters had lived in Loch Ness for centuries why then had no traces of them turned up in the form of carcasses or bones? Gould decided that it was a 'misconception'[1] to assume that the creature was indigenous to the loch. It was all quite simple: a sea-serpent (which could not logically be a plesiosaur and was therefore probably a giant newt) had swam up the River Ness during a wet night and become trapped in the loch. Gould was not greatly interested in anecdotes about the monster being seen before 1933, remarking 'Although interesting, such stories are of no great value as evidence.' He also commented, coldly, that he had 'neither the space nor the inclination' to discuss the water-beast episode in Adamnan's *Life of Columba*. Likewise he tersely dismissed the Highland water-horse tradition:

> Such tales are, no doubt, of great interest to students of folk-lore; but in the present instance I regard them as more or less beside the point – except in so far as they provide sceptics with excellent ground for contending that the stories of the 'Loch Ness monster' are merely a temporary revival of an old and deep-rooted superstition.[2]

Mrs Whyte had no such qualms. It was she who laid the foundations of the monster 'tradition' examined later in this book. It was she, too, who originated the myth of the lonely loch, and who first made the wildly inaccurate but immensely influential statement that 'Before the year 1933 no motor road existed beside Loch Ness.'[3]

1 *The Loch Ness Monster and Others*, p. 102.
2 *The Loch Ness Monster and Others*, p. 27.
3 *More Than a Legend*, p. 21.

More Than a Legend ended with a ringing appeal 'Some day the truth must surely be known. Why not start the investigation now?' It did not fall on deaf ears. This book alone revived the flagging fortunes of the monster, encouraging a new generation of monster-watchers to make their way north to the loch's fabled waters. But before the heady excitements of the nineteen-sixties got properly under way however there appeared one other figure on the scene. This was Dr Maurice Burton, a man whose name is anathema to believers in the monster, a man who committed the worst offence of all. He changed from being a believer to a non-believer. What was worse Burton was a professional zoologist and an influential author, a critic not lightly to be dismissed.

What motivated Maurice Burton to write *The Elusive Monster: An Analysis of the Evidence from Loch Ness* (1961) was not, at the time, very clear. Burton had been fascinated by the Loch Ness mystery from its inception. For years he favoured the giant eel theory, but changed his mind after reading *More Than a Legend*. In 1959 he published an article in the *Sunday Express* (3 August 1959) arguing that the monster was probably 'something like a plesiosaur. If a few plesiosaurs have survived a likely home for them is in Loch Ness.' The following year Burton published another article announcing that the monster was 'a reality ... probably in the nature of a very large shell-less terrapin or fresh-water turtle. Since such a creature would come very near to a plesiosaur this brings me very near to the conclusions reached by Commander Gould and Mrs Whyte' (*Illustrated London News*, 20 February 1960).

Four months later Burton led a team of five watchers to Loch Ness for an investigation which lasted eight days. No large unknown animal manifested itself, and Burton returned south and wrote *The Elusive Monster*, which debunked much of the evidence and argued that most sightings of the monster simply involved mats of rotting vegetable matter propelled by gas. Burton offered no explanation for his sudden and spectacular change of mind.

In his haste and passion to demolish the bulk of the eye-witness sightings Burton had overlooked one rather crucial fact. The humic acids present in Loch Ness prevent rapid putrefaction occurring. Vegetable remains on the floor of the loch simply crumble to a powder, and no gas is generated. This feature of the loch was noted by the Royal Geographical Society's Bathymetrical Survey of 1903–4. Burton had blundered badly and produced an 'explanation' for which there was no supporting evidence whatsoever.

This is not to say that *The Elusive Monster* is as bad a book as believers often claim. Though Dr Burton's main theory was demonstrably absurd, many of his secondary interpretations of monster sightings were persuasive. The behaviour of otters and mergansers, Burton argued, often resembled the reported activities of the monster. The handful of 'horned monster' reports he attributed to people sighting roe deer swimming in the loch. Burton also drew attention to some of the inadequacies and contradictions of eye-witness evidence, and stressed how subjective were most people's estimates of size in unfamiliar environments.

The monster fraternity has had a great deal of sport with Maurice Burton's changes of mind and the flaws in his vegetable mat theory. But few of the believers seem actually to have read *The Elusive Monster*. Elizabeth Montgomery Campbell shared a common misconception when she wrote that Burton's aim was to prove that the monster did not exist.[1] On the contrary, Burton *still believed* in the monster's existence when he published *The Elusive Monster* in 1961. The book was actually the unhappy product of a man torn in two. Rationally, as an experienced zoologist, Burton found the notion that an undiscovered giant species thrived in a small Scottish lake was offensive to good sense. In 1951 he had admitted on television that the existence in Loch Ness of some huge unknown marine animal was 'very, very unlikely'. But at the same time there was the eye-witness

1 See Elizabeth Montgomery Campbell, *The Search for Morag* (London: Tom Stacey, 1972), p. 43.

evidence which seemed to allow no other interpretation. *The Elusive Monster* marks only the first stage of Burton's disenchantment with the monster. Most of the evidence he brushed aside as involving natural phenomena. Some (such as Lachlan Stuart's photograph of three humps) he found frankly inexplicable. The remainder – particularly the land sightings – pointed in the direction of something which resembled a plesiosaur but which Burton believed was actually more like an otter. At the end of *The Elusive Monster* Burton put forward the bizarre conclusion that the solution to the Loch Ness mystery lay in the existence of a twenty-foot-long otter, which lived along the lonely shores of the loch and only rarely took to the water.

As an explanation this seemed almost as extreme as the plesiosaur theory, and the same objections could be levelled against it. If there was a giant unknown land animal in the Loch Ness region, why had it not been spotted before 1933? Though otters are among the shyest and most elusive of animals, the idea that specimens twenty feet in length could escape notice for long was preposterous. Burton in fact had very little knowledge of the Loch Ness region and greatly exaggerated its isolation.

In the years following publication of *The Elusive Monster* Burton's position hardened. As each new piece of evidence for the monster's existence appeared, Burton stepped forward to pour scorn on it. Just as Alex Campbell was regularly called upon to speak on the monster's behalf, so Burton became the media's resident sceptic.[1] The note of caution which Burton had half-heartedly tried to sound in *The Elusive Monster* was quickly forgotten as a new generation of monster-hunters arrived at the Loch. His book could not have come out at a worse time. In 1960 someone reported seeing the monster on land – the first such sighting for over a quarter of a century. Someone else took a dramatic piece of

1 Campbell launched a rambling attack on *The Elusive Monster* which sidestepped almost all of Burton's evidence and arguments. See 'No, Dr Burton!', *The Scots Magazine*, May 1962, pp. 95–100.

film of the monster swimming across the loch near the village of Foyers. A sensational new photograph of the monster, taken by flashlight at a range of only twenty-five yards, was published. Maurice Burton had tried to bring the Loch Ness story to an end. In fact it had only just begun.

3   The Tradition Investigated

> It will be seen that this mere painstaking burrower and grubworm of a poor devil of a Sub-Sub appears to have gone through the long Vaticans and street-stalls of the earth, picking up whatever random allusions to whales he could anyways find in any book whatsoever, sacred or profane. Therefore you must not, in every case at least, take the higgledy-piggledy whale statements, however authentic, in these extracts, for veritable gospel cetology. Far from it.
>
> Herman Melville, *Moby-Dick* (1851)

The first sentence of Alex Campbell's historic *Courier* news report of 2 May 1933 began on a note of confident authority. 'Loch Ness,' he asserted, 'has for generations been credited with being the home of a fearsome-looking monster ...'

It was a fascinating piece of information to spring on the world. Certainly, if a species of giant unknown animal lived in Loch Ness one would expect people to have reported seeing the creatures before 1933. And this, according to the books about the monster, is just what happened. For centuries, they say, the loch has been regarded as a strange place, inhabited by something odd and mysterious. There is so to speak a monster 'tradition' at Loch Ness. According to the books it goes like this:

> For as long as recorded history Loch Ness has always possessed a sinister reputation and been associated in one way or another with a monster. A neolithic carving found at Balmacaan, near Loch Ness, appears to depict the monster and incorporates numerous features reported by

witnesses, including vertical undulations and a wide head. Significantly a Roman historian, Dio Cassius, reported that the Caledones, the tribe which lived around Loch Ness in Roman times, had a taboo against eating fish from the lake.

The earliest recorded sighting of a monster in Loch Ness is to be found in Book 2, Chapter 27, of *The Life of St. Columba*, written around 565 A.D. Its author, Adamnan, a highly reputable writer, describes how Columba came upon the funeral of a man who had been attacked by the monster. Columba promptly ordered one of his men to swim out into the loch after a boat, whereupon the monster re-appeared and swam towards the man. Columba commanded the beast to depart, and upon hearing the saint's voice the creature swam off at high speed.

Since the sixth century reports have continued to this day. A Scottish chronicle mentions the monster being 'lately seen' in 1520. Hector Boece's sixteenth-century *History of Scotland* describes how a 'terrible beast' came out of the loch 'early one morning about mid-summer', demolishing trees and killing three men. Richard Franck's *Northern Memoirs* (1694) mentions 'a floating island' in Loch Ness, probably a reference to the monster's single hump showing above the surface. The seventh edition of Daniel Defoe's *Tour Through the Whole Island of Great Britain* (volume four) contains an account of the 'Leviathans' in the loch, which were frequently disturbed by General Wade's men blasting the military road along the lochside in 1726. Some years afterwards, in 1771, Patrick Rose heard about a monster 'which was a cross between a horse and a camel with its mouth in its throat' which had recently been seen in Loch Ness.

A century later, in the summer of 1885, 'stories were circulated about a strange beast being seen by many people about Loch Ness.' The monster was even well enough known to be mentioned in the *Glasgow Evening News* in 1896. In November of the same year an article about the

Loch Ness mystery, complete with a realistic woodcut of the monster, appeared in the Atlanta *Constitution*.

The loch's sinister reputation again hit the headlines in 1932 when the wife of a prominent banker was drowned there after a boating accident. Although only yards from the shore and despite being an excellent swimmer Mrs Hambro simply disappeared. Had she been snatched by the monster? Divers were never able to find the body, and rumours leaked out that they had discovered gigantic underwater caverns. A year later the monster hit the headlines in a big way and became nationally famous for the first time.

Even when public interest in the monster slackened in the nineteen-fifties, the loch's sinister reputation came to prominence again. In September 1952 John Cobb was killed on Loch Ness while attempting to break the world waterspeed record. His jet-boat *Crusader* disintegrated when it hit a patch of disturbed water at over 200 m.p.h. People watching the record-breaking run from high up on the north shore claimed to have seen the monster's wake at the very moment *Crusader* approached the area. The dark and sinister monster-haunted loch had claimed another tragic victim ...[1]

The Loch Ness 'tradition' is spinechilling. Unfortunately it absolutely fails to stand up to scrutiny. Some of the stories are untrue, others involve wild misinterpretation or wilful distortion of the evidence. For example, the alleged references to monsters in Defoe's *Tour Through the Whole Island of Great Britain* and the *Glasgow Evening News* of 1896 exist as nothing more than unsubstantiated rumour. No-one has ever been able to identify the references. Likewise, there

1 This 'tradition' has been compiled from: F. W. Holiday, *The Great Orm of Loch Ness* (1968); Peter Costello, *In Search of Lake Monsters* (1974); Tim Dinsdale, *Loch Ness Monster* (1961); Roy Mackal, *The Monsters of Loch Ness* (1976); Nicholas Witchell, *The Loch Ness Story* (1974); F. W. Holiday, *The Dragon and the Disc* (1973); and Tim Dinsdale, *The Leviathans* (1966) and *Project Water Horse* (1975).

is no article on the Loch Ness monster in the Atlanta *Constitution* for November 1896. That story first appeared in John Keel's sensationalist *Strange Creatures From Time and Space* (1975), a book riddled with lamentable inaccuracies and exaggerations.

The stories of the monster being seen in 1520, 1771 and 1885 derive from an eccentric letter which appeared in *The Scotsman* on 20 October 1933, and which has been quoted *ad nauseam* ever since. The monster books omit to mention that the letter's author, one D. Murray Rose, failed to supply either his address or any specific references to the chronicles or publications wherein his weird and wonderful stories could be found. Judging by Rose's garbled account of the St. Columba episode his scholarship ought not to be relied upon too seriously. The monster books also omit to quote Rose's letter in full, which shows him to be a harmless crank. Rose's pet theory for the monster was sharks: 'throughout the ages,' he wrote, 'sharks may have got into Loch Ness.' Quite how they achieved this, and why they did not immediately die in the loch's fresh water Rose did not explain.

As for the neolithic monster carving, this story first appeared in F. W. Holiday's *The Great Orm of Loch Ness* (1968). Holiday came across a photograph of the carving in a book about the region, and describes how he devoted some time 'searching the grounds of derelict Balmacaan House for a view of the ancient carved stones on which an unidentified creature is depicted.' Had Holiday been a little more informed about archaeology he would have learned that he was wasting his time. His mysterious neolithic monster carving – actually a Pictish Class 1 symbol stone – was excavated, along with another stone, in 1864, near Drumbuie, and has for many years been in the National Museum of Antiquities, Edinburgh. It is only one of a number of Pictish symbol stones found in the region. The serpent design is one of the more frequent of the fourteen different Pictish symbols, and is common in other parts of Scotland. Holiday's claim that the Drumbuie stone shows a monster is empty speculation. Archaeologists themselves have warned against attempts to interpret the symbol stones, since 'Little is known about the Picts and the symbol stones attributed to them are as enigmatic as the racial history is obscure ... It is not known whether they were painted or not, nor why they were made, nor anything about them whatever.'[1]

The story about the Caledones' Loch Ness 'taboo' is equally without foundation. Dio Cassius was actually a Greek historian, who wrote a history of Rome some time between A.D. 201-222. A large part of his *Roman History* has been lost and survives only in an abridgement produced by Joannes Xiphilinus in the eleventh century A.D. In his *Dictionary of Greek and Roman Biography and Mythology* (1849) Sir William Smith commented that this work 'is executed with the usual carelessness which characterises most epitomes.' The story of the Loch Ness 'taboo' has been extracted (with wild exaggeration) from the following passage:

> There are two principal races of the Britons, the Caledonians and the Maeatae, and the names of the others have been merged in these two. The Maeatae live next to the cross-wall which cuts the island in half, and the Caledonians are beyond them. Both tribes inhabit wild and waterless mountains and desolate and swampy plains, but live on their flocks, wild game, and certain fruits; for they do not touch the fish which are there found in immense and inexhaustible quantities.

No mention of Loch Ness; no mention of a monster. So much for the Loch Ness taboo.

The most important anecdote in the entire monster 'tradition' is undoubtedly the episode of St. Columba and the water beast. Unfortunately anyone who bothers to consult Adamnan's *Vita Sancti Columbae* will quickly discover that Adamnan is not talking about *Loch* Ness at all, but about the *River* Ness – two very different stretches of water. The River

1 Stewart Cruden, *The Early Christian and Pictish Monuments of Scotland* (Edinburgh: H.M.S.O., 1964), p. 5.

Ness is wide and shallow and flows through Inverness into the Moray Firth. It is separated from Loch Ness by another lake, Loch Dochfour. It has never been accessible to shipping because of its shallowness. When Cromwell wanted a patrol boat put on Loch Ness his troops had to trundle it overland on logs. The idea that a monster could live in the River Ness is improbable. Facts have never stood in the way of monster enthusiasts, however. Tim Dinsdale assures us in *Loch Ness Monster* that 'there is a very clear report in Latin of an encounter with a terrible water monster on Loch Ness fourteen centuries ago.' But there is no ambiguity about Adamnan's text. Adamnan clearly describes the episode occurring in the *River Ness*, and tells how 'a water beast' melodramatically appeared in front of Columba, and 'with gaping mouth and with great roaring rushed towards the man swimming in the middle of the stream.' Therefore the excited speculation which some authors have indulged in – whereabouts in the loch did Columba see the monster? was it Foyers Bay? by Urquhart Castle? – is absurd and pointless. The way in which almost all writers on the monster have exaggerated this episode says little for their objectivity or scholarship. St. Columba's 'sighting', mentioned in virtually every publication on the monster, has been totally misrepresented.

Few writers on the monster seem actually to have bothered to examine a copy of Adamnan's biography for themselves. Most simply copy out at secondhand the version of the episode presented by Father J. A. Carruth in his little tourist booklet, *Loch Ness and its Monster* (1950). Carruth characterises Adamnan's life of Columba as 'trustworthy', and quotes Bede's description of Adamnan as 'A good and wise man.' This impressed Tim Dinsdale, who wrote 'The case for the original appears to be fairly sound, and once recorded the truth owes nothing to the passage of time.' Frank Searle added his voice to the general chorus of praise: 'In those far-off days, the Church wasn't too keen on people who told weird stories so the good Bishop would have looked closely at these stories before accepting them. But he did accept them and furthermore, wrote about them. That seems pretty good evidence.'[1]

Carruth's opinion one can disagree with but nevertheless respect, since he is a Catholic monk, and for him the lives of the Saints have, literally, the force of holy writ. There is less excuse for other commentators since they ought to have been aware of the narrative conventions governing the genre of saints' biographies.

The *Life of St. Columba* is in fact, like other saints' biographies, crammed with amazing events and miracles. A saint's biographer had to conform to certain narrative conventions. The major task of such a biographer was to prove the sanctity of the individual he was writing about. In the words of the editors of a recent edition of the *Life*,

> Sanctity meant the merit that God rewarded with miracles and therefore it was necessary for Adamnan to devote his book to miraculous occurrences. It was not necessary to follow chronological order, and he makes little attempt at writing a consecutive narrative. His purpose was to show Columba as a saint.[2]

The episode involving Columba and the water beast in the river does not occur in the context of an account of the saint's travels in Scotland in the sixth century A.D., but in an inventory of episodes describing Columba's miraculous powers over animals.

No-one but a devout believer could possibly take the fantastic incidents of the saint's life seriously. Columba's biography was designed to impress a naive audience with tales of the saint's supernatural prowess. Adamnan wrote his book almost a century after the death of Columba, and so obviously had no direct knowledge of his life.

Columba's river-beast also rather embarrassingly contradicts the reported behaviour of the Loch Ness monster. Nessie is a shy creature, not given to rushing about with its

1 Frank Searle, *Nessie* (London: Coronet, 1976), pp. 15–16.
2 Alan Orr Anderson and Marjorie Ogilvie Anderson, ed. and trans., *Adamnan's Life of Columba* (London: Thomas Nelson, 1961), p. 18.

mouth open, roaring hideously and attacking people swimming in the loch. 'It would of course be wise to allow some poetic licence in the telling of this tale,' Tim Dinsdale concedes. In other words, what doesn't fit the Loch Ness legend can be discarded as embellishment, what does seem to fit can be accepted as 'reasonably accurate'. Dinsdale makes great play with the river-beast's frightened reaction to Columba's shouted command:

> Now St Columba, it is known, had a powerful voice with which he taught his Christian faith to the warlike men of the Highlands, and the Monster, it is known, reacts immediately to sound, diving at once when frightened.[1]

The editor of the 1894 Oxford edition of the *Life* was less impressed by the episode, remarking 'This highly imaginative touch is very characteristic' and pointing out that Columba came from Ireland, and Irish folklore is full of dreadful 'wurrums' which lurk in rivers and lakes waiting to roar at the unfortunate traveller. Moreover as anyone who bothers actually to read the *Life* quickly discovers, the power of Columba's words is a recurring feature of the narrative. It is only necessary to look at the episode which immediately precedes the river-beast incident to see this:

> At another time when the blessed man was for some days in the island of Sci [Skye], being alone for the sake of prayer, and separated from the brothers by a considerable distance, he entered a dense wood, and encountered a boar of remarkable size, which was being pursued by hunting dogs. The saint saw it a little way off, and stood still, regarding it. Then he raised his holy hand, with invocation of the name of God, and praying intently said to the boar: 'You will approach no further; in the place to which you have now come, die.' When these words of the saint rang out in the wood, not only was the wild beast

1 *Loch Ness Monster*, p. 37.

unable to advance further, but before Columba's face it
immediately fell, slain by the power of his terrible word.

The parallels with the river-beast episode immediately
following are obvious. The significance which Dinsdale
attaches to Columba's voice in relation to the Loch Ness
monster collapses like a pack of cards. Columba's saintly
voice was constantly frightening the life out of all manner of
weird and wonderful beasts. The water-beast of the River
Ness was no exception.

Tim Dinsdale has also made much of a monster described
in Hector Boece's *History of Scotland*. Dinsdale refers to the
sighting, which occurred at Loch Ness in the early sixteenth
century, as 'consistent with modern reports obtained from
reliable sources.'[1]

This terrible beast – issuing out of the water early one
morning about mid-summer, he did very easily and
without any force or straining of himself overthrow huge
oaks with his tail and there with killed outright three men
that hunted him with three strokes of his tail, the rest of
them saving themselves in trees thereabouts whilst the
aforesaid monster returned to the loch.[2]

Unfortunately Dinsdale failed to check his source. Had he
done so he would have discovered that the text of *Scotorum
historia* is not, as its title might seem to imply, a
straightforward narrative of Scottish events, but rather a
collection of myths and legends almost as fantastic as those to
be found in Adamnan's biography of Columba. One modern
historian has commented that Boece 'confuses the natural
with the supernatural, the credible with the incredible, in a
wild welter ... Boece must be described as a careless worker
– lazy, credulous, undiscerning ... he not only wrote fables
about the past, but when sources of information failed him,

1 Dinsdale, *Loch Ness Monster*, p. 38.
2 Ibid.

did not scruple to invent them. Marvels on land and sea crowd his pages. Hardly an important event occurs without its supernatural accompaniments.'[1] All this is bad enough in itself. What is worse is that the episode quoted by Dinsdale did not, as he leads the reader to believe, occur at Loch Ness at all! Dinsdale omits to give the opening part of the sentence which he quotes, which actually begins:

> It wes said be Schir Duncane Campbell to us, that out of Garloll, ane loch of Argyle, the yeir of God M.DX yeris [i.e. 1510], came ane terrible beist ...[2]

Dinsdale's account of the episode is a travesty – which has not prevented Professor Roy Mackal falling for it hook, line and sinker and solemnly assuring *his* readers that reliable land sightings of the Loch Ness monster go back precisely 436 years.[3]

This leaves only one historical source left: Richard Franck's mysterious and exciting reference to a 'floating island' in Loch Ness. Franck served in Cromwell's cavalry, and toured Scotland in the 1650s. He subsequently wrote an account of his travels, with the wordy title *Northern Memoirs, calculated for the meridian of Scotland. Wherein most or all of the cities, citadels, seaports are described. Together with various discoveries, remarkable observations, theological notions. To which is added, The contemplative and practical Angler, with a narrative of that art experimented in England, and perfected in Scotland. Writ in the year 1658* (1694).

Franck's book is not in fact a straightforward travel book but is cast in the form of a florid dialogue between 'Arnoldus' (Franck himself) and 'Theophilus' (his alter ego). It is hard to disagree with the editor of the nineteenth-century edition of the volume who irritably complained, 'The rage of fine writing had unfortunately seized on Richard Franck – with inveteracy unparalleled. Instead of acquainting us with what

1 J. B. Black, 'Boece's *Scotorum Historia*' in *Quatercentenary of the Death of Hector Boece* (Aberdeen: University Press, 1937), 30ff.
2 John Bellenden, trans., *The History and Chronicles of Scotland by Hector Boece*, Vol. I (Edinburgh: W & C Tait, 1821), p. xxxi.
3 See Roy Mackal, *The Monsters of Loch Ness* (1976).

actually befell him, like a man of the world, he generally renders himself obscure, and sometimes altogether unintelligible, by his affected pedantry and obscurity.'

The first draft of *Northern Memoirs* was probably completed in 1658, but Franck then rewrote it, adding more and more flowery observations and 'reflections' over the next thirty years, until the book was finally published. As for the 'floating island', quoted out of context the reference to 'The famous Lough-Ness, so much discours'd for the supposed floating island' certainly sounds mysterious. But anyone who actually bothers to read Franck's almost unreadable book will quickly discover that it was *Loch Lomond* which was 'so generally discours'd for the floating island.' This makes sense, since other writers have referred to the Loch Lomond floating island tradition. Franck however was anxious to score a point, and denounced the Loch Lomond island: 'it floats not here in these solitary Western Fields, as fictitiously supposed by the ignorant reporters.' No, the floating island, according to Franck, was actually to be found in Loch Ness. Could it have been, as some writers have suggested, the monster's back, just breaking the surface? Franck didn't think so: 'Nor is it any other than a natural plantation of segs and bullrushes, matted and knit so closely together by natural industry.' It remains unclear whether Franck had seen the island himself, though his detailed description suggests he probably had. The role of 'floating islands' in Scottish lochs remains obscure, though it should be remembered that even today some primitive societies still construct them (they can be found on lakes in Peru). It is even possible that Franck was confusing the artificial island at Loch Ness with the Loch Lomond 'floating island' tradition. This tiny man-made island, today known as Cherry Island, can be seen off the north shore of the loch, just outside Fort Augustus.

It may safely be said that the legend of the Loch Ness monster was quite unknown in the Renaissance. The classic accounts of animal lore and legend at that time are by Konrad Gesner in his *Historiae Animalium* (Zurich, 1551–8) and Ulisse Aldrovandi in his *Historia Naturalis* (Frankfurt, 1623) and

Monstrorum Historia (Bologna, 1642). These were massive surveys which drew on hundreds of printed sources and also on verbal reports. They discussed not only real animals but also mythical ones such as the unicorn and the hydra. Neither makes any mention of Loch Ness.

The entire Loch Ness monster tradition crumbles at the first sceptical probe. It is simply untrue that the loch has been, as Roy Mackal claims, 'the site of strange observations for over 1400 years.' No-one began seeing 'monsters' in Loch Ness until the nineteen-thirties. Moreover, tragedies like those involving Mrs Hambro and John Cobb provide interesting examples of the way in which rumours spread and legends spring up. There was nothing especially mysterious about Mrs Hambro's death. Loch Ness, at 42^{0}F, is shockingly cold, and for even an experienced swimmer jumping overboard fully-dressed is a risky proposition. A moment's panic and Mrs Hambro would have drowned almost immediately. There is no reason whatever to assume that a monster came along like the shark in *Jaws* and devoured her. The fact that the body was never recovered is not unusual. Sometimes drowned bodies are recovered from Loch Ness, sometimes they are not. Mrs Hambro drowned in a particularly deep part of the loch, making it impossible for divers to explore more than a fraction of the area. No underwater caves were found, nor have any ever been located at Loch Ness since. Since its walls are composed of igneous rock it seems highly improbable that any ever will be.

The theory that John Cobb's speedboat frightened a monster which swam off at high speed, causing his boat to crash, was told to Tim Dinsdale by his friend Torquil Macleod. Dinsdale duly published the theory in his second book, *The Leviathans* (1966). It has since been repeated in numerous other publications, including Nicholas Witchell's best-selling tourist brochure *Loch Ness and the Monster* (1976). It is a sensational theory which adds a certain morbid interest to the Loch Ness mystery. The theory is however absolutely without foundation. It is certainly true that John Cobb's boat disintegrated when it hit a pattern of ripples at high speed.

But these ripples were caused by one of Cobb's own pilot boats. The loch surface was flat calm that day, and the way in which boats' wakes 'live' for twenty minutes or more in such conditions has regularly been noted.

What happened was that Cobb was signalled to proceed when the wake from one of his own guide boats was still travelling across the loch. Cobb sped forward and smashed into the wake sideways. At the speed he was travelling the impact of this very minor encounter was catastrophic, and *Crusader* shot into the air and disintegrated. We have spoken to two witnesses who were actually there in 1952 and who saw the accident happen. They are in no doubt at all that Cobb's own pilot boat was the unwitting cause of the tragedy.

Under scrutiny, the legends of Loch Ness all vanish into thin air. It would be uncharitable to assume that the monster tradition was knowingly falsified. Although one or two cases must have involved fraud or leg-pulling, there is no reason to suppose that writers on the subject have been guilty of anything other than laziness. Monster-experts tend to be enthusiastic amateurs, seeking evidence which reinforces a belief already held, not disinterested enquirers after the truth.

In late 1933 and 1934 when the Loch Ness monster had become internationally famous, some stories were produced testifying to sightings by local people which had occurred in previous years but which were never reported at the time. This evidence remains scanty and carries little conviction. Some of these early 'sightings' flatly contradict the consensus image of the monster established by students of the mystery, and have been quietly discarded.

Finally, it is curious that the *Inverness Courier*, so quick to publicise 'The Sea-Serpent in the Highlands' reported from the Outer Hebrides in March 1856, should have ignored the monster on its own doorstep for so long. This, and the widely-publicised case of the Stronsa carcase washed up in the Orkneys in 1808, show that unusual happenings in the north of Scotland were brought to public attention in the nineteenth century. Had a monster been sighted in Loch Ness during those years the matter would surely have been reported.

4 Loch Ness Before The Monster

> Our geographers seem to be almost as much at a loss in the description of this north part of Scotland, as the Romans were to conquer it; and they are obliged to fill it up with hills and mountains, as they do the inner parts of Africa, with lions and elephants, for want of knowing what else to place there. Yet this country is not of such difficult access, as to be passed undescribed, as if it were impenetrable.
>
> Daniel Defoe, *A Tour Through the Whole Island of Great Britain* (1724–26)

The fact that the Loch Ness monster 'tradition' collapses under scrutiny does not necessarily mean that there cannot be an unknown species in the loch. If Loch Ness was a remote, lonely stretch of water, unvisited by man for centuries, then it does not seem surprising that reports of the monster only emerged in the twentieth century.

This is exactly what the monster books argue. Loch Ness was, they say, a strange and isolated lake. Only a handful of crofters ever watched over its grey, desolate waters, and the crofters, speaking only Gaelic, rarely if ever communicated with strangers. Only in 1933, when a road 24 miles long was blasted out along the craggy north shore of the loch, did the monster hit the headlines. People were then able to drive the entire length of the loch for the first time. Ever since then there have been numerous other sightings of the mysterious creatures.

The argument is a convincing one. If no-one ever visited Loch Ness then how could anyone be expected to see the monsters there? Unfortunately the legend of the lonely, unvisited loch is nonsense. There are times when it seems almost everyone has visited Loch Ness – including Queen Victoria, Prince Albert, Dr. Johnson and Boswell, James Watt (inventor of the steam-engine), Robert Southey (poet laureate and Coleridge's brother-in-law), the novelist Daniel Defoe, the great engineer Thomas Telford, the poet Robert Burns, the actress Ellen Terry, John Bright (the Quaker), the great Victorian naturalist Charles St John, the magician and writer, Aleister Crowley, and Sir James Barrie, creator of Peter Pan. None of these figures ever saw or heard about a monster in Loch Ness.

But obviously none of them had the benefit of travelling along the new north shore motor road. Peter Costello refers scathingly to the old military road between Dores and Foyers, and explains that Loch Ness can hardly be seen at all from it: 'Since this was the only road until 1933, it is not surprising that nothing strange was noticed in the loch by travellers.'[1] Tim Dinsdale agrees; in his latest book about the monster he refers to the first 'discovery' of the monster 'in the early 1930s, when the north shore road was built at Loch Ness.'[2] Costello, Dinsdale and everyone else who has ever written about the monster agree on this point. The source of their information about the road is Constance Whyte's book *More Than a Legend* (1957). A contemporary reviewer thanked Mrs Whyte for clarifying

one important point which sticks in most of our gills and underlies our impression that the Loch Ness Monster was some kind of newspaper stunt. Why, if it had always been there, did it not get into the headlines until 1933?

Mrs Whyte reminds us that it was in this year that the motor road along the north shore of the loch was constructed; so that for the first time many curious pairs of eyes, not inhibited by superstition from reporting what

1 *In Search of Lake Monsters*, p. 123.
2 *Project Water Horse*, p. 189.

they saw, scanned its surface. She suggests that one of the reasons why the Monster has been less often in the public eye since 1933–34 is that trees and scrub have grown up here and there between the road and the loch and have thus reduced the chances of the Monster being spotted on its rare, brief and unpredictable appearances. I do not know the road myself, but this makes sense.[1]

The 'new' 1933 motor road was however a fiction of Mrs Whyte's own devising. In fact there had been a road along the north shore of Loch Ness *since the end of the eighteenth-century*. Tourists and motor vehicles had been passing along it well before 1933. The 1906 edition of Ward Lock and Company's 'Red Guide' to *Oban, Fort William and the Western Highlands* contains a section entitled 'Oban to Inverness' which recommends the north shore road. From Fort Augustus, the guide explains, the 'road runs near shore of Loch Ness' as far as Invermoriston. After Invermoriston 'the road again runs by the side of the loch' as far as Strone. Passing through Drumnadrochit the traveller comes to Temple Pier, where 'the road gets to the shore of the loch. Pass through Brachla on good road to Lochend Inn and Dochgarroch.' In other words the road followed just the same route that it does today. Further evidence for the road's existence is provided by the Automobile Association's *Scotland for the Motorist* (1925) which recommends the route 'along the shores of Loch Ness.' Drumnadrochit is praised as 'an ideal summer resort' and the Guide adds, 'From Drumnadrochit the route proceeds by a winding road along the sylvan banks of Loch Ness.'

The Great Glen Exhibition at Fort Augustus includes an old large-scale Bartholomews map of Loch Ness which clearly shows the road running along the north shore. Ironically, the Loch Ness Exhibition at Drumnadrochit itself exhibits a much older 'General Map of the intended Caledonian Canal or Inland Navigation from the Eastern to the Western Sea' based on the original survey by John

1 *The Spectator*, 5 April 1957, p. 439.

Howell, dating from the end of the eighteenth-century. Here, too, the road along the north shore is clearly marked.

Mrs Whyte has never lived at Loch Ness and only became interested in the mystery during the nineteen-forties. All that happened in 1933 was that sections of the north shore road were *improved*. The road was resurfaced along its entire length and there were a number of repairs carried out; this work was finished in September 1933, at a time when there were only a handful of reported sightings of the monster. The popular idea that the building of a new road disturbed the monsters lurking in the depths is without substance.

Far from being a lonely, uninhabited spot before 1933 Loch Ness was extremely popular with the leisured English middle-classes during the previous hundred years. The *Inverness Courier* itself commented on the new tourist boom.[1] This flood of visitors increased after the reconstruction of the Caledonian Canal in the 1840s.[2] Excursions by steamer through the Canal (which took in the entire length of Loch Ness) became fashionable and popular. The Highland lochs became 'almost as well known to the English as Regent Street or Hyde Park.'[3] Queen Victoria herself travelled on Loch Ness in September 1873, belatedly following in the wake of Prince Albert, who had sailed from Fort William to Inverness some twenty-six years earlier. After this great event Macbrayne's offered 'Summer Tours in Scotland' following 'The Royal Route'. Loch Ness was full of steamers catering to the tourist traffic. The *Lochiel* and *Lochness* operated between Inverness and Fort Augustus, picking up and putting down passengers all along the loch, at Temple Pier, Inverfarigaig, Foyers, Invermoriston and Fort Augustus. The *Glengarry* and the *Gondolier* offered a daily service up the canal in either direction, and the *Glengarry* was also

1 See 'Visitors to the Highlands', *Inverness Courier*, 28 August 1833.
2 According to the Earl of Malmesbury 1833 'was the first year that the Highlands became the rage ... At that time a stranger could fish and shoot over almost any part of the Highlands without interruption.' *Memoirs of an Ex-Minister* (London: Longmans, 1885), p. 41.
3 Charles St. John, *Short Sketches of the Wild Sports and Natural History of the Highlands* (London, 1846).

used for weekend pleasure excursions to Invermoriston (where a river walk was open to 'respectable, well-conducted persons'). These two veteran paddle steamers were still operating daily trips up the loch in the 1920s. The *Glengarry* left Fort Augustus at 6 a.m. each day, carrying mail, cargo and passengers, and called at various piers along Loch Ness, returning from Inverness in the afternoon. Not all travellers were pleased with the way the Highlands had been opened up to tourism. The Victorian naturalist Charles St. John wrote,

> I well remember being one bright summer's day on the shore of Loch Ness, and enjoying the surpassing loveliness of the scene. The perfectly calm loch was like a mirror; here and there a trout rising at a fly dimpled the smooth water, and in my idle mood I watched the circles as they gradually widened and disappeared. I was suddenly aroused by a Glasgow steamer passing within a hundred yards of me, full of holiday people, with fiddles and parasols conspicuous on the deck, while a stream of black sooty smoke showered its favours over me, and filled my mouth as I opened it to vent my ill temper in an anathema against steam-boats, country-dance tunes, and cockneys.[1]

In the first thirty years of the twentieth century Loch Ness remained a popular and busy place, so much so that the Highland Railway was extended to the lochside on a new line from Spean Bridge to Fort Augustus. The line was opened in July 1903, and in the words of the railway company's advertisement provided 'new ground for visitors in a most interesting and romantic part of the Highlands.' Today the remains of this old line, including the pillars of the former bridge across the Oich, and the decaying, overgrown pierhead station beside Loch Ness can still be seen.

By the late 1920s and early 1930s the tourist trade at Loch Ness began to dry up in the face of slump and the

1 *Op. Cit.*, pp. 7–8.

international economic recession. The boom years of the
Caledonian Canal were coming to an end, and it was being
used less and less. In 1927 the *Glengarry* was withdrawn from
service and broken up. In 1929 the Fort Augustus-Inverness
steamer run was abandoned. The piers at Invermoriston and
Foyers and Drumnadrochit which had once been alive with
the bustle of passengers and luggage fell into disuse. In 1933 it
was announced that the railway line to Fort Augustus would
be closed down. Public meetings protesting about this
threatened closure were reported in the *Inverness Courier* on 20
and 27 October 1933. But not even the sudden appearance of
a prehistoric monster in Loch Ness could spare Fort Augustus
or Drumnadrochit from the effects of recession, and the line
duly closed down at the end of the year.

The question arises of how the myth of the timeless,
lonely, unvisited loch ever came to be believed in the first
place. The answer lies in the kind of people who became
interested in the monster enigma. Monster experts are
usually enthusiastic amateurs with a chauvinistic ignorance
of Scottish social history. To the English, Scottish culture
remains largely a matter of clan tartans, malt whisky, Bonnie
Prince Charlie, bagpipes, haggis, jokes about kilts, and at
best – the paperbacks of John Prebble. It is an attitude
enthusiastically aided and abetted by the Scottish tourist
industry.

Scotland remains one of England's oldest colonies, and
ignorance or sentimental paternalism still characterises the
English attitude to Scotland. There is a revealing comment in
Tim Dinsdale's *Loch Ness Monster* where he mentions his first
visit to Loch Ness in 1960. After a melodramatic description
of himself 'driving all alone into this land of rock and ice'
Dinsdale tells how he arrived at Inverness: 'a mellow tidy
place, with shops and banks and all the outward signs of life
of a modern thriving township; *so different from the outpost I had
imagined*'[1] (our italics). Exactly. After 'researching' the Loch
Ness mystery Dinsdale had convinced himself that the

1 *Loch Ness Monster*, p. 79.

Highlands were still as remote and unvisited as they had been in the middle ages. His attitude of mind was identical to that of the geographers Daniel Defoe had attacked two centuries earlier, quoted at the beginning of this chapter.

Loch Ness has always been of central importance in Scottish history, largely because of the important communications role played by the Great Glen. From prehistoric times this great natural avenue across Scotland has functioned as a vital route for travellers. In the Neolithic era it was the path taken by the chambered-cairn builders of Argyll as they moved north. There are numerous ancient settlements around Loch Ness, including the forts at Dun Scriben, Craig Mony, Craig Phadrig, Ashie Moor, Castle Kitchie, and Dun Dearduil. Urquhart Castle was itself built on the site of an Iron Age vitrified fort, and occupies an important observation point.

Traditionally, monsters and dragons have long been supposed to maintain guard over hoards of underwater treasure, and many archaeological finds have been made in rivers and on the beds of lakes. No evidence has emerged that primitive man regarded Loch Ness as the home of a water serpent or held it in any awe. There is even a piece of negative evidence which suggests the very opposite. This is Cherry Island, an overgrown and partly-submerged crannog just outside Fort Augustus. Dating from the first century A.D. Cherry Island is artificial, built upon boulders and wood, providing the foundation for a round farm homestead. There are at least a dozen crannogs in the Inverness area, and many remained in occupation into the late medieval period. It seems unlikely that men would have built such a construction had the loch been known as the haunt of huge and terrifying water-beasts.

Much of the early history of Scotland is still obscure, but Inverness was geographically of great importance from ancient times, situated as it was near a river mouth and surrounded by the fertile lands of the Moray Firth. Urquhart Castle was equally significant in its location, since it provided the major observation post overlooking the whole upper part of the Great Glen. It would be reasonable to expect the first written reports of monsters to filter out of Urquhart Castle, in view of its panoramic views of the loch. The castle site seems to have been permanently settled from prehistoric times, transforming over the centuries from a primitive vitrified fort to a sophisticated Norman fortress with towers and citadel. There was probably a royal castle at Urquhart in the reign of William the Lion, but not until the outbreak of the Wars of Independence at the end of the thirteenth century do specific and contemporary records of the castle begin to appear. The castle was captured by Edward I, and eventually retaken by Robert the Bruce in about 1308. It subsequently changed hands on numerous occasions, during a protracted series of clan wars. During the English civil war the castle was plundered yet again, causing the Lady of Urquhart to write a complaint that she had been left 'without a serviette to eat my meal on'.

The first recorded letter to be written from Urquhart Castle is dated 25 July 1297, and numerous other contemporary records and items of correspondence made over the following five centuries have survived. None, however, makes any reference to a wondrous serpent in the loch.

English authority returned to Loch Ness at the time of the civil war. Cromwell built a major citadel at Inverness, and placed a galley on the loch. As one contemporary observer put it, the Roundheads 'carried a bark, driven uppon rollers of wood to the Lochend of Ness and there enlarged it to a statly friggott, to sail with provision from one end of the Loch to the other.' At the time of the Revolution of 1689 the castle received a Whig garrison, which stayed on after the collapse of the legitimist uprising for a period of two years. After evacuating it they blew up some of the castle buildings, and before long the local people had begun stripping the ruins of stone and lead. In February 1715 a severe storm brought more of the castle crashing down, and it has remained a deserted, roofless shell ever since.

During the Restoration era the Highlands slowly began to

open up to English influence. Daniel Defoe described how cosmopolitan and 'English' the Inverness area became after Cromwell.

Defoe apparently visited Scotland around 1698, and returned again in 1706, living there for most of the next four years. He made it clear in the title of his *Tour Through the Whole Island* that he would give 'a particular and diverting account of whatever is curious and worth observation.' Despite this Defoe still managed to travel the length of Loch Ness with Scottish guides without anyone telling him about a monster in its waters.

The peace which Defoe found in the Highlands proved short-lived. The first fifty years of the eighteenth century were times of crisis for Scotland, culminating in the Jacobite risings of 1715 and 1745, and the bloody massacre at Culloden. The troubles brought the English army flooding back to the area. Three important forts were established: Fort William, Fort Augustus, and Fort George (at Inverness). Communications overland up the Great Glen were unsuited to the movement of armies, and General Wade was ordered to construct a series of military roads. Under the General's direction a road linking Inverness and Fort Augustus was built in 1726. This road (often confused with the Loch Ness road) followed the high route from Inverness by Essich and Bochrubin, crossing the Farigaig by a ford and so across the moor to Loch Garth-side and Whitebridge. It was not until 1732 that the road along Loch Ness was constructed, requiring much rock-blasting and the construction of a bridge at Inverfarigaig (still visible today, beside the modern bridge). Captain Edward Burt visited Loch Ness after the construction of this new road and described the scene in his classic travel book *Letters from a Gentleman in the North of Scotland* (1754): 'Now, for the space of twelve miles, it is an even terrace in every part, from whence the lake may be seen from end to end.' But although the trees had been cut down and the undergrowth cleared no-one, it seems, saw any monsters. General Wade himself visited the road works, staying at a wooden hut which was afterwards converted into an inn and named after him. The site is now occupied by the Foyers Hotel

With the building of the Wade military roads the opening up of the Highlands began. It was along the new road by Loch Ness that Dr Johnson and Boswell came in 1773. Johnson was impressed by the 'horrid' scenery and puzzled why the loch never froze. Though the two men had a Gaelic-speaking guide and spoke to local people on the way, no-one mentioned anything about a monster to the good doctor. Boswell subsequently published his account of their visit in his *Tour of the Highlands with Dr Samuel Johnson* (1785).

It was around this time that ships became a regular sight on Loch Ness. General Wade had put a galley on the loch for patrol purposes, and by the end of the century it was reported that 'a sloop of sixty tons burthen is continually sailing on this lake to supply Fort Augustus from Inverness.'[1] By 1820 the first paddle steamer had arrived at Loch Ness, taking over from the sailing ship.

By the end of the eighteenth century however Scotland was in crisis. A handful of wealthy landowners who had backed the winning English side at the time of the rebellions used their privileges to dispossess the nation. Crofters and farmers were driven from their homes with great cruelty, and the land was turned over to highly-profitable sheep-farming. Emigration soared and Scotland became threatened by depopulation.

At this point Thomas Telford appeared on the scene. Telford, one of the great engineers of the nineteenth century, was brought in to remedy the situation. He produced a report for the government which argued that Scotland needed to revitalise its agriculture and fishing industry. New roads, bridges and harbours would be required to drag the country into the nineteenth century. Most ambitiously of all Telford proposed that a canal be built

1 John Phillips, *A General History of Inland Navigation, Foreign and Domestic* (London: Fifth edition, B. Crosby, 1805), p. 560.

along the length of the Great Glen, linking the east and west coast fishing grounds.

This idea was not a new one. James Watt, later to become famous as the inventor of the steam engine, had previously surveyed the Great Glen for a canal system in 1773. Three reasons combined to encourage the English government to finance the construction of the Caledonian Canal in 1803. Firstly it would enable shipping to avoid the dangerous passage round the north coast of Scotland. Secondly it would bring work to the Highlands and help check the emigration. Lastly there was a war with France going on at this time, and the canal would be strategically valuable.

Work began almost immediately from both ends, at Clachnaharry and Corpach. By 1818 the canal workers were approaching Loch Ness and completion. The resident engineer for the eastern section wrote that year to his son, proudly remarking, 'Vessels are now daily and regularly passing to and from Fort Augustus with stone, coal, meat and provisions etc., there were one day last week 10 vessels on Loch Ness at the same time.'

As the canal's eastern division neared completion the foreman mason, John Cargill, moved his headquarters to Fort Augustus, where he had a house built. By this time the western division was also nearing completion, so that in the years 1819–20 almost the entire labour force was concentrated upon the remaining eleven miles of the central section of the canal, between Loch Ness and the east end of Loch Lochy. Great problems were encountered in deepening the approach to the canal from Loch Ness, but after the combined efforts of the first steam bucket dredgers ever built the task was finally completed.

The poet Robert Southey visited the Great Glen at this time and was much impressed by the landscape and the canal.

Between the General's Hut and Fort Augustus the road is carried full 1500 feet above the sea, that is, half the height of Skiddaw! When we came in sight of our journey's end the view was very impressive; it commanded the head of

Loch Ness, the river Oich which enters it, the bridge, the fort standing alone, and the two villages, or suburbs, if so they may be called which have grown up in consequence of the establishment of the Fort, one to the West, the other beyond the river.[1]

Southey visited the Fort Augustus canal excavations and found them 'a most impressive and rememberable scene. Men, horses and machines at work; digging, walling and puddling going on, men wheeling barrows, horses drawing stones along the railways ...' But despite the great influx of English visitors, engineers and labourers no-one reported sighting huge unknown animals in Loch Ness. In October 1822 the canal was opened and the first ships sailed through.

With the opening of the Caledonian Canal we return to the great era of Victorian tourism with which we began. As the years rolled by more and more visitors came to the Great Glen. Robert Burns arrived at Loch Ness and visited the Falls of Foyers, the sight of which encouraged him to scribble a dozen lines of uninspired romantic doggerel. Charles Darwin came to the Great Glen in the summer of 1838, spending 'eight good days' in Glen Roy, investigating the mysterious 'parallel roads'. Aleister Crowley, the legendary black-magician, writer and self-publicist, lived at Loch Ness between 1900 and 1918. His home, Boleskine House, can still be seen above the road between Inverfarigaig and Foyers. Crowley was obsessed by the paranormal, but the news that a monster inhabited the loch just below his house seems to have eluded him. Nowhere in his extensive writings is there any reference to the beast.

One could go on multiplying examples of this sort almost indefinitely. There are two other pieces of negative evidence which are perhaps worth mentioning. One is the Bathymetrical Survey of Loch Ness carried out by the staff of the Research Department of the Royal Geographical Society,

1 Robert Southey, *Journal of a Tour in Scotland in 1819* (London: John Murray, 1929).

who made an intensive investigation of the loch's geography and natural history during 1903 and 1904. Around 1700 soundings of the loch were taken, and sixty dredgings made from the bed. In the words of the Royal Society Report, 'Loch Ness was made the subject of a more thorough, though still far from exhaustive biological investigation than any other Scottish loch.'

In 1912 another kind of expert arrived at the lochside, when the ruins of Urquhart Castle were handed over by the owners to the government's Ancient Monuments Department. A complete excavation and repair of the vast ruin was immediately begun. Interrupted in 1914 by the war, the extensive diggings were resumed in 1919 and completed in 1922.

During all this time and all this activity no-one ever reported seeing monsters in Loch Ness. The loch's waters have been open to the public gaze for two centuries, and it seems odd that the monster was never seen by English troops or by the men on the sailing boats which silently plied the loch, or even by Victorian tourists out fishing. The negative evidence against the existence of a herd of giant unknown animals in Loch Ness seems overwhelming.

5 The Man Who Discovered Monsters

'Did you come into contact with the Loch Ness monster at all?'
'I was up in Inverness for a fortnight last year, sir,' Brownsworth replied, 'but I wasn't lucky enough to see it.'
'Ah, pity. I believe I've seen it oftener than anybody. Twelve times, to be exact. It's a great sight.'

Compton Mackenzie, *The Rival Monster* (1952)

The Loch Ness myth is about many things, but perhaps its most fascinating aspect is the human one – the role played by a handful of individuals in promoting the legend over fifty years. Alex Campbell's part in originally publicising the discovery of a monster, and his continuing role in the Loch Ness story over half a century make him a figure of great significance in any investigation of the myth. The part he has played has been curious and remarkable. He was the man who first drew attention to the beast's existence; he claimed to have had one of the earliest and most dramatic sightings of the monster; he has provided a number of anecdotes of monster sightings occuring before 1933. Finally, he has seen the monster more often than anyone else, without ever photographing it.

In 1933 Campbell was employed by the Ness Fisheries Board as water bailiff of the loch. He was guardian of the waters and had a proprietorial interest in it; Loch Ness was 'his' loch.

Alex Campbell was brought up believing in a monster in Loch Ness. When he was a child his parents warned him never to swim there in case the water-kelpie seized him. There is a rather obvious reason why his parents should say such a thing, which is that Loch Ness is a very dangerous place for the inexperienced. Its banks and shoreline shelve steeply, and around much of the lochside even the tallest of men would be out of his depth within a matter of a few steps. The water remains at an almost constant 42°F throughout the year. Anyone falling into the loch would succumb to exposure within a few minutes if unable to reach the shore. The Great Glen is like a gigantic wind-tunnel, and climatic conditions at Loch Ness can change with alarming suddenness. One moment the loch can seem tranquil and idyllic, the next its surface may be transformed into a terrifying Atlantic-like immensity of surging eight-foot-high waves driven by winds sweeping at speeds. Loch Ness is no place for amateur boatsmen or children. Elementary child psychology would suggest that telling a young boy not to swim in the loch because of the fearful water-kelpie would be a very effective way of putting a taboo on its waters.

Loch Ness is black and opaque at the surface, owing to the density of the peat particles washed down from numerous rivers and burns and suspended in its waters. The inky impenetrability of the loch's appearance can certainly seem sinister, and it is not hard to understand that the suggestion of a fearsome beast in its depths would work far more effectively on a child's imagination than an adult's reference to something as abstract and incomprehensible as 'drowning' and 'death'. Such a simple explanation has not however occurred to monster enthusiasts, who regularly cite Campbell's childhood memory of water-kelpie tales as proof of the continuity of a monster tradition. Actually all it does is reinforce the impression that Campbell was brought up in a household with a fondness for superstition and Highland folklore. That this is the case is confirmed by a little-known article which Alex Campbell wrote for *The Scots Magazine* (May 1962). In it Campbell describes his family's long connections with the district and 'the wealth of folk-lore' he had inherited. His maternal great-great-great grandmother had, as a girl, witnessed the Battle of Culloden. Campell adds that 'The Highlander is noted for the meticulous way in which he passes his folk-lore down, generation after generation,' and mentions that one of his own forebears had heard water-kelpie tales 'as far back as 1802'. Interestingly in his last book *Raven Seek Thy Brother* Gavin Maxwell noted the powerful grip which superstition, folklore and the supernatural still exerted over local people in the West Highlands, even in the nineteen-sixties. He mentioned Loch na Beiste (Loch of the Beast), which is near the popular tourist crossing at Kyle of Lochalsh. The loch is said to contain 'a creature that some describe as having a head covered with a mane, while others who claim to have seen it refuse utterly to give any description whatsoever.'

The previous water-bailiff at Loch Ness, Campbell's own father, apparently never saw the monster once during his lifetime. Campbell himself made no claims to have seen a monster in Loch Ness prior to his newspaper reports of 1933. Then, in October, just as the *Courier* reports began to be taken up by the national press, Alex Campbell stepped forward and claimed his first sighting of the beast. The story of Alex Campbell's 'sighting' is so extraordinary that it deserves wider consideration.

His claim to have seen the monster first appeared, anonymously, in the *Scotsman*, 17 October 1933. The paper's reporter, the first representative of a national newspaper to arrive at Loch Ness in pursuit of the monster, described how he had met a local man whose sighting of the beast must

to anyone who is at all sceptical appear to be very fantastic. It was given recently by a man who up to that time had refused to believe of the existence in the loch of anything other than a seal or a large marine animal of some kind. He stated that one afternoon a short time ago he saw a creature raise its head and body from the loch, pause, moving its head – a small head on a long neck – rapidly from side to side, apparently listening to the sound of two drifters coming from the Caledonian Canal, which was out of its sight, then take fright and sink into the water. While it was above water, he said, he could see the swirl made by each movement of its limbs, and the creature seemed to him to be fully 30 feet in length. The description he gave of its form was like that of a plesiosaurus, and when shown a sketch of a 'reconstructed' plesiosaurus he stated that it was very like the animal he had seen.

The man was Alex Campbell, and clearly he was being a little disingenuous in passing himself off as a former sceptic who was now forced to believe the evidence of his own eyes.

Then, suddenly and inexplicably, Campbell retracted his 'sighting'. In a letter to his employers, the Ness Fisheries Board, Campbell claimed an identical monster sighting in the same place, in identical weather conditions. 'But the light was improving all the time, and in a matter of seconds I discovered that what I took to be the Monster was nothing more than a few cormorants.'

Campbell's motive in writing this letter remains obscure, but on the evidence available it would appear that his formidable role in promoting the monster had come to the ears of his employers. The Ness Fisheries Board, it seems, was not amused. Unfortunately for Campbell his letter came to the attention of Rupert Gould, a monster-investigator and author, who promptly splashed it across the pages of his book *The Loch Ness Monster and Others* (1934).[1] Ironically Gould regarded Campbell's letter as 'an interesting and valuable piece of negative evidence'. Gould interviewed Alex Campbell and commented: 'the element of "expectant attention" was, in my opinion, certainly present.' By 'expectant attention' Gould meant that those who expect to see a monster will, sooner or later, 'see' one, most probably

1 See Rupert T. Gould, *The Loch Ness Monster and Others* (London: Geoffrey Bles, 1934), pp. 110–13.

through the misinterpretation of some known object – like a cormorant.

Campbell's discomfiture at finding himself quoted *against* the existence of a monster must have been immense. But presumably it was some consolation when he persuaded Gould that two of his neighbours, Commander Meiklem and the local schoolmaster, had both had separate sightings in 'perfect conditions for observation'. Gould duly included the two men in his inventory of 42 'classic' sightings, coming down strongly in favour of the beast's existence.

Alex Campbell was also interviewed about his monster 'sighting' by Dom Cyril Dieckhoff, O.S.B., one of the monks at the nearby Abbey. Dieckhoff planned to write a book about the monster which had so dramatically appeared in the neighbourhood (though he was to die leaving the book unfinished; his notes later fell into the hands of Mrs Constance Whyte, who used them extensively in her book *More Than a Legend* (1957)). Campbell told Dieckhoff that he had seen the monster on 22 September (contradicting the account given in Gould's book, which refers to one sighting on 7 September, and another in October). This 'monster' was similar to the one which he had described to the *Scotsman* journalist, and later retracted in the letter to the Ness Fisheries Board. A few days after telling Dieckhoff about his sighting of a thirty-foot-long monster Campbell changed his mind. The monk wrote down in his notes: 'Later modified his statement to say that sun was in his eyes and a misty haze on the water, so that visibility was poor or only moderate – light not too good – gave impression that for some reason was anxious to minimise what he had previously said and absolutely refused to allow his name to be mentioned to anyone.'[1]

We have shown earlier how Campbell's original 1933 news report of the monster was written from the viewpoint of a passionate believer, and how it drew attention to the curious,

---

1 Quoted in Constance Whyte, *More than a Legend: The Story of the Loch Ness Monster* (London: Hamish Hamilton, 1957), p. 75.

anonymous 'monster' reports of 1930. What is equally curious is Campbell's role in promoting the notion of a monster 'tradition' at Loch Ness. Commander Gould, though convinced that the monster was a solitary specimen which had only arrived in the loch via the River Ness in 1933, sceptically included in his book a handful of anecdotes concerning much earlier sightings. One of these was drawn from the *Northern Chronicle* (12 August 1933) which reported how 'some forty-four years ago an Abriachan mason, Alexander Macdonald, often saw a strange creature disporting itself on the loch in the early hours of the morning.' Mr Macdonald was unable to substantiate the story because he had, alas, died 'a good many years ago'. What Gould did not know was that the source of this anecdote was none other than Alex Campbell. The story had, it turned out, been handed down in the Campbell family. Campbell retold it and introduced some new pre-1933 sightings in his *Scots Magazine* article, mentioned earlier.

In 1934, when interest in the monster began to ebb away, Alex Campbell remained energetically committed to the beast's existence, tracking down witnesses wherever he could find them. By the end of the year he had collected the names of eighty-two people who claimed to have seen the monster, including himself.

These efforts were to no avail. For two decades little happened. Throughout the nineteen-forties there were only seventeen recorded sightings, throughout the fifties only twenty-one. These were the depression years for the monster industry, with barely two sightings a year during a twenty-year period. Then, in 1957, Constance Whyte's *More Than a Legend* was published, triggering a revival of interest in the mystery.

Not long afterwards Alex Campbell reported his latest sighting. On 16 July 1958, he claimed, he had seen – not for the first time – two monsters simultaneously. Later he remembered another odd experience which he had had on 'a beautiful summer day in 1955 or 1956'. He was, he said, rowing his boat in the middle of the loch when suddenly there was a commotion in the water and his boat *began to rise up in the air* – then fell back on to the water. It was, he hinted darkly, his closest and most frightening encounter with the monster. (Zoologist Maurice Burton subsequently dismissed this anecdote as being quite absurd and fantastic, and impossible to reconcile with the behaviour of any known marine creature which suddenly finds itself with a rowing-boat on its back.)

Over the years Campbell has alleged many other sightings of the monster (making a grand total of eighteen, at the latest count). Undaunted by his terrifying experience on the beastie's back Campbell pluckily went on fishing in the loch and was duly rewarded by another astonishingly close sighting, this time of an immense hump which rose slowly from the loch 'only a few yards distant'.[1] On another occasion Campbell had the good fortune to see 'two separate Monsters, rolling and splashing about on the surface, one of which clearly exhibited a pair of forward flippers.'[2]

There are five remarkable features to Alex Campbell's sightings. The first is the *frequency* of them. No other individual at Loch Ness (apart from Frank Searle, of whom more later) can claim to match Campbell's astonishing sightings record. The second is the *closeness* of his sightings. Few have ever got as close to the beast as Alex Campbell. The third is *the curious absence of supporting evidence* for Campbell's sightings. It seems very odd that a man with such a passionate commitment to the monster's existence should never have had a camera with him on any of these occasions. The fourth is *the remarkable detail* of his sightings. Most monster-hunters would count themselves lucky if they saw a hump. Campbell's sightings have rarely been so banal. He has seen the head and neck, the flippers, and the creature with its head stuck in something. ('Doubtless,' comments Peter

1 Tim Dinsdale, *Loch Ness Monster* (London: Routledge & Kegan Paul, 1961), p. 95.
2 *Ibid.*

Costello, 'Campbell's animal had got itself covered in weeds, grubbing along the bottom.'¹ Doubtless). On one occasion Campbell even heard the monster's *heavy breathing*: 'What he described,' remarked Tim Dinsdale, much impressed, ' – or rather the sound he copied by breathing in and out loudly, making a low hissing noise through his teeth, was almost identical to the sounds made by a giant sea turtle. Great sighs, taken in as though on a deep-breathing exercise.'²

Lastly there are the curious inconsistencies which abound in Campbell's sightings record. After a quarter of a century, when everyone had forgotten about the peculiarities surrounding Campbell's 1933 monster-that-wasn't, he announced that his first sighting of the beast had actually occurred the following year, in 1934. The 1934 sighting turned out to be identical in every respect with the sighting which Campbell had given the *Scotsman* and shortly afterwards retracted. This dramatic new evidence of the monster's existence was broadcast to the world through the pages of *Everybody's Magazine* (21 February, 1959):

The early morning mist was clearing fast as I came out of my cottage on the banks of Loch Ness. It was a June morning in 1934. Then as the mist shredded away under the warm sunlight I witnessed the most incredible sight I have seen in my forty years as a water bailiff on Scotland's biggest loch. Something rose from the water like a monster of pre-historic times, measuring a full thirty feet from tip to tail.

Campbell has subsequently told this story many times, calling it his 'best' sighting. It is identical with his sightings of 7 September 1933, 22 September 1933, and October 1933, each of which he previously explained involved the observation of cormorants in bad light. The more he has told

1 *In Search of Lake Monsters*, p. 82.
2 Tim Dinsdale, *Project Water Horse* (London: Routledge & Kegan Paul, 1975), p. 42.

the story, the more Campbell has begun to contradict himself (though the basic framework of the anecdote remains the same, culminating in the arrival of two trawlers on the scene). In one version the monster bursts from the depths before Campbell's startled eyes, in another it is already there on the surface as the mist thins. To one interviewer Campbell vividly described the animal's 'front paddles', to another he stated firmly that no flippers were visible. In one version the monster dives, creating a huge disturbance in the water, in another it sinks silently away below the surface. Campbell then (you can take your pick) ran for his camera, ran to his boat, or ran back to his cottage to thumb through his picture-book of prehistoric monsters.

Alex Campbell is a man at home with the Loch Ness monster, despite his terrifyingly close encounters of the third kind. The monster is something he *knows*. As the legend revived in the nineteen-fifties he became the self-appointed high priest of the loch's mysteries, always at hand with advice and inspiration for new devotees of his fabulous beast. In 1962, after publication of Maurice Burton's *The Elusive Monster*, which dared to question some of the evidence from Loch Ness, Campbell angrily broke into print in *The Scots Magazine* and wrote an impassioned defence of the monster. The article is full of extraordinary fallacies (e.g. 'It is an old and well-established fact that Loch Ness never gives up anything – not even its dead').

It would be unfair to call Campbell a hoaxer. He has never been involved in the construction of fake monsters, peddled dubious photographs, or gone out of his way to make money from the mystery. At the same time his role in originally publicising the monster cannot be ignored, nor can the strange blindness of the monster fraternity to the inconsistencies and question-marks which surround Campbell's sightings.

In the nineteen-sixties and seventies Alex Campbell became the man everyone went to when they wanted to learn more about the monster. When Tim Dinsdale made his first pilgrimage to Campbell's home in 1960 and showed him his pictures of prehistoric animals, the Scotsman pointed confidently at an Elasmosaurus. 'That's it,' he said, 'only with a shorter neck.' Dinsdale immediately rushed off in a state of high excitement and shot some motion film of a 'monster' – a monster which he afterwards sheepishly realised was nothing more than waves plus a little imagination.

Dinsdale's best-seller *Loch Ness Monster* gave Campbell an honoured role in the Loch Ness story, treating him as one of the most important witnesses of them all, and greatly helping in the process of turning Campbell into a celebrity of sorts. Campbell is now an old man, but he remains a charismatic, legendary figure whom monster enthusiasts speak about in tones of awe and respect.

He has always had a great zest for publicity. Campbell has given numerous interviews to television, radio and the press and has always been on hand to offer advice and encouragement to monster-hunters. When the Loch Ness Investigation Bureau first considered night-time searchlight sweeps of the loch Campbell rushed to their defence:

Apparently it is this particular and hitherto untried method that the unbelievers scoff at. But is it so mad? To give one instance only of a night appearance – never before published – let me tell of what a cousin of mine and his friend saw one evening about ten o'clock in Urquhart Castle Bay.

(*Scots Magazine*, May 1962)

The two men, whom Campbell did not name, had seen, he claimed, 'a huge black body, distinctly humped'.

There is one final twist to the Alex Campbell story. The monster is not the only enigma associated with Loch Ness which he has tried to publicise. According to Campbell Loch Ness is haunted by the spectre of St Columba's ship, which appears once every twenty years. Campbell has even named witnesses. The latest sighting (1962) was by an Irish tramp;

the previous spectral appearance (1942) was witnessed by Campbell's brother Colin:

> It was pitch black and I could not see even the trees or rocks around me. But there, 30 yards from the shore, was the ship. It had no light of its own. It was spotlighted by something fluorescent, whitish and bluish and magical. The ship was stationary, as though at anchor. I saw ropes coiled on the deck and every line of her. She looked like an ancient craft from Biblical times.

The episode of St Columba's spectral ship remains a curious one, and suggests something of the grip which superstition and folklore held over the Campbell family. In our view it startlingly reinforces the view that Alex Campbell's role in the birth and evolution of the Loch Ness mystery needs to be regarded with extreme caution. When Tim Dinsdale dedicated his book *Project Water Horse* 'To Alex Campbell, who started it and who has stood firm ever since' the words perhaps carried an unintended irony.

6 Credulity and Fraud

i

something happened yes
                    Samuel Beckett, *How It Is* (1959)

The credit for putting the idea that there were monsters in
Loch Ness into people's minds may have to go to an obscure
but imaginative water-bailiff, but obviously one man alone
cannot be held responsible for what followed. Something
happened in 1933 at Loch Ness. What happened was that
people started 'seeing' monsters there. To understand what
opportune coincidence of factors led to those sightings we
need first to go back a few years earlier, to the late 1920s. It
was then – probably 1928 – that H. V. Morton motored down
the Great Glen, past Loch Ness. Morton was a much-
travelled man who had written a bestseller about a journey
through England, followed it up with *In Search of Scotland* and
achieved his greatest prominence with *In the Steps of the Master*,
an account of a trek to the places in the Middle East
associated with the life of Christ.

What struck Morton about the Great Glen was its
stunning romantic grandeur. It was, he exclaimed, quite
simply the most romantic valley in Europe – 'The Rhine
cannot hold a candle to it.'

What scenery, what primeval wildness, what splendid
solitudes, what lonely mountain-crests, what dark gloom
of pine and larch, what sudden bright glimpses through
trees of deep water reflecting the curves of guardian hills
... the Great Glen through which the Caledonian Canal

runs is a luscious extravagance in landscape, rich in its variety, almost terrible in its wild splendour.[1]

Loch Ness is undeniably a stark, craggy landscape of the kind made popular by the Romantic movement. Around its shores are mountains, waterfalls, thick pine forests. It resembles the landscape of a Gothick novel – it even has a ruined castle towering over its waters, complete with dungeon.

Loch Ness thrilled Morton:

> The road to Fort Augustus runs for twenty-four miles beside the northern bank of Loch Ness. This is my idea of a perfect Highland loch. It is never greater than a mile in width, so that, unlike some lakes, it cannot pretend to be the sea. Here for twenty-four miles is a changing beauty of hill, woodland and water. I have never seen inland water which looked deeper: it is actually black with fathoms – 130 fathoms, I am told.
>
> The deepest, most sinister portion of the loch is that opposite the ruined shell of Urquhart Castle. Here the water is 750 feet in depth! And the old castle sits grimly on a bluff overlooking the deep water and sings a song of battle and siege. Weeds grow over it and try to press apart its massive stones, but the old building gazes steadily down to Loch Ness, and Loch Ness gazes back with rarely a ripple on her black face; and it seems to you that both of them have appropriate secrets ...[2]

What is fascinating about this description is that Morton wrote it before anyone had ever mentioned the idea of monsters lurking in the loch's depths. Loch Ness was a blank, an area of darkness, possessed of sinister qualities. It was, in a sense, a loch waiting for something to happen, waiting for someone to come along and inscribe its blackness with a terrible meaning. The landscape cried out for meaning, and

1 H. V. Morton, *In Search of Scotland* (1929), p. 182.
2 *In Search of Scotland*, p. 185.

that meaning was finally supplied. Once the idea of a 'Loch Ness monster' was born the landscape itself produced the appropriate atmosphere of mystery and expectation. What is surely significant is that Morton regarded the area of the loch around Urquhart Castle as the most sinister and enigmatic, the most full of 'secrets'. This is precisely the area where most monster sightings are made, and which has attracted most attention from monster hunters.

In an intriguing and revealing comment Percy Cater, one of the first London journalists to visit Loch Ness in 1933, wrote after a second visit in the fifties:

The Loch oppresses me as much as it did when I first saw it twenty years ago. It remains as enigmatic as the face of the Mona Lisa. Its surface, suggestive of its sinister depths, is as forbidding as anything I know. In this harsh landscape it is easy to think of strange goings on in the loch.

A 'sinister landscape' is culturally produced. Loch Ness is not sinister to a salmon or an otter. If it seemed sinister to Morton and Cater it can only have been because of certain inherited cultural responses, whether drawn from literature, painting, poetry or the cinema.[1]

Obviously a landscape on its own, no matter how mysterious, does not simply produce monsters of its own accord. The idea first had to be put into people's minds, and this is why the role of the press was so important in giving the monster credibility.[2] Significantly Loch Ness hit the headlines during a period of intense competition among the popular press. In 1900 only about 19% of the adult population

1 Ironically the wheel has now turned full circle, and the romantic elements in the Loch Ness mystery have inspired Peter Tremayne's *The Curse of Loch Ness* (Sphere Books, 1979), a formula Gothick novel.
2 Nowadays the monster fraternity are almost as caustic in their criticisms of the Press as they are of Science. Nicholas Witchell attacked the mass media in *The Loch Ness Story* – and then went on to become a reporter with BBC television news. In his new role he has, oddly enough, been criticised for misrepresentation and bias; see Liz Curtis, 'Back View,' *City Limits* (29 January – 4 February 1982), p. 44.

of Britain read a newspaper; by 1930 the proportion had rocketed to 75%. In the early thirties there were five popular newspapers with circulations in excess of one million copies a day. The *Daily Mail* led the field until 1932, when it was overtaken by the *Daily Herald* and *Daily Express*. It was this last paper which proved to be the most influential in terms of style and lay-out, and the *Express* was itself deeply influenced by the conventions of American newspaper practice – large black type blaring sensational headlines, and page-composition staggered and fragmented with photographs and minor items. Lengthy political analysis gave way to shorter, more frivolous news coverage. In a decade of international crisis, the era of Hitler, Franco, Stalin and Mussolini, the sudden appearance of a prehistoric monster in Scotland came as marvellous news to the popular press.

It took some time before the potential of the Loch Ness monster was fully grasped. On 9 June 1933 the *Scottish Daily Express* carried a small news item:

MYSTERY FISH IN SCOTTISH LOCH
Monster Reported at Fort Augustus

A monster fish which for years has been somewhat of a mystery in Loch Ness was reported to have been seen yesterday at Fort Augustus.

A 'monster fish' is not especially newsworthy. Indeed, fishermen who boast about the size of the one that got away are a traditional source of humour. Size has always fascinated the human race (the palaeontologist Stephen Jay Gould in his study of the giant Irish elk refers to 'the curious anecdotes and the sheer wonder that immensity always inspires'). But giant fish are not remarkable. Besides, in Britain 'fish' is a word with homely associations (most notably, chips). There is nothing particularly compelling about a 'monster fish'. But a *monster*, especially a prehistoric one, is something altogether different. The word 'monster' is powerfully charged with a variety of meanings. It can refer to evil ('An inhumanly cruel or wicked person'), to size ('Animal or thing of huge size'), or to something repellent and out of the ordinary ('Misshapen animal or plant'). In practice these are the three major meanings of the term when it is used in relation to Loch Ness. The loch's 'sinister' qualities had, at last, in 1933, found an appropriate focus: a huge, unknown, misshapen animal.

By the end of that year the popular papers were frantically competing for scoops. The Scottish *Daily Record* snapped up the first photograph in December, but the *Daily Mail* had its revenge the following April with the famous 'surgeon's photograph'. Two months later the *Scottish Daily Express* published its own monster photo, and before long the *Daily Mail* had come up with another sensational 'head and neck' snapshot of the beast. It was not for nothing that *Punch* magazine ran a cartoon which showed the monster writing 'DAILY M ...' on the loch's surface.

Recalling the unfortunate affair of the hippopotamus hoax Peter Fleming acidly commented, 'It was a few days later that the Monster was seen for the first time on land by a witness whom Mrs. Whyte [in *More Than a Legend*] calls "reliable."'[1] Fleming's reference to the Arthur Grant sighting is not quite accurate (the first people to see the monster on land were Mr and Mrs Spicer the previous July), but his scepticism seems in retrospect wholly justified. Throughout the fifty years of the monster's existence there is a startling correlation between 'sightings' and press publicity.

There are four classic 'land sightings' enshrined in monster lore which look increasingly dubious once they are put back into their contemporary contexts. The legendary Spicer sighting is perhaps the most dubious of them all. Mr Spicer was clearly a man who enjoyed publicity. His rambling, eccentric letter to the *Inverness Courier* dramatically announcing that he had seen 'a dragon or pre-historic animal' crossing the road in front of his car is scarcely very

1 'Monster in Aspic,' *The Spectator* (5 April 1957), p. 440.

convincing. It was also rather devious of Spicer to ask what the creature could have been, since he had already heard about the Loch Ness monster when he wrote his letter. In her book *More Than a Legend*, which did so much to revive the Loch Ness mystery, Constance Whyte wrote,

> Reports were circulated that the Monster had been seen 'with a lamb in its mouth'; this and other distorted or incomplete accounts were common at the time and, much to the annoyance of Mr and Mrs Spicer, were frequently repeated afterwards.[1]

Quite why Mr and Mrs Spicer should have been so annoyed is hard to say. After all it was Mr Spicer himself who wrote in his original *Courier* letter (4 August 1933), 'It crossed my road about fifty yards ahead and appeared to be carrying a small lamb or animal of some kind.' In December the Spicers' story was taken up by the national papers, and Spicer became a temporary celebrity. He appeared on the popular radio programme In Town Tonight, afterwards boasting, 'I broadcast to twenty million people from the BBC and have letters from all over the world.' On the radio Spicer repeated his claim that he had seen the monster carrying a sheep or small deer in its mouth. Months afterwards the Spicers changed their story:

> it entered Mrs Spicer's mind for a moment that something was being carried on the creature's back. On reflection, Mr and Mrs Spicer decided that it must have been the end of the tail. It was only on second thoughts, too, for the whole event was over in a matter of seconds, that they identified the thing like an elephant's trunk as a neck.[2]

Their estimate of the monster's size also changed dramatically. From being between six and eight feet in length it

1 *More Than a Legend*, p. 79.
2 Ibid.

grew and grew as Spicer retold his story until it was twenty-five, even thirty feet long.

Within a month of the Spicers' story being taken up by the national press the monster was seen again on land. The witness was Arthur Grant, a twenty-one-year-old student. He was driving along the north shore road at one o'clock in the morning when a mystery animal lurched across the moonlit road in front of him:

> To my astonishment it moved and then rose up and came a little towards me. Suddenly it swerved round, crossed the road, and plunged down the bank into the loch. The tail was long, thick and strong, and carried well off the ground. The end was rounded. When the creature crossed the road it did not walk but seemed to bound, springing from its hind feet.[1]

Grant was clearly acquainted with the dramatic details of the Spicer sighting, since he emphasized to the *Daily Mail* that the monster's 'long jaws would easily hold a lamb or a goat.' Returning to the spot next day Grant came across 'what might have been the footprints of a three-toed monster.' For something which happened with frightening suddenness and speed Grant was nevertheless able to provide remarkably detailed accounts of the episode. He drew no less than six different drawings of the mystery animal, which contradicted each other on important points of detail.

The last land sighting from the 1933–34 period came on 5 June 1934 at 6.30 a.m. when the monster was allegedly seen on the beach at Fort Augustus by a teenage girl in a house two hundred yards away. She examined the monster for twenty-five minutes through binoculars, before it disappeared into the loch. Oddly, in view of this stunningly close sighting, the girl's account said nothing new about the monster at all, apart from reinforcing the popular impression of the beast's general shape. Her description of the

1 *Daily Mail*, 6 January 1934.

creature's 'giraffe-like neck and absurdly small head' seems to have been much influenced by the so-called 'Surgeon's photograph' which, very significantly, had been published for the first time only shortly before the girl's sighting.

No-one else saw the monster on land until 1960, and no-one has seen it out of the water since. In February 1960 a man called Torquil Macleod had pulled up in his car while travelling from Invermoriston to Fort Augustus when his attention was 'attracted by a slight movement on the opposite shore.' Examining the object through binoculars he saw 'a large, grey black mass ... at the front there was what looked like an outsize in elephants' trunks.' It was of course the monster. Macleod was not quite sure whether he was watching the animal's head and neck or the tail, though he felt it was 'obviously scanning the shores of the loch in each direction.' He watched the creature for eight or nine minutes, then it turned, exposing 'a large squarish ended flipper forward of the big rear paddles – or flippers.' It then flopped into the water and disappeared. Macleod later met veteran monster hunter Tim Dinsdale and the episode received wide publicity as a result of its detailed discussion in Dinsdale's best-selling book *Loch Ness Monster* (1961).

Macleod was not a neutral witness, but a man passionately committed to a belief in monsters. Indeed Macleod and his wife had actually moved to the Loch Ness area for the sole purpose of monster-hunting. This may seem an extraordinary thing to do, but there is a special pathos surrounding the whole affair. Macleod was a sick man, dying from a rare form of cancer. Before his life ended he wanted, desperately, to see the loch's legendary beast.

In *More Than a Legend* Constance Whyte described the remote southern shore of the loch between Fort Augustus and Foyers:

Beyond the Abbey the road leaves the lochside and there is, on the south side, between Fort Augustus and Foyers, a 10-mile length of shore which is not overlooked, for rocks and precipices rise high from the water's edge. Perhaps, who knows, there is here at night-time a sequestered rendezvous for these enormous creatures; here perhaps, even during the day-time there are places where they can bask in peace, while across the water buses and cars, like beetles with folded wings, creep along against the massive background.[1]

More Than a Legend was a book which Macleod knew well; indeed, the first person he told of his sighting of the beast on land in just this area was none other than Constance Whyte. Sadly, Macleod's account of his sighting is unsatisfactory on a number of counts. The sketch which he produced of how the monster appeared through binoculars at a distance of about a mile is an impossible one. A monster, even a monster fifty feet long, could not have appeared through the lenses of low-powered 7 × 50 binoculars with the dramatic size Macleod showed. The object would in fact have appeared relatively small. Macleod's 'monster' bears some resemblance to the object seen and sketched by Dr Kirton in November 1933, which was almost certainly nothing more than a man in a fishing boat (see illustration).[2] As time went by Macleod elaborated his story, contradicting himself in quite major ways. The version given in Dinsdale's *Loch Ness Monster* fails to tally with Macleod's description of the animal's features and behaviour given in David James's booklet *Loch Ness Investigation*. Even the weather is different in these two accounts. In the earlier version Macleod claimed that 'The weather was dull and overcast, with a drizzle drifting down the loch.' Later, however, he described how 'The animal kept turning itself in the sunshine.'[3]

The evidence for the Loch Ness monster coming ashore is highly dubious, riddled with inconsistencies, and provides important clues to the solution of the mystery. It has not prevented credulous writers from offering spinechilling

1 *More Than a Legend*, pp. 59–60.
2 See *The Loch Ness Monster and Others*, pp. 79–80.
3 *Loch Ness Investigation*, p. 18.

Figure 2

(i) Monster seen by Dr J. Kirton at a distance of 1¼ miles with the naked eye.

(ii) Monster seen by Torquil Macleod through 7 × 50 binoculars at a range of one mile.

(iii) How Macleod's 'monster' would actually have looked through 7 × 50 binoculars at a range of one mile.

warnings that visitors to Loch Ness may find themselves unexpectedly face to face with the largest land animals in the world.

In the beginning the Loch Ness monster myth perhaps only involved a harmless combination of expectation and imagination, fuelled by a Press hungry for sensation, which in turn found individuals who willingly craved publicity. But when the first photographs of the beast began to appear a new element entered the story – deliberate deception.

ii

'I wish you wouldn't keep appearing and vanishing so suddenly: you make one quite giddy.'
'All right', said the Cat; and this time it vanished quite slowly, beginning with the end of the tail, and ending with the grin, which remained some time after the rest of it had gone.

    Lewis Carroll, *Alice's Adventures in Wonderland* (1865)

When the photographic evidence for the Loch Ness monster is examined two things stand out. One is the sheer paucity of film evidence gathered over fifty years. The other is how dissimilar all the photographs are. Considering the extraordinary numbers of people who have lurked at the lochside, cameras in hand, it does seem odd that so few have managed to photograph the monster. There is an immense disparity between the volume of eye-witness sightings and the number of photographs obtained on these occasions. So many of the original 'classic' monster photographs were taken by people who claimed they were not even looking for the creature. The good fortune of such individuals is in perplexing contrast with the fruitless results of a decade of intensive observation of Loch Ness between 1962 and 1972.

What photographic evidence there is resembles the eye-witness evidence by virtue of its contradictions and ambiguities. Believers would argue that this is because the monster exhibits a variety of shapes and behaviour patterns. A more obvious solution would be that a variety of phenomena have been photographed. Once the monster photographs are submitted to critical examination it is surprising how many of them collapse as evidence for an unknown animal in the loch.

To start with perhaps the most famous monster snap of them all, the so-called 'surgeon's photograph.' (*Plate* 1.) This was actually the first of two snaps (for the second see *Plate* 2.) taken in April 1934 by Lieutenant Colonel Robert Kenneth Wilson, a London gynaecologist. It purports to show the head and neck of the monster, just before it dived out of sight. Writers on the subject, while admitting that the circumstances in which the photographs were obtained have never been entirely clear, repeatedly emphasize Dr Wilson's *respectability*. A hoax, they imply, is simply out of the question, even though Wilson himself was later very cagey about the whole affair. This, they state, was simply the proper and understandable discretion of a medical man. For a man who didn't want publicity however Dr Wilson did two curious things. Firstly he took his film to an Inverness chemist and announced that he believed he had photographed the Loch Ness monster. Secondly, he sold the film to the *Daily Mail*. But there is one other circumstance of Wilson's photograph which is so remarkable that it is strange that no-one has ever commented on it before. This is the date on which it was taken. When was that? 'April of 1934,' says Tim Dinsdale in *Loch Ness Monster*; 'early one morning in April 1934,' adds F. W. Holiday in *The Great Orm of Loch Ness*; 'early April,' agrees Witchell in *The Loch Ness Story*; 'April 1934' says Costello in *In Search of Lake Monsters*. Although clearly identified in Gould's *Loch Ness Monster and Others* (1934) the date was not mentioned again until forty years later, in Professor Mackal's *The Monsters of Loch Ness*: April 1st, 1934.

Mackal appears not to grasp the cultural significance of April 1st in British life. The fact that the most famous photograph of the monster was produced on All Fools Day must inevitably cast doubts on its authenticity as evidence for an unknown animal in Loch Ness.

According to all the books about the Loch Ness monster

Wilson took his photograph almost by accident, when he stopped his car at approximately seven o'clock in the morning. Wilson told a very different story to the *Daily Mail* (21 April 1934), remarking 'at about mid-day I decided to stop and enjoy a quiet smoke at the lochside. I got my camera out of the car and made it ready in case I should see the monster. After a few minutes stroll I saw a sudden commotion in the water.' The object was, he estimated, between 100 and 300 yards away. The angle of the shadow cast by the object certainly suggests that it probably was photographed at noon.

The question of what Wilson actually photographed will perhaps never be answered. The ring of ripples around the object in the first photograph certainly gives the impression of life and animation, and it just possible that it shows an otter's tail or a diving bird such as a cormorant. Alternatively it may simply have been a model which Wilson threw into the loch. Maurice Burton has perceptively observed that 'The ripples in the Wilson photo are typical of an object entering water rather than something being thrust up from below.' There is also the question of scale. If the object was photographed on a telephoto lens at a range of only one hundred yards then it was clearly something quite small – possibly only ten or twelve inches in height.[1]

The available evidence points strongly in the direction of a hoax. Apart from the date on which the photographs were taken there is the fact that in later years Wilson's youngest son bluntly admitted that his father's pictures were fraudulent. All this ties in with Maurice Burton's experience: 'When I contacted Wilson himself, in quest of further details, he replied tersely that he made no claim to having photographed a monster and did not believe in it anyway.'

1 One problem in dealing with this famous photograph is the large variety of prints which have been published. The print shown in Gould's and Dinsdale's books is a partial enlargement. On a postcard stall in Inverness we purchased a print with a slightly wider field of vision than in the most commonly reproduced version, and even this may have been subject to enlargement and trimming.

To show how easy it is to create a photograph of this sort *Plate* 3 shows a fake made by the author.

If Wilson's intention was to pull legs his success was, and has been for half a century, spectacular. Two days after publishing the first photograph the *Daily Mail* reported, 'Yesterday thousands of people visited the loch hoping to catch a glimpse of the monster. A line of motor cars travelled down both sides of the loch.'

Ultimately the 'respectability' of the photographer remains an irrelevance. As Ronald Millar has shown in his fascinating study *The Piltdown Men*, the greatest hoax of twentieth-century British science, the notorious 'Piltdown man' skull, was perpetrated by at least one eminent professional figure with a string of qualifications.[1]

There is even a curious resemblance between the way in which Wilson afterwards covered himself by saying in effect 'here is an object photographed in Loch Ness – make of it what you will' and the care which Grafton Elliot Smith took to cover himself against the charge of credulity by carefully emphasizing that he had only ever worked with a plaster cast of the Piltdown skull.

There is one other feature of Wilson's photographs which renders them worthless as scientific evidence for an unknown animal in Loch Ness. This is simply that there is no land background in either of them: the objects might have been photographed in Hyde Park's Round Pond for all anyone can tell. The same objection can be levelled against the first photograph of the monster ever taken, Hugh Gray's 1933 snapshot. (*Plate* 4). It shows an area of water on the surface of which a blurred and indistinct serpentine shape appears to be thrashing around. The film was taken to a chemist in Inverness on 1st December 1933 by Hugh Gray's brother. It may or may not be significant that this was just

1 See Ronald Millar, *The Piltdown Men* (London: Gollancz, 1972). An astonishing inventory of modern scientific frauds has been compiled by T. J. Hamblin in his article 'Fake!', *British Medical Journal* (19–26 December 1981), pp. 1671–4.

after Commander Gould's dramatic press communiqué announcing that Loch Ness contained a sea-serpent had appeared in the *Inverness Courier* (29 November 1933). Gray claimed that the monster had surfaced only a hundred yards or so from where he was standing. Unfortunately he did not have an opportunity to observe the creature closely because of the spray, and because he was busy with his camera. The photograph was sold to the *Daily Record*, and the original negative lost. It remains an inconclusive and unsatisfactory piece of evidence. We have been to the site of the Gray sighting and taken comparative photographs. The absence of any shoreline foliage in Gray's picture is slightly surprising. For the mystery object to have been where Gray claimed it was in the loch its dimensions would truly have been enormous to have appeared in such a way on his film, especially if (as seems likely) he was using a simple camera with a lens of ordinary focal length.[1]

It would be interesting to know, too, whether Hugh Gray was related to 'A. Gray', another inhabitant of Foyers, whose efforts to catch the monster using wire, hooks, and a barrel were reported in the *Inverness Courier* of 30 May 1933, at a time when scarcely anyone apart from Alex Campbell gave the monster any credence at all. Hugh Gray subsequently had the good fortune to see the monster on five more occasions, but failed to obtain any more photographs.

No-one can complain that Lachlan Stuart's world-famous photograph of a three-humped monster lacks background (*Plate* 5). Taken in July 1951 the photograph clearly shows the shoreline in the region of Urquhart Castle, with the castle promontory itself visible in the middle of the picture. The picture has proved something of a problem to monster believers, not least because of the peculiarly sharp angles of

1 Even a fervent believer like Tim Dinsdale has, over the years, changed his mind about the Gray photograph. He is noticeably cool about it in his children's book *The Story of the Loch Ness Monster*, where he remarks, 'It does not show very much of anything. The print has either been touched up, or light has spoiled the picture. There are other features in it which are peculiar.'

the humps. Peter Costello finds it 'an unlikely picture of a live animal'; F. W. Holiday, unable to reconcile Stuart's monster with his own 'great orm' theory ignores it altogether. Whatever the objects are they are certainly astonishingly close to the shore. When pressed as to what he thought he had photographed, thirty-year-old Stuart replied, 'perhaps a prehistoric monster.'

There are serious objections to regarding Stuart's photograph as evidence for an unknown animal in the loch. Firstly there is nothing in the photograph which shows the humps to be animate, for example leaving a wake. Secondly, the humps are, when examined closely, out of alignment. The middle hump is closer to the camera than the one on the right, and the base of the hump on the left fails to align with the other two. Thirdly, the objects photographed are extremely close to the shore and in shallow water. Rather naively Constance Whyte wrote, 'Apparently the camera cannot lie.' She also mistakenly believed that rocks at Loch Ness 'are all within a yard or two of the shore.' In fact, as our own photographs demonstrate, it is remarkably easy to produce ambiguous pictures of objects such as rocks in Loch Ness (*Plates* 6(a) and (b)).

It is always interesting to consider the context in which photographs of the Loch Ness monster appear. For example, in autumn 1958 H. L. Cockrell produced a new photograph of what he half-heartedly asserted 'could' have been 'Nessie'. In 1958 however the loch was ripe for a new photograph. The previous year the mystery had been revived by the publication of Mrs Whyte's *More Than a Legend*, which rescued the monster from over twenty years of neglect and obscurity. Soon a number of expeditions were announced, the BBC came up with a documentary, 'The Legend of the Loch', broadcast in May 1958, and the British film industry made *Behemoth the Sea Monster*, allegedly inspired by the Ness enigma. Cockrell was leaping on a bandwagon which had already begun rolling when he announced to the press details of his own one-man expedition. On his third day at the loch Cockrell claimed to have experienced a terrifyingly close encounter with the monster. His 'monster' greatly resembles a floating stick; in some prints of the photograph it is even possible to see *through* the curving 'hump'. Cockrell described how a squall blew up and he lost sight of the object. When he paddled to the spot in his canoe he did indeed find a stick. (*Plate* 8).

The photograph provided Cockrell with a convenient climax to a series of articles which he published that autumn in the *Weekly Scotsman*. Within days a reader had sent in *his* monster snap, which also showed an ambiguous, low dark object on the surface of the loch. This was the MacNab photograph, sent in by the photographer himself, and allegedly taken three years earlier (*Plate* 7). MacNab claimed that while standing on the road above Urquhart Castle his attention had been caught by 'a movement' in the water. 'Naturally I thought of the monster,' he wrote, a suspicion confirmed by 'a quick glance' which 'showed that some black or dark enormous water creature was cruising on the surface.' He then took his photograph. Unfortunately no-one else in the vicinity saw this enormous beast.

> My son was busy under the bonnet of the car at the time and when he looked in response to my shouts there were just ripples on the water. Several cars and a bus stopped but they could see nothing and listened to my description with patent disbelief.

MacNab's photograph is certainly a remarkable one. Without question it shows a section of Loch Ness around Urquhart Castle. The height of the castle proved useful in measuring the length of the object. The 'monster' was actually longer than the sixty-four feet high castle tower! One hump alone appeared to be at least fifty-five feet long, and that was only the section showing above the surface. Perplexed by the size of MacNab's monster some believers have concluded that he must have photographed two animals, swimming chummily along, one behind the other.

We know the area shown in the Macnab photograph well, and we have both spent many days observing the loch at this point from the old Loch Ness Investigation Strone camera station. It seems to us that the phenomenon which MacNab photographed could easily be a wave effect resulting from three trawlers travelling closely together up the loch. In some prints of this photograph a wake effect appears to be visible *ahead* of the 'monster', suggesting that it was indeed caused by a boat or boats travelling toward Fort Augustus, and hidden from view beyond Strone point. The only thing that is odd about MacNab's photograph is the density which the body of the wave appears to possess. Wakes can produce the illusion of solid bodies, but rarely in such a pronounced fashion. A solution to this mystery may be provided by Roy Mackal's curious discovery that there are two versions of the MacNab photograph.[1] As Mackal comments, 'If the object did, indeed, appear on the water in the original negative exposed of the scene, why was it necessary to rephotograph the "original" print, with the resulting two different versions?'

Two years later the *Weekly Scotsman* came up with another sensational photograph which was equally unconvincing as a photograph of a living animal. This was the O'Connor photograph. Peter O'Connor was a publicity-seeking twenty-six-year-old Gateshead fireman who dramatically announced to the *Sunday Express* that he intended to lead an expedition of sixty people to Loch Ness to kill the monster, using an arsenal of weapons which included Bren-guns and a bomb. In the event the sixty expedition members and the weapons failed to materialise, nor was any organisation prepared to finance such an obviously crackpot scheme. O'Connor subsequently claimed to have visited Loch Ness in May 1960 with a tent, a friend, and a Brownie camera. Within four days O'Connor claimed he had seen the monster twice. His second sighting was the most spectacular and occurred at 6.30 a.m., when no-one else was about. According to O'Connor the monster swam past his campsite, only yards from the shore, whereupon he waded in up to his waist and took a flashlight photograph. When asked why the

1 See *The Monsters of Loch Ness*, Appendix C, pp. 273–6.

monster had not reacted to his presence O'Connor's reply 'was simple and straightforward. He *didn't* splash. Trained as a Royal Marine Commando, and as a frogman, he said that he had been taught how to move through water without a sound.'[1]

O'Connor also explained that the light-meter setting on his camera was wrong, so that unfortunately the background of the photograph was in complete darkness. The monster could be forty feet long and in Loch Ness; alternatively it might be three feet long and in the Serpentine. The object which O'Connor photographed greatly resembles the top half of a large brown loaf.[2] It appears to be motionless, and there are no signs of the wake which one would certainly expect to be generated by a huge animal swimming through water at extremely close range.

Oddly, O'Connor did not immediately announce his great achievement but waited three weeks, until 16 June. Significantly this was just three days after Tim Dinsdale had been interviewed by the *Daily Mail* on the subject of his sensational motion film of the monster, shown on BBC television the same day. The Loch Ness monster was once again hitting the headlines, and the moment could not have been more opportune for O'Connor to step forward and reap the publicity which he so evidently craved. Subsequently O'Connor received further publicity in Dinsdale's best-selling *Loch Ness Monster*, which treated his photograph and various sightings with great seriousness. For many years O'Connor's photograph was prominently displayed at the public exhibition maintained by the Loch Ness Investigation Bureau. In the nineteen-seventies the O'Connor photograph increasingly fell into disrepute. Roy Mackal (in *The Monsters of Loch Ness*) and Nicholas Witchell (in *The Loch Ness Story*) both identified it as dubious; Tim Dinsdale cautiously deleted all mention of O'Connor in later editions of *Loch Ness Monster*. O'Connor's photograph is conspicuously absent

1 Tim Dinsdale, *Loch Ness Monster*, p. 156.
2 O'Connor refused permission for his photograph to be reproduced in this book.

from the Loch Ness Monster Exhibition recently set up at Drumnadrochit.

In her book *The Search for Morag* (1972), published when the Loch Ness Investigation Bureau was still at Loch Ness, Elizabeth Montgomery Campbell explained that the Bureau was only interested in movie film of the beast:

> The Bureau has never set out to obtain still pictures as these would be unacceptable as evidence. Too many fakes have already been offered to the Press and sometimes published. I recall one which was produced by photographing the loch with a cut-out paper 'monster' dangled on thread in front of the camera. The result was far too crude to have deceived any experienced person, and of course the Bureau was not consulted, the picture was published, and one more hoaxer had his moment of triumph.

Mrs Campbell's image of the monster fraternity's sturdy scepticism is difficult to substantiate, as the case of Frank Searle shows. Searle, an ex-soldier, arrived at Loch Ness in 1969 and led a squatter's existence in a makeshift tent at the lochside, surviving frugally on his army pension. For three years he watched the loch, reporting a number of sightings but failing to obtain any photographs. Although not officially a member of the Loch Ness Investigation he was regarded by the Bureau as being sympathetic with its main aims. Searle acquired a growing reputation as a dedicated independent investigator. In July 1972 L.N.I. members received a newsletter from David James, head of the Bureau, announcing that

> The Dores area is now officially covered by Frank Searle who has been living in a tent near the shore at Balacladaich Farm for nearly three years. He has recorded at least 14 sightings of wakes and humps and is an experienced and reliable watcher.

No-one was more pleased than the Loch Ness Investigation when, the very same month, Searle suddenly produced a sensational monster photograph. The picture received widespread publicity, including a full-page spread in the *Daily Mirror* of 1 September 1972, which commented,

> Yesterday it was hailed as a classic by the Loch Ness Phenomena Investigation Bureau. The Bureau's young American secretary, Miss Holly Arnold, 25, said: 'This is a really good picture – most exciting indeed. It's the first one in years to show any kind of detail.' .

Searle was suddenly a celebrity. Afterwards he boasted, 'Reporters from the big national dailies, and a television unit, were dashing round the loch looking for me. Next day I and my picture appeared in all the big dailies, and I was on television. People started coming to see me. I began to get letters.' Before long he had erected a sign at the roadside directing visitors to 'the Frank Searle Loch Ness Investigation', where a prominently-displayed jamjar solicited donations for 'further research'.

The Searle photograph was unimpressive; indeed it greatly resembled a tree trunk. There was even what looked very much like a branch sticking out to the right of the second 'hump'. But Searle's puritan dedication to the cause had established his credibility with the monster faithful. In their eyes his long and fruitless sojourn had at last been rewarded with what seemed to be a well-deserved success. At the end of the year Searle featured prominently in the Bureau's list of authenticated sightings.

It was embarrassing therefore when Searle went on to produce a series of increasingly clumsy photographs purporting to be of the monster. The objects portrayed were clearly neither animate nor very large. If Frank Searle had restricted the number of his sightings and been less prolific and inept in producing his Nessie pictures he would probably have won himself a place in the annals of classic monster photography. As it was his celebrity lasted for about a year, after which it became clear he had over-reached himself. Few believers could seriously accept that Searle's photographs showed a huge unknown living animal. In *The Loch Ness Story* Nicholas Witchell launched a bitter attack on Searle, unhesitatingly identifying him as one of 'the fakers', but diplomatically omitting to mention the way in which the Bureau had allowed itself to be fooled.[1]

In recent years other photographic evidence has been published, all of it characterised by ambiguity and a failure to provide clear proof of an immense unknown living animal surging along the loch's surface. The 1977 Anthony Shiels photograph has been widely reproduced, and appears on the cover of the latest edition of Dinsdale's *Loch Ness Monster*. It is an unconvincing picture of a motionless 'head and neck'. The photographer, 'Doc' Shiels, is a professional Punch and Judy man and self-styled 'psychic entertainer'. He told *Titbits* magazine, 'I am sure Nessie appeared as a result of my psychic powers.' Shiels has also had the good fortune to photograph 'Morgawr, the monster of Falmouth Bay'.[2]

Of the various hoaxes related to monsters over the years photographic hoaxes tend to be the ones that endure the longest. The classic monster photographs yield a multiplicity of interpretations, and there is nothing monster buffs enjoy more than scrutinising these photographs and discovering exciting new details which no-one else has spotted. Unfortunately it is all too easy to fake monster pictures, and at the close of the nineteen-fifties one man came to realise that still photographs on their own would never convince a sceptical world. That man was Tim Dinsdale, who went to Loch Ness for the first time in April 1960, armed with a movie camera and telephoto lens. The sensational result of Dinsdale's expedition was to inspire an extraordinary revival of the mystery and trigger two decades of intensive surveillance of the loch's baffling surface.

1 A highly entertaining account of the human side to the Loch Ness story at this time is provided in Dan Greenburg's 'Japanese Come to Catch Loch Ness Monster: A Penetrating Account of a Big-Game Hunt That Never Quite Got Beneath the Surface', *Oui* (May 1974), pp. 51–122.
2 For more about Shiels's wearisome exploits in the world of the bizarre and fantastic the reader should consult Janet and Colin Bord's *Alien Animals* (1980).

7 The Dinsdale Film

The countenance of Ben Nevis was darkened by an angry flush. 'Loch Ness Monster imaginary?' he exclaimed in stupefaction. 'Imaginary? I don't know what the world's coming to. I really don't. Oh, I see this expedition of mine is going to be absolutely necessary.'

Compton Mackenzie, *The Rival Monster* (1952)

Tim Dinsdale came to the monster relatively late in life, when he was in his mid-thirties. Only months before taking his dramatic piece of movie film he had barely heard of the Loch Ness monster.

In 1959 Dinsdale was an aeronautical engineer on the brink of redundancy. The spark which lit the fire of his curiosity was an article about the monster in *Everybody's Magazine* (21 February 1959). That night Dinsdale found himself tossing restlessly in his sleep, brooding about the enigma. He dreamed he was at Loch Ness, on its steep jutting shores, peering down into its inky depths, waiting for the legendary beast to burst into view.

In the weeks and months that followed Dinsdale became increasingly obsessed by the mystery. He sat late into the night, poring over the published sighting reports. 'I could scarcely believe it because it was like proving that a Unicorn existed!' he commented afterwards, '*And yet, I could not doubt the truth of what I had read.*' (Our italics.)

Alex Campbell's 'classic' sighting, quoted extensively in the *Everybody's Magazine* article, seems to have exerted an immense influence upon Dinsdale. He subsequently gave it pride of place at the beginning and end of *Loch Ness Monster*, the book which he subsequently wrote about his first visit to the loch. This, of course, was the bogus sighting which, unbeknown to Dinsdale, Campbell had retracted, attributing his 'monster' to a line of cormorants.

As far as Dinsdale was concerned, having studied the literature on the subject he 'no longer had any doubt at all' about the monster's reality. Without having visited Loch Ness, spoken to a single eye-witness or having examined the curious origins of the myth Dinsdale had persuaded himself of the creature's existence.

The following spring he drove north to the loch, and there, at the end of a week's exploration, on the very morning of his departure, Dinsdale shot a brief piece of film of a mysterious object churning its way across Loch Ness.

The Dinsdale film remains famous as the only piece of movie film of the monster which is at all credible. The film itself is not all that spectacular. Shot on 16mm equipment, using black and white film, Dinsdale's footage shows a dark indistinct blob moving across Loch Ness at a distance of one mile, then changing course and travelling parallel with the shore.

The film is important in various ways. Firstly it is the one piece of motion film to show a large unidentified object moving on the surface of Loch Ness. There can be no quarrel with the fact that *something* is present on the loch, or with the fact that it was shot at Loch Ness. A hoax can be ruled out. Secondly Tim Dinsdale is a man of great sincerity, and his passionate devotion to the cause has been without parallel. Since 1960 he has devoted his entire life to proving that the monster exists. It says something for his integrity that after two decades of questing he willingly admits that he has drawn a blank. In almost a quarter of a century he has had only two further brief, inconclusive sightings. He has failed absolutely to obtain any further photographs or film.

Dinsdale's fruitless quest starkly highlights the unreliability of other figures at Loch Ness who have claimed numerous sightings or peddled ridiculous and obviously-faked snap- shots of the beast.

In 1966 the status of Dinsdale's film soared when it was analysed by R.A.F. photographic experts at the Joint Air Reconnaissance Intelligence Centre (JARIC) who commented that what the film showed was 'probably an animate object'. Believers greeted the report with rapture. Here, at long last, was conclusive proof of the monster's existence. It was a turning point in the investigation.

Impressive as all this sounds, the truth is that there is nothing about Dinsdale's film to support the belief that he filmed a large unknown animal. Ironically, Dinsdale's own detailed account of the circumstances in which he took his film (given in his book *Loch Ness Monster*), combined with JARIC's analysis, help to reveal just what did happen at Loch Ness that bright April morning all those years ago.

Tim Dinsdale arrived for the first time at Loch Ness on 16 April 1960. He was in a state of considerable fatigue, having spent twenty-five hours out of the previous two days driving alone from London to the Highlands (this was in the days when motorways and fast dual-carriageways were still things of the future).

Dinsdale was in such a condition of stress and nervous excitement that upon first arriving at the loch he immediately saw a 'monster':

incredibly, two or three hundred yards from shore, I saw two sinuous grey humps breaking the surface with seven or eight feet of clear water showing between each!

Dinsdale jammed on the brakes and skidded to a halt in a shower of gravel. Hurling himself out of his car he began to fix his Bolex camera onto its tripod. Then, at the very last moment, he reached for his binoculars. The 'monster' was close enough for Dinsdale to recognise that it was simply a floating tree-trunk. Sheepishly he put the camera equipment away and drove on.

The problem of fatigue and tension was to worsen as Dinsdale's time at the loch wore on. He slept badly, and his mood alternated between bouts of black depression and elation. He visited local hierophants of the monster myth – authors J. A. Carruth and Constance Whyte, and Hugh Gray, the first person to photograph the beast – and his excitement began to mount when he heard of Torquil Macleod's dramatic land sighting eight weeks earlier. Later, back at the Foyers Hotel where Dinsdale was staying, two of the other guests reported seeing a strange V-wake moving down the middle of the loch. What was more there was blasting going on in the hills, and it was widely believed that the dynamiting of the new road in 1933 had stirred the monster from its subterranean slumbers.

By now Dinsdale was deeply excited. Inside him he had been nursing the fear that the monster might have died. Now he knew it still existed. Furthermore conditions for a sighting seemed perfect. At the same time he felt oppressed by despair and frustration. He had been at Loch Ness *three days* and *still* hadn't seen the beast. 'I knew that unless [the loch] gave up its secret soon I must fail in my quest; because within twenty-four hours I would be making unwilling preparations for the long and tedious journey home.'

Dinsdale was, by now, a man on the brink of nervous exhaustion. He had had no relaxation since his shattering two-day drive from London at the beginning of the week. In five days he had driven almost a thousand miles, alone. Afterwards Dinsdale confessed to the *Daily Mail* that he had slept only three hours each night.

At this point Dinsdale made his final pilgrimage. Ironically the person he set out to visit was none other than Alex Campbell. Dinsdale was overwhelmed with excitement to be talking at last to someone 'who had *actually* seen the Monster's head and neck protruding above the water. I knew without any last tremor of doubt that the huge back that people so often reported could not be that of a whale, or a porpoise, or seal, or any other type of ordinary creature.' No, Alex Campbell had confirmed the most important thing of all, that the monster really was a monster, huge in size and extraordinary in its anatomy.

Filled with new hope Dinsdale drove back through the evening dusk to the Foyers Hotel. By now it was eight o'clock and the light was poor, but Dinsdale, *'exhilarated by the thought of this last minute reprieve from failure'* (our italics) quickly set up his camera, 'and for the thousandth time scanned from left to right with every conscious effort.' And then, suddenly, at the very last moment, a thousand yards away at the mouth of the river below, there it was. The monster! Shaking with excitement Dinsdale pressed the button and began to film.

The huge animal was thrashing the surface of the loch in a manner familiar from a hundred eyewitness reports. Finger still pressed firmly on the trigger, Dinsdale was in no doubt about the beast's movements: 'I could see a violent disturbance – a churning ring of rough water, centering about two black shapes, rising and falling in the water!'

Then, with the monster still splashing about at the surface, Dinsdale decided on a bold gamble. Ceasing filming he ran for his car and drove at breakneck speed down the winding zig-zag road to Lower Foyers. He jumped from his car and ran along the shore to the river mouth, expecting to meet the monster at close quarters. But when he reached the tip of the delta all he found was the smooth-flowing river and a deserted loch. The monster had vanished into the depths again.

Dinsdale had planned to leave the very next morning, Friday 22 April. But Alex Campbell's words had had 'a remarkable effect' upon him, influencing him to delay his return by twenty-four hours. Dinsdale still felt frustrated. He had succeeded in filming the monster but the light had been bad and the creature had shown little of its body. Dinsdale was after bigger game: conclusive, incontrovertible proof of the beast's existence. For that he would need good film of the creature's head and neck.

His extra day at Loch Ness turned out to be wasted. Dinsdale watched the loch in vain. In the evening he gloomily began to prepare for his departure the next morning. It was, he knew, impossible to delay his return any longer.

Despite the long drive ahead of him that day Dinsdale nevertheless rose at dawn on the morning of Saturday 23 April and excitedly drove to the Fort Augustus end of the loch, for one last enthusiastic surveillance of Borlum Bay (where Alex Campbell had seen his 'monster') and the Horseshoe scree, scene of Torquil Macleod's extraordinary land sighting.

It was in vain. Three and a half hours later Dinsdale gave up and drove back toward the hotel. The situation was now *identical* to the circumstances of the previous Thursday evening when he had dreamed of *a last minute reprieve from failure*. As Dinsdale drove back across the hills, out of sight of the loch, he seems to have had a curious premonition that he might yet see the fabulous beast. He pulled up and went through the complicated motions of setting up the tripod and camera.

Sure enough, as Dinsdale cruised through Upper Foyers and slowly downhill to the hotel, he looked down at the loch in the few 'fleeting seconds' that it came into view and saw the monster. There it was, as if by a miracle – the monster's huge hump breaking the surface.

It had 'a curious *reddish brown* hue' which could be seen distinctly with the naked eye. Thrilled, Dinsdale began filming the monster as it moved away across the loch and then headed south-west towards Invermoriston. But a glance at the footage indicator told him that there was only fifteen feet of film left in the camera. Dismayed, he stopped the camera. He needed that precious supply of film in case the creature came back across the loch, head and neck held high. By now the animal was moving away from him and Dinsdale was faced by an agonizing predicament. On a sudden impulse he decided to shorten the distance between himself and the beast. He knew that he could drive to the water's edge in just a very few minutes, 'two or three at most'. Arriving at the lochside a brief glance was enough to tell him that he had lost his gamble. The monster had once again dived from view. There was nothing to be seen anywhere on the water surface. For an hour he waited there, watching, but the animal did not re-appear.

Dinsdale returned to the hotel. After breakfast he arranged to film the hotel proprietor's dinghy in roughly the same place where he had seen the monster, so that a 'scientific' comparison of size could be made. Dinsdale then had lunch and set off on the long journey south to Reading, mission accomplished.

At Fort Augustus he stopped briefly at the post office and despatched a lengthy cable to the British Museum, dramatically informing them that on 21 and 23 April 1960 he had exposed several hundred feet of film of a large unknown animal in Loch Ness. The Museum authorities were not, it seems, very impressed.

The rest of the story is well known. On 13 June Dinsdale gave an exclusive interview to the *Daily Mail*, telling the paper's readers that there was definitely *one* monster in Loch Ness. There might even be *two*, 'possibly three ... Each monster would probably live more than 200 years.' He did not reveal the logic or the evidence which led him to these remarkable deductions.

Stills from the film shot on 23 April were sold to numerous newspapers, both in Britain and abroad. The film itself was first shown on BBC television's 'Panorama' programme (invited guest: Alex Campbell) and released to TV news services around the world. Excitedly, Dinsdale told the *Mail*, 'My film could be the key at last to starting a proper scientific expedition. I would like to go back. But funds will have to be raised first.'

These words were prophetic. The film did indeed inspire a host of new expeditions, ranging from amateur one-man vigils to the more sophisticated endeavours of the Loch Ness Phenomena Investigation Bureau, which in its heyday in the late sixties had over one thousand members, and which mounted a massive surveillance of Loch Ness over a ten year period.

Dinsdale's film was important in persuading the uncommitted that there really was something in the Loch Ness mystery. As Roy Mackal has admitted, these early expeditions were not encouraging:

> No results, and nothing to make me decide anything – except to forget the whole matter. If this had been all there were, I am convinced that at this point I would have washed my hands of Loch Ness permanently.
>
> The one thing that would not go away was the Dinsdale film sequence. Although it was grainy in quality because of the great distance involved in the photography I could not explain it, try as I would. It alone was sufficient for me.[1]

In all the excitement one ambiguous aspect of Dinsdale's sensational achievement had been forgotten. The film which appeared on television and propelled Dinsdale to fame was the *second* film of the monster which he had taken. What, then, of the first film, which had shown the monster thrashing about at the mouth of the River Foyers?

In *Loch Ness Monster* Dinsdale abruptly dismisses this embarrassing matter. His first 'monster' was, he explains, 'no more than the wash and swirl of waves around a hidden shoal of rocks; caused by a sudden squall of wind!' He had, in fact, as he ruefully admitted 'been fooled completely', which was unfortunate since he had used up most of his film on this phoney monster.[2]

1 *The Monsters of Loch Ness*, p. 13. Mackal later retracts this, commenting 'Before sonar contact with a large animate target was first made in 1968, we had often doubted if there really *were* unexplained creatures in Loch Ness' (p.53).
2 In quoting the circumstances of the sighting earlier we deliberately omitted Dinsdale's retrospective qualifying phrases ('I *thought* I could see ... what *appeared* to be ...') in order to capture the flavour of his original certainty and excitement. Throughout *Loch Ness Monster* Dinsdale plays down the significance of his false sighting, and the film he shot has never been reproduced in any of his books.

It remains a curious coincidence that Dinsdale filmed his second 'monster' just two days later from almost the same spot, in much the same location, and in an identical condition of psychological tension and excitement. He even repeated his earlier impulsive action of rushing off down to the loch shore, only to find by the time that he arrived there that his 'monster' had gone.

Could Tim Dinsdale also have been 'fooled completely' on the second occasion of his sighting and filming a monster? Zoologist Maurice Burton certainly believed so. Burton pointed out the undeniable fact that the object in Dinsdale's film *could not be identified for shape*. It was just a blob, moving on the loch's surface at extreme range. Dinsdale claimed to have been able to make out details of the monster's back, but in Burton's opinion his description was consistent with 'a row of sou'-westers worn by several men sitting in a line from stem to stern in a 15-foot dinghy – no uncommon sight on Loch Ness.'[1] This explanation seemed farfetched and unsatisfactory, since the fishermen of the loch almost always fish alone or in pairs.

Dinsdale responded to Burton's criticism with a prickly comment in his Postscript to the second impression of *Loch Ness Monster*: 'there had been,' he said, 'some fatuous criticism of the film, brushing it aside as a simple case of mistaken identity involving a local motor boat – blandly ignoring the fact that I had deliberately included a local motor boat afterwards to provide this comparison.'[2]

What neither Burton nor Dinsdale mentioned was that their opinions of each other's judgement were coloured by strong personal feelings. Though few were to realise this

1 *The Elusive Monster*, p. 74.
2 According to Peter Costello (*In Search of Lake Monsters*, Panther edition, p. 91) Burton later alleged that Dinsdale had filmed a motor boat owned by a local man, Jack Forbes. From our own enquiries at Foyers we have learned that there was a man living there in 1960 called *Jock* Forbes, but he was a farmer and did not own a boat. Burton still insists that in 1960 'a local farmer was in the habit of crossing from Foyers on a Saturday at that time with cargo.'

afterwards the two men actually knew each other *before* Dinsdale headed north to Loch Ness in the Spring of 1960. In a long-forgotten article in the *Illustrated London News* (20 February 1960) Burton discussed the Surgeon's photograph, remarking that if it could be put 'beyond reasonable doubt' that it was genuine then 'everything else drops into place.' This, he went on,

> is where Mr T. K. Dinsdale comes into the arena.
>
> Mr Dinsdale is an aeronautical engineer by profession, experienced in the study and interpretation of photographs, and he has made a very detailed analysis of this picture.

There then followed a lengthy quotation from Dinsdale's extremely subjective and unconvincing analysis of 'barely discernible' ripples in the photograph, much the same as the one subsequently incorporated in *Loch Ness Monster*. Dinsdale had sent his 'analysis', unsolicited, to Burton, who had been deeply impressed, concluding that he was 'now convinced beyond all doubt' that the photograph was genuine and the monster a living reality. By this time the two men were on such good terms that Dinsdale actually borrowed the camera which he later used to film the monster from the Burton household.

The break between them was not long in coming, and it seems to have been caused by nothing more than the Dinsdale film itself. While Dinsdale basked in glory, became a celebrity and was commissioned to write a book about Nessie, Burton seems to have been undergoing a violent revulsion from the monster. While Dinsdale cheerfully worked at completing *Loch Ness Monster*, Burton hurriedly set about reversing all his previous opinions and doing his level best to demolish the case for the monster's existence. Dinsdale appears not to have known about his friend's sudden change of mind, since the first edition of his book obliquely referred to Burton's former enthusiasm for 'the Plesiosaur theory; to which, in all probability, many practising zoologists subscribe in private – and one, at least, openly.'

Burton meanwhile had hurried up to Loch Ness and based himself at Foyers for a few days. His luck was not equal to Dinsdale's, and he returned home and quickly wrote *The Elusive Monster*, which debunked much of the evidence – particularly evidence of the monster *in the water* – and ended with the icy comment, '*The Loch Ness Monster* (sic) by Tim Dinsdale appeared after this book had gone to press. It contains nothing to make me alter any of the opinions expressed here.'

In correspondence at this time Burton privately explained that one of the factors which had caused him to revise his former belief in the monster was the extraordinary transformation which he had witnessed in Dinsdale after his 'sighting'. This may well have been true, but Burton's own disenchantment with the monster was so abrupt that the suspicion seems reasonable that it was in no small part motivated by sour grapes.

Burton was undoubtedly wrong in identifying the mystery object in Dinsdale's film as a local fishing boat. But, equally, Dinsdale's defence of his film rested on some very dubious assertions. Dinsdale did not, as he frequently claims, film a 'motor boat' for comparison. He filmed a dinghy with an outboard motor. The difference is an important one, since although a dinghy's wake appears different from the wake of Dinsdale's 'monster', a motor boat's does not (*Plate* 14).

What is odd about Dinsdale's emphasis on the monster's wake is that it ignores his own much larger claim to have watched the beast through binoculars before beginning to film. Through his X7 binoculars Dinsdale claims he saw,

a long oval shape, a distinct mahogany colour and on the left flank a huge dark blotch ... like the dapple on a cow. For some reason it reminded me of the back of an African buffalo – it had fullness and girth and stood well above the water, and although I could see it from end to end there was no visible sign of a dorsal fin upon it; and then, abruptly, it began to move.[1]

Dinsdale's binocular evidence is crucial in deciding his reliability as a witness. Ironically the JARIC analysis contradicted Dinsdale's testimony on a number of important points and revealed his account to be inaccurate. Dinsdale produced a sketch of what he claimed he saw through his binoculars of the monster's back. The first thing to be said about this sketch is that it is not a true picture of what one sees through binoculars. The hour-glass shape which Dinsdale portrays owes more to the conventions of the cinema than to what anyone sees when looking through binoculars, which is simply a circular image. Secondly, even if Dinsdale was telling the truth about seeing the monster's back in the loch, he could not possibly have seen it with the size and detail which he portrays in his sketch. Dinsdale was using X7 binoculars, which are rather low-powered. Melodramatically, he told the *Daily Mail* his binoculars were 'powerful German ones used on espionage work'. With or without thrilling war-time associations they were still only of a X7 magnification. This is crucial, because as the JARIC analysis revealed, Dinsdale was much further away from the 'monster' than he believed at the time, and subsequently described in *Loch Ness Monster*. Dinsdale's estimate of the object's distance from himself was 1300 yards, but as JARIC showed it was almost a quarter of a mile further away.[2] Dinsdale's own map in *Loch Ness Monster* is wildly out of proportion, and JARIC commented that Dinsdale's mapping of the monster's route was grossly inaccurate. *On JARIC's own analysis the 'monster' could not possibly have appeared as Dinsdale claimed.*

There is a simple test which anyone can carry out for

1 *Loch Ness Monster*, p. 100. Dinsdale's description and sketch bear an uncanny resemblance to the plesiosaur. In the book Dinsdale admits that he took pictures of prehistoric animals with him to Loch Ness in 1960. It seems odd that he himself has never remarked on this resemblance.
2 See the Joint Air Reconnaissance Intelligence Centre (U.K.) Photographic Interpretation Report No. 66/1 (24 January 1966). The JARIC Report is published in Peter Costello's *In Search of Lake Monsters* (1974).

Figure 3

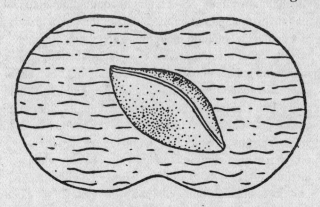

(i) The monster Tim Dinsdale saw through × 7 binoculars in 1960, at a range of one mile.

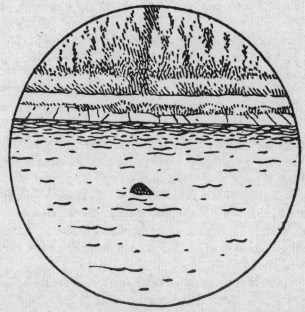

(ii) How the object would actually have appeared through × 7 binoculars at that range.

themselves, which is to go to Foyers, stand on the road where Dinsdale shot his film, and examine the area through X 7 binoculars. It is impossible to examine the area where Dinsdale's mystery object was through binoculars of this magnification and not capture within the lens a broad sweep of Loch Ness, including the opposite shore.

The conclusion must be that Dinsdale did not see the monster's back in the way that he claimed. What, then, *really* happened that Saturday morning in April all those years ago?

As Tim Dinsdale drove over the hill, half-expecting to see the monster, knowing it was his last chance to film it, his eye was caught by an object on the surface of the loch – an object which had 'a curious *reddish brown* hue about it which could be distinctly seen with the naked eye!' Thanks to JARIC we now know that this object was almost exactly *one mile* away. An object which appears reddish brown at such a distance is clearly something which is relatively brightly coloured. Reddish brown is a reasonable colour for a motor boat, but an unusual one for the Loch Ness monster (which is usually described by witnesses as being black or grey). This is an aspect of Dinsdale's film which is easily forgotten, since he used black and white film.

It is our belief that on seeing the distant motor boat Dinsdale screeched to a halt in a state of nervous excitement and immediately began filming. The object, which was following a course from the general direction of Foyers pier, then changed direction and moved parallel with the opposite shore at a speed of about 10 m.p.h.

Dinsdale claims that his film shows the monster submerging, but all that actually happens is that the object enters a band of shadow and becomes indistinct, a point confirmed by JARIC's analysis. This dark shadow had gone when Dinsdale later filmed the dinghy.

There is another remarkable feature of the Dinsdale film which has been left quietly undiscussed. This is the astonishing fact that as the 'monster' swam along the opposite shore a vehicle drove by on the road above. According to JARIC the vehicle has a length of 14 feet and is

1. and 2. The famous 'surgeon's photographs showing the
monster's head and neck. Taken by R. K. Wilson in April, 1934.

3. Fake photographed by the author.

4. The earliest photograph of the monster, taken by Hugh Gray in November,

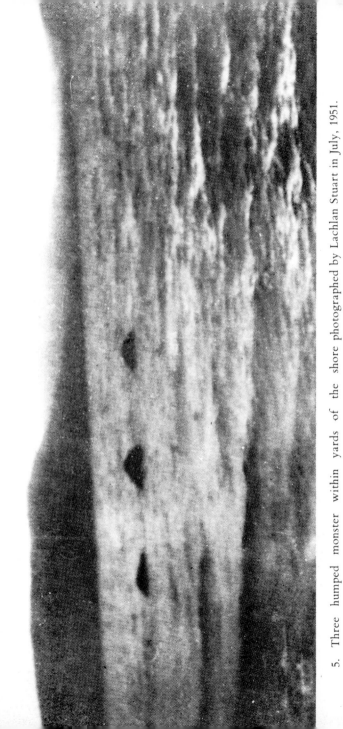

5. Three humped monster within yards of the shore photographed by Lachlan Stuart in July, 1951.

6. (a) and (b). A rock off-shore at Whitefield and a close-up of the same rock.

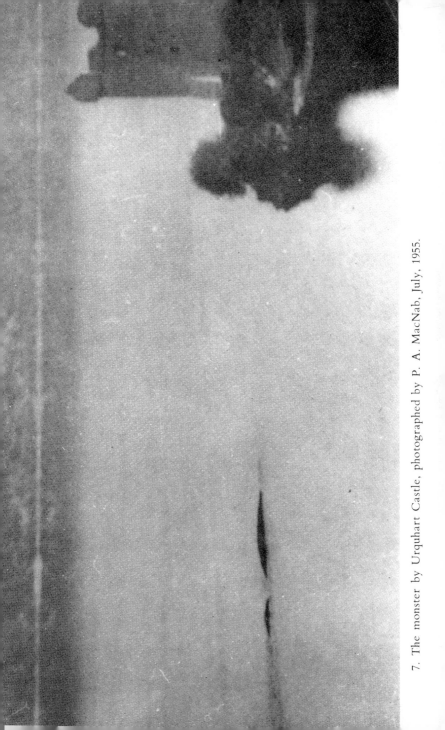

7. The monster by Urquhart Castle, photographed by P. A. MacNab, July, 1955.

8. H. L. Cockrell's photograph 1958.

9. A computer-enhanced photograph of the monster's flipper, taken underw
by Robert Rines/The Academy of Applied Science, August, 1972.

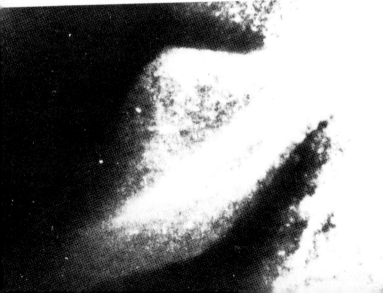

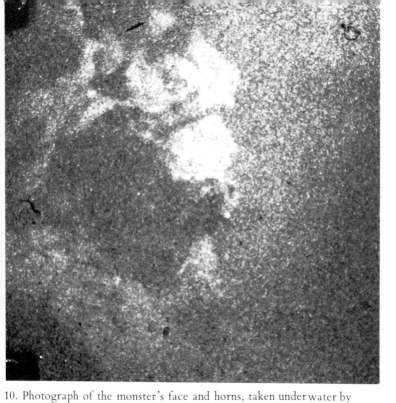

10. Photograph of the monster's face and horns, taken under water by Robert Rines/The Academy of Applied Science, June, 1975.

11. (a) and (b) Driftwood photographed on the shore of Loch Ness by the author.

11(b). Driftwood photographed on the shore of Loch Ness by the author.

12. The Lehn and Schroeder theory of the sea monster as an optical illusion (*see also opposite*).

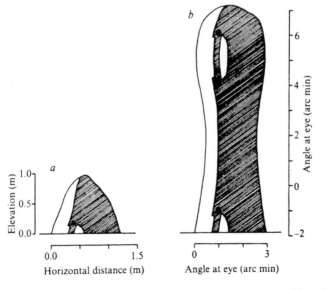

(a) The back of a killer whale. (b) The distorted image of the whale seen from a distance of 1.4 kilometres under mirage conditions.

Above. Lake Winnipeg, 28 May 1980. The boulder in centre foreground was identified as the source of the image below. It is about 68 cm wide and should show 30–35 cm above water on a calm day. *Below*. The boulder distorted into a merman shape, 3.17 pm. CDT (central daylight time), 2 May 1980. The image subtends 5.4, vertically and 2.2, horizontally. The photograph was made from a distance of 1.10 km using a mirror lens (focal length 1, 250 mm). The merman image of this boulder lasted for only a few minutes. Such conditions occur almost every spring on Lake Winnipeg.

13. Log floating in Loch Ness.

14. The wake of a motorboat on Loch Morar.

15. (a) Otter swimming.
    (b) Otters showing backs breaking surface.

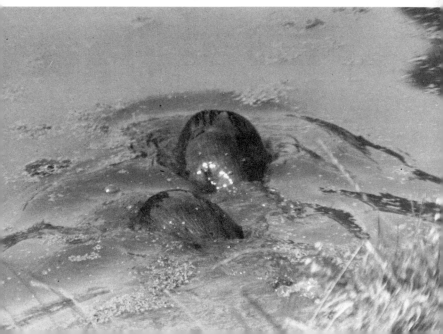

(c) and (d) Otter's tail breaking the surface.

(e) Otter on land.

(f) Otter making a long neck.

16. (a) A roe-deer swimming just off-shore at Loch Ness, 1975.
    (b) A roe-deer emerging from Loch Ness, 1975.

17. A great crested grebe

18. A cormorant

travelling at a speed of 39 m.p.h., 'possibly a family saloon or a small truck.'

The appearance of this vehicle in the film is extremely revealing. Traditionally the monster has always reacted violently to noise (car doors slamming, commands shouted by saints etc.). Dinsdale's mystery object merely continues on its way, unperturbed by the sound of a motor vehicle driving past *only one hundred yards away*. Secondly, the response of the driver is interesting. He (or she) *doesn't stop*. As Dinsdale's film shows the roadside along the opposite shore was bare of trees in 1960, giving drivers an unrestricted view of the loch at this point. The idea that a driver travelling at moderate speed along an empty road could have failed to have his or her attention caught by a huge monster swimming past a hundred yards away seems highly unlikely. The fact that the driver just kept going suggests that this was because the object passing by was something perfectly ordinary – a motor boat.

Finally, although the motor vehicle was only slightly further away from the camera than the 'monster' itself, JARIC were quite unable to identify it or even say whether it was a car or truck. The vehicle appears only as a blob. In the same way the motor boat that Dinsdale filmed at a range of one mile likewise lost definition and appears as a blob. A single frame of 16mm film measures only .4 × .3 inches at the film gate, so that when Dinsdale began filming the field of vision was already four hundred feet wide. His 'monster' consequently 'almost disappeared into the negative – the image, in fact, being only about .012 inches long.'[1]

With the film in his camera running low Dinsdale panicked, revved up his car, and raced down the hill to Lower Foyers. Missing his turning he drove round a small council estate (it would have been quicker to brake and reverse) and arrived back at the turning along which a dirt track led towards the loch shore. This impulsive action cost Dinsdale a good four or five minutes in wasted time

1　F. W. Holiday, *The Great Orm of Loch Ness* (London: Faber, 1968), p. 63.

(misleadingly in *Loch Ness Monster* he makes it all sound as if it happened in a matter of seconds).

By the time Dinsdale had run on to the pebbled shore of the loch the object, travelling at about 10 m.p.h., would have travelled about a mile, gaining Dinsdale nothing. The entire exercise was a complete waste of time. Despite the gloss of cool logical decision-making which Dinsdale put over the episode it suggests rather the state of excitement he was in. Indeed, although Dinsdale claims that shortage of film motivated his impulsive action this is contradicted by his admission earlier in his book that he had with him two back-up cameras, an 8mm cine and a 35mm still, for just such an eventuality.

Tim Dinsdale's claim that he could see the loch surface for miles in both directions from the point on the shore which he drove to is also deeply misleading, as anyone who bothers to visit the location can discover for themselves. His view up and down the loch was actually severely restricted by a rocky headland to the west, and by the delta of the river to the east. The 'monster' could have crossed the loch or returned to Foyers Bay and Dinsdale would not have been able to see it. *Significantly, he neither saw the mystery object appear nor disappear on the loch's surface.*

Contrary to the fond belief of the monster fraternity there is nothing in the JARIC Report to contradict the idea that Dinsdale merely filmed a motor boat. Just as few believers seem to have actually read Burton's *The Elusive Monster*, so few seem to know the JARIC Report in its entirety. Instead the phrase 'probably an animate object' is repeated time and time again, always wrenched from its context. It is time to put that phrase back where it belongs, in paragraphs 14 and 15 of the Report, which state:

> The object is travelling at 10 m.p.h., and it is doubtful if a 'non-planing' hull of under 16 feet could achieve this speed. A power boat shell with planing hull could easily achieve and exceed this speed, and the design is such that it could appear to have a continuous surface. However,

these craft are normally painted in such a way as to be photo visible at any time, and in any case the existence of such a craft would scarcely be missed by an observer. The assumption is, therefore, that it is NOT a surface vessel.

One can presumably rule out the idea that it is any sort of submarine vessel for various reasons, which leaves the conclusion that it probably is an animate object.

What is JARIC saying here? Simply that the object which Dinsdale filmed is, in terms of its speed and appearance, quite consistent with a motor boat with a planing hull, except that such boats 'normally' are painted in such a way as to be visible as such. The key phrase in JARIC analysis is the statement that 'the existence of such a craft on the loch would scarcely be missed by an observer. The assumption is therefore that it is NOT a surface vessel.' In other words, the value of Dinsdale's film as evidence for a monster *rests on his own testimony*.

In *Project Water Horse* Dinsdale heaps praises on JARIC for being 'expert', 'unprejudiced', and 'Heir to a famous wartime tradition, when they had first spotted the German Peenemünde rocket launching sites.'[1] Ironically the RAF Photographic Interpretation Unit did *not* first discover the Peenemünde rockets. It was actually R. V. Jones, the man in charge of Scientific Intelligence at the Air Ministry, who discovered them, after the 'experts' had spent five days peering at the aerial photographs and spotting nothing. Jones

1 Although it is not part of our argument that the JARIC measurements are wrong it is worth pointing out that they may have been, and that JARIC's 'expert' interpretation rests on a number of dubious assumptions. It seems unlikely that Dinsdale was able to identify the exact spot from which he shot his film, since immediately afterwards he drove off in a state of great excitement. Dinsdale assumed that he was three hundred feet above the loch surface, and JARIC accepted his assumption. JARIC admit that if Dinsdale was not 300 feet above the surface 'then all measures require adjustment, i.e. if the height is 290 feet all measures will be in error by + 10%.' The film was not submitted to JARIC until five years after it was taken, and the Report makes no mention of the RAF analysts bothering to visit Loch Ness in order to shoot film for comparative purposes, or of them making on the spot measurements. The scientific

himself points out that photographic analysis is not an objective science: 'what one could see in a photograph was often a matter of subjective interpretation.' It was this factor which actually led JARIC's predecessors to bungle their analysis:

> the principal interpreter assigned to the task supplemented his powers of observation by a remarkably fertile imagination. What were in fact catapults for flying bombs were, for example, interpreted as 'sludge pumps', a theory perhaps coloured by the interpreter's previous experience as an engineer with a river Catchment Board.[1]

So much for Dinsdale's proud wartime tradition.

Dinsdale has recently called in other anonymous 'experts' to back up his claims. He now insists that computer-enhancement reveals a second 'hump' on his film. The evidence for this is extremely dubious. By juxtaposing a frame showing the hotel-owner's dinghy from the *side* with the mystery object moving directly *away* from the camera Dinsdale once again indulges in a bogus comparison. The

value of the JARIC Report in sustaining a belief in 'monsters' is further undermined by the breathtaking admission contained in paragraph 18: 'Further discussion of wake and wash patterns should be left for those more familiar with fluid dynamics.' This appears never to have been done. Believers never tire of pointing to the different wake created by Dinsdale's 'monster' and the boat he afterwards filmed. The comparison was a bogus one, however. Firstly Dinsdale did not film the boat immediately afterwards, but some two hours later. The weather can change surface conditions dramatically, and the same boat can create quite different wake-effects under different surface conditions. Secondly Dinsdale compared his fast-moving 'monster' wake with that of a slow-moving dinghy with an outboard motor. A fast-moving motor boat creates a wake which much resembles that left by Dinsdale's 'monster'. The JARIC Report ends with discussion of another dubious 'assumption'. Paragraph 19 states: 'Dinsdale suggested comparing the apex angle [of the mystery object] with that on the [Lachlan] Stuart photograph. If, in the Stuart photograph, the three humps are part of the same beast then the view is most likely a side view.' The assumption that Stuart photographed a 'beast' now seems very questionable.

1 R. V. Jones, *Most Secret War* (London, 1978), p. 339.

so-called second hump, which is perfectly visible on the original film, could be a shadow, a wave or simply a blob on the film. There is a good-quality reproduction of some frames from the Jet Propulsion Laboratory's computer study in Anthony Harmsworth's glossy brochure *The Mysterious Monsters of Loch Ness*. Fascinatingly, they show the contours of the mystery object to be lumpy and irregular. This is not at all what one would expect from computer-enhancement of the image of a single huge half-moon-shaped hump, but is entirely consistent with the theory that what is shown is the irregular outline of a motor boat. When examining these computer-enhanced frames (which include Dinsdale's bogus dinghy comparison) Roy Mackal's observation is well worth bearing in mind: 'the object was not filmed at right angles to its long axis; the view in the film is neither purely a side or rear view but some intermediate aspect.'

There is a final curious twist to the story of Dinsdale's encounter with the monster. He shot his film on 23 April, St George's Day, a day devoted to a hero who slew a dragon. Dinsdale seems to have had this heroic analogy floating around in his subconscious, remarking that up until the time of his expedition the monster had become 'no more than a childhood fairy tale, half forgotten and about as real as St George's Dragon.'[1]

It was only some months later, in April 1960, when he 'reached out ... to grasp the Monster by the tail' that 'battle' really commenced for Dinsdale. From then on he began 'a sort of private crusade' to persuade the world that monsters really did exist in Loch Ness. It is a role he has maintained ever since – the modern knight-in-armour, riding his 'great white steed'[2] across the loch, armed to the teeth with powerful cameras, a hero of our times.

1 *Loch Ness Monster*, p. 50.
2 *Project Water Horse*, p. 166.

8 Surveillance and Science

The one thing I am anxious about now is that you really get this letter and give the facts to the Natural History Museum. If only my camera had not been swept up in the whirlwind I might possibly have got a snap of him on his throne, but I don't know. Somehow I didn't want to do anything except look and look and look.

Mervyn Peake, *Letters from a Lost Uncle from Polar Regions* (1948)

Shortly after his appearance on television in June 1960 Tim Dinsdale was commissioned to write a book about the monster, which duly appeared in 1961. This first edition of *Loch Ness Monster* – a book which quickly became the classic book on the subject and which is still in print today – ended with a dramatic last chapter entitled 'What next?'

Dinsdale concluded that the solution to the mystery still lay in photographic surveillance of the loch. The odds against success were high, but they were not impossible. After all, 'Sir Edward Mountain's expedition had shown that if one individual watched the loch for 30 days, during the hours of daylight, he might, with luck, see the Monster on one occasion!' And Dinsdale himself had been lucky enough to see the beast after only six days at the loch! All that was needed was more people prepared to keep watch over Loch Ness and the mystery would be solved:

if the Monster's surface appearances are rare (and they are very rare in daylight) they *must inevitably* yield their full secret if a sufficient number of people are prepared to watch the loch for long enough. This is a simple fact.

Exciting words. Even more excitingly Dinsdale's sober analysis of the sightings record showed that the animal elevated its head and neck above the surface on 42% of all the occasions it put in an appearance. The head and neck had only to be filmed *once* in good light, at close quarters on colour ciné film for its existence to be established once and for all. Modestly referring to his own celebrated footage of the monster Dinsdale concluded, 'I hope there will soon be better film to take its place.'

The year that his book was published Tim Dinsdale returned to Loch Ness, full of enthusiasm. 'In the Spring of 1961,' he later wrote, 'there was every reason to suppose that close-up ciné film would at last be obtained.' At the end of March he spent day after day, watching the loch from a variety of places along the sixty miles of shoreline. He returned home empty-handed, in a state of depression, under 'the crushing influence of defeat.'[1]

1961 had drawn a blank, but Dinsdale put a brave face on his failure. It was also a great boost to his morale to learn that some important people had been greatly impressed by both his film and his book. In 1962 the Loch Ness Phenomena Investigation Bureau was formed by various prominent public figures, including Peter Scott and David James, a Conservative MP. Dinsdale joined as a 'Field Associate' and began a collaboration which was to last for over a decade.

1962 promised to be a very exciting year indeed. There were three major expeditions to Loch Ness, together with a number of one-man investigations. Ted Holiday, another author and veteran monster-watcher, was at the loch during the summer of 1962, and Dinsdale himself carried out two further expeditions there in the spring and autumn. Both men failed to obtain any film of the monster.

1 Tim Dinsdale, *The Leviathans* (Revised edition: London, Futura, 1976), p. 16.

The major effort came from the three big expeditions. The first was under the command of Lt. Colonel H. G. Hasler, O.B.E., D.S.C., famous as one of the 'Cockleshell heroes' of World War Two and later well-known as a trans-Atlantic yachtsman. It involved some sixty volunteers who took it in turn to maintain a continuous day and night patrol of the loch from a yacht. It was thought that a silent sailing boat might be just the thing for a close-up sighting of the beast. The search went on for two months, making a series of successive sweeps of the loch. After four weeks at Loch Ness Hasler announced that he was concerned at the total lack of results. The very next day – success! Of sorts. Three expedition members reported an inconclusive sighting of some 'humps' just two to three inches high.

Having failed to film the monster the Hasler expedition eventually packed up and went home. At this point a university expedition under the leadership of Peter Baker and Mark Westwood arrived at Loch Ness. The group maintained a surveillance of the loch lasting, in all, 480 hours. Ciné-cameras were positioned along the shore and echosounding equipment was used. The results were inconclusive. There were sightings of unidentified objects in the loch, but no film was taken. Tim Dinsdale ruefully observed, 'the lake was probed and peered at as never before, and yet both these expeditions retired exhausted, with results which barely compensated for the huge expenditure of energy.' Perplexed by their expedition's failure Baker and Westwood commented, 'No large fast-moving objects were seen, and only [boats'] wake effects compared in size with the huge manifestations of the 1930s.'

These first signs of a 'revisionist' attitude to the Loch Ness monster were soon lost sight of in the excitement created by the Loch Ness Phenomena Investigation Bureau taking to the field for the first time. This happened in October 1962, when a team of 26 volunteers maintained a day and night vigil at the loch, under the command of David James. There were a number of sightings, the most dramatic of which occurred on the afternoon of 19 October. James subsequently described in the *Observer* (17 May 1964) how 'Eight of us saw a length of back six to eight feet long break the surface about 200 yards away and cruise slowly after [some] fish. We shot about fifty feet of film and eyewitness statements were taken from all concerned that evening.' Whatever the film showed however it was clearly not the conclusive footage which the monster hunters had sought.[1]

In June 1963 the Bureau returned to Loch Ness with financial support and the loan of equipment from Associated Television. A two-week vigil produced one piece of tantalising footage, showing a dark log-shaped object very close to the opposite shore. David James dramatically announced that 'the head and neck are in the can.' It soon turned out that this was a wild exaggeration. The mystery object had been filmed at a range of 2¼ miles, far too far away to permit identification. It might have been the Loch Ness monster. It might equally have been a tree trunk. The film was subsequently analysed by JARIC who commented that any signs of motion which the object seemed to possess might well have been caused by either wave motion or halation.

Excited by its dramatic near-misses the Bureau (by now known simply as L.N.I. – the Loch Ness Investigation) returned to the loch in 1964. This new expedition was organised on bigger and better lines. Special observation platforms were constructed on opposite sides of the loch. One was bolted to the wall of Urquhart Castle, offering a dramatic viewing post over the deepest portion of the loch. The other was constructed on the southern shore, near Whitefield. Together, it was thought, they would eliminate the recurring problem that mystery objects always seemed to appear on the opposite shore of the loch to where the watchers were. Each viewing platform housed a sturdy

1 Over the years David James's opinion about the episode seems to have radically altered, since in his Foreword to William Owen's tourist brochure *Scotland's Loch Ness Monster* (1980) he comments, 'I have spent many weeks by the lochside ... without ever seeing anything. All the same I must admit I am a firm believer.'

tripod mounted with an impressive battery of photographic equipment, including 35mm movie cameras with powerful telephoto lenses. Tests were carried out which showed that the cameras were capable of recording an object only a foot wide at a range of one mile. The Bureau planned to maintain a continuous watch from Whitsun to October. 'It was hard not to feel excited at this news,' wrote F. W. Holiday, joining the expedition:

> No longer would the laws of optics stand in the way of our obtaining detailed pictures of the [monster], for the two camera-rigs under construction were almost certainly the most formidable photographic tools that had ever been used for natural history purposes in Britain.[1]

The monster mystery was surely on the brink of being solved. 'Given average luck success seemed assured,' Holiday commented. Even though the monster was an elusive creature 'it was not unreasonable to suppose that dawn till dusk watching, seven days a week for five months, would produce results. After all, if you watch a given area of sky for long enough, you are bound to see a rainbow.'

What was more, the Bureau's volunteers were not the only ones watching the loch. Dinsdale was continuing his own vigils from the south shore and Holiday was keeping a sporadic surveillance from random points around the loch. 1964 was also the year in which one of the authors of this book first travelled to Loch Ness, maintaining a vigil from the old pier overlooking Foyers Bay. Despite all these activities the monster proved elusive. 1964 turned out to be a bad year for monster-watchers. No film was obtained by the L.N.I. cameras, and the Bureau logged only eighteen sightings for the whole year. Only four of these were by expedition members.

In 1965 the Bureau set up its headquarters at Achnahannet, in a field at the roadside. It was decided that operating

1 F. W. Holiday, *The Great Orm of Loch Ness* (London: Faber, 1968), p. 65.

cameras from both sides of the loch was impractical and different tactics were employed for the new monster-hunting season. The main observation rig commanded a panoramic view of the loch, stretching from Foyers in the west to Whitefield and beyond in the east. Each day a mobile camera unit mounted on a Bedford van was sent out to Strone Point, covering the area around Urquhart Castle. Another mobile unit went out each day and manned a camera set up on a wooden platform built on the shore below the Drumna-drochit-Lochend road. The entire central section of Loch Ness was kept under surveillance in this way between 17 May and 18 October. The results of this epic vigil were depressing. One nine-second film sequence had been shot, showing two wakes moving parallel with one another at a speed of around 1 m.p.h. The wakes were 1300 yards away and could have been caused by otters, birds or possibly even fish. It was not the conclusive film evidence which the L.N.I. was after. What was even more demoralising was that the more the loch was watched the less the monsters seemed to show themselves. Only nine sightings were logged for 1965. Tim Dinsdale made two expeditions to the loch that year, continuing his lonely vigils from the south shore, but he, too, drew a blank.

1965 was an important year for the Loch Ness mystery in that the L.N.I. activities attracted the attention of a man who was destined to become the first of a succession of prominent American investigators. This was Dr Roy Mackal, an Associate Professor of Biochemistry at the University of Chicago. Mackal's growing interest in the monster coincided with publication of the JARIC Report on Tim Dinsdale's film in February 1966. The Report created a sensation, not least in Fleet Street which misinterpreted the findings and splashed the news that the RAF were convinced Loch Ness held a monster over ninety feet long.

Morale among the monster-hunters soared once again, and as Mackal shrewdly pointed out, the JARIC Report 'made money raising easier.' Newly-inspired the L.N.I. returned to the loch for the 1966 season. Though it was the best year to date for volunteers, equipment and coverage the investigation once again proved a failure. Over 4000 hours of sustained photographic surveillance of Loch Ness resulted in no new film. Undaunted, Mackal held a news conference on 19 September at which he affirmed his belief in the existence of a large unidentified species in Loch Ness. 'He added that, although it was premature to be dogmatic, the balance of probability lay in the direction of an invertebrate of the gastropod class, possibly somewhat between the giant squid and the slug in appearance.'[1]

Wearily L.N.I. returned to the loch the following year. Then, on 13 June 1967, the expedition achieved its first important photographic success. A volunteer on mobile patrol filmed a large wake cutting across the loch near Dores. The film was quickly submitted to JARIC, who produced a cautious report observing that although 'precise measures are impossible' it seemed probable that the object causing the wake was travelling at not less than 5 m.p.h. Unfortunately it was '*not* possible to detect the shape or nature of the object causing the disturbance, though varying optical enlargements of up to × 38 [were] used.' Nevertheless, JARIC concluded, 'a possible length for that part of the object which seems to break the surface is in the order of seven feet.' This was exciting news for monster-hunters, since JARIC's estimate of length was just that bit larger than was possible for any of the known species of the loch. Inconclusive as this piece of film was it turned out to be the best photographic evidence the L.N.I. was ever able to come up with to support the belief that a species of monster between 30 feet and 50 feet in length inhabited the loch.

No-one foresaw this at the time. Morale was once again high, and the number of sightings reported by Bureau personnel was the highest since the investigation had begun. 'This may well be a direct outcome of the extended coverage of the loch which the Bureau is now able to provide,'

1 L.N.I. Annual Report, 1966.

concluded David James, optimistically, in the 1967 L.N.I. Annual Report.

Crouched alone amid bracken high up on the south shore Tim Dinsdale did not share the Bureau's mood of jubilation. By the end of the 1967 monster-hunting season he felt deeply depressed. His twelfth successive expedition to the loch in seven years had ended, yet again, in defeat. The confidence and certainty displayed in the conclusion to *Loch Ness Monster* were now ebbing rapidly away. 'I began to feel the odds were hopeless,' Dinsdale confessed.

Dinsdale was right. Though nobody knew it at the time 1967 was to be the climax of the hunt for the beast using movie film. The following year the Bureau returned, but obtained no film. David James remained unshaken, quietly confident of success. 'Time, luck and the extraordinary pertinacity of our volunteer watchers will ultimately produce the missing piece of our jigsaw puzzle,' he wrote in the 1968 Annual Report. Meanwhile, to whet the appetite of the monster fraternity Roy Mackal had come up with a new theory as to the beast's possible identity. An extinct form of air-breathing mammal known as Steller's Sea-cow should, he felt, 'be seriously considered.' Admittedly there were objections. The Sea-cow had been an air breather, lived off the coast of Alaska, had a short neck, and was a herbivore. Also it was extinct. But some of the odd features of the creature seemed to resemble the Loch Ness monster. 'An adapted Sirenian presents fewer incongruities than any other solution on the basis of the evidence available,' David James informed L.N.I. members.

The only problem was that the evidence available didn't add up to much. A further summer of surveillance in 1969 produced no new movie film, and the following year it was the same story. For the first time the Bureau failed to produce an Annual Report. The same thing happened in 1971: massive surveillance of the loch, nil photographic results, no Annual Report. By now, short of money and exhausted by his lonely vigils, Dinsdale had thrown in his lot with the Bureau and become 'Director of Surface Operations'. In the 'Final

Operations Newsletter' for 1971 Dinsdale addressed his troops:

> We still need clear ciné photography, and the hunt must go on until we get it. In this tremendous battle with the odds, and the difficulties at Loch Ness and Loch Morar – we must take heart from the fact that our target of 'credibility' is coming inexorably within range of our determined skills and technical equipment. It is easy to become despondent, because results each year appear meagre in relation to the huge effort expended – but, in fact, they accumulate; are valid, and impressive. We need only to 'dot the i's and cross the t's' with photography.

Dinsdale was putting a brave face on the situation, but the negative results of nine years' intensive surveillance of the loch could scarcely conceal the fact that these were only words. The stark reality of defeat was overwhelming, and in seeking to deny it Dinsdale was beginning to sound like a German general in 1918. A bit more effort and victory would be inevitable.

The hollowness of Dinsdale's optimism was highlighted a few months later when, after one more fruitless summer of observation, the Loch Ness Investigation effectively collapsed. The headquarters site at Achnahannet was abandoned, the camera equipment sold, and the watchers went away. Only Tim Dinsdale remained, and has remained ever since, still patrolling the shores of the enchanted loch, pursuing his ancient dream of a close-encounter. Twenty years after his first dramatic 'sighting' that goal now seems as far away as ever.

ii

Mercy, mercy! This is a devil, and no monster: I will leave him.

Shakespeare, *The Tempest* (1611)

The failure to obtain close-up motion film of the monster had a catastrophic effect on the monster fraternity. Nor was it just movie film which had failed; as Dinsdale observed, 'Between 1960 and 1972 no-one seems to have taken a good still photograph in spite of the attempts made to do so.'[1] This was, thought Dinsdale, 'incredible'.

Up until 1960 there was a basic consensus about what the Loch Ness mystery was. The loch was inhabited by a solitary sea-serpent (Gould), not more than two or three monsters at the most (Dinsdale), or by a small family of the creatures (Whyte). When the monster appeared at the surface it was immense in size, created huge waves, and moved at speeds of up to 50 m.p.h. Often the creature raised a long thin swan-like neck into the air. Sometimes it remained on the surface for half an hour or more. A number of classic still photographs had been obtained of the monster's head and neck, humps and back. The difficulties of proving the monster's existence did not seem insurmountable. All that was required was more people to keep the loch under surveillance, armed with powerful movie cameras.

In *More Than a Legend* Constance Whyte had advised that the best time to see monsters was at dawn. Tim Dinsdale agreed: 'At least 80% of appearances are recorded between dawn and about 9.30 a.m.'[2]

But from 1962 Loch Ness was subjected to intensive surveillance which began from first photographic light. After ten years the loch yielded no dawn monsters, and the Bureau's baffling 1967 film of a wake was taken at 11.40 a.m. The myth of the early-morning monster (further demolished by the sighting reports which the Bureau logged over a ten-year period) was simply the first of the legends which began to disintegrate in the face of empirical research. As the years went by a long list of cherished beliefs about the monster began to crumble and need re-thinking.

Zoologists pointed out that if monsters had existed in the

1 *The Story of the Loch Ness Monster*, 81.
2 *Loch Ness Monster*, p. 243.

Figure 4
The Changing Monster

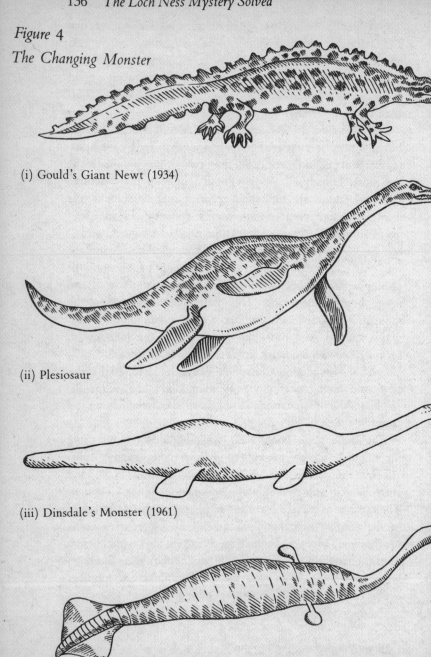

(i) Gould's Giant Newt (1934)

(ii) Plesiosaur

(iii) Dinsdale's Monster (1961)

(iv) Holiday's Great Orm (1968)

loch for centuries then there would clearly have to be a breeding herd of them, otherwise extinction would have overtaken the animals long ago. It was suggested that there must surely be around *two dozen* monsters in the loch at the very least. But this raised another embarrassing point of logic: why did the monsters take it in turns to come to the surface? If certain conditions favoured monster-surfacings then why didn't all twenty-four animals rise to the surface and sport in the sunshine? If Dinsdale, believing only in three monsters, believed the chances of success were so good then why were so many monsters elusive?

The failure of the great monster watch of 1962–72 resulted in a number of revisionist interpretations of the monster mystery. As early as 1962 the university expedition led by Baker and Westwood had concluded that the monster was far, far smaller than generally believed, and that people who reported seeing large humps were mistaken and were only seeing wake-effects produced by trawlers and other shipping on the loch. At the time such radical ideas were unacceptable to the monster fraternity, but found an echo fourteen years later in Roy Mackal's *The Monsters of Loch Ness*. After putting forward a number of exciting theories about the beast's identity Mackal eventually concluded that 90% of sightings were false, and that the monster was at most twenty-five feet long and did not create anywhere near as much turbulence as witnesses often claimed. The beast was, he thought, either a giant eel or some weird descendant of an embolomer.

The long years of failure at Loch Ness eventually took their toll on Mackal. Having helpfully included the design for a monster-trap in his book Mackal drew the conclusion that surface photography was unproductive and lost interest in the mystery. The Professor now devotes his spare time to looking for prehistoric dinosaurs in Africa. According to the *Sunday Telegraph* (1 November 1981):

Dr Mackal said pigmies who had actually seen the strange creature all reported the same kind of animal in detail. 'It had a long head and neck, a long thin tail, and a body as big as a hippopotamus. Some have a frill down the back of the neck.'

In the nineteen-sixties and seventies the failure to obtain close-up photography of the monster encouraged a number of extravagant guesses as to the creature's identity. In his book *In Search of Lake Monsters* (1974), Peter Costello revived Oudemans's theory that the monster was a giant long-necked seal. By a dexterous reading of the eye-witness evidence Costello argued that everything pointed to a hairy mammal, and not a newt, plesiosaur, or eel. The same objection can be levelled against Oudemans's disciple as against the master himself: 'upon his not exactly trustworthy foundations [he] has erected a vast superstructure of theory which they are in no way fit to support.'[1]

Concocting new theories about the identity of the Loch Ness monster is a harmless and entertaining pastime. But since each writer claims to prove his or her case from the same evidence obviously they cannot all be right (unless, of course, Loch Ness is inhabited by giant newts, giant seals, giant otters, giant eels, and twenty-four plesiosaurs – which seems unlikely).

Perhaps the most spectacular revisionist of them all was F. W. Holiday. In *The Great Orm of Loch Ness* (1968) Holiday devoted many pages to his theory that the monster was a giant marine worm (or as he preferred to call it, an 'orm'). In 1966 the Chicago Field Museum of Natural History published an article about a recently discovered fossil, *Tullimonstrum gregarium*. What excited Holiday was the way in which the fossil's shape seemed to resemble that of the Loch Ness monster. There were however a number of serious objections to the idea that the monster was a giant descendant of the *Tullimonstrum*. The most fundamental was that the largest known fossil was only fourteen inches long. Secondly, what Holiday interpreted as parapodia (fleshy lobes which squirt out water) were in the Museum's opinion

1 R. T. Gould, *The Case for the Sea-Serpent*, p. 8.

probably eyes, not round and rubbery but attached to a single stiff transverse bar, so that if one eye moved forward the other automatically moved backward. The Museum also pointed out that the *Tullimonstrum* fossils were all preserved in flat silhouette, like tracings on paper, and that opinions about the creature's shape in cross-section could only be empty conjecture.

Holiday's hypothetical 'great orm' did not even fit the evidence from Loch Ness. He was obliged to ignore Lachlan Stuart's photograph of three sharply-pointed humps as well as Tim Dinsdale's description of the monster's bony, ridged back.

The recurring failure of investigations at the loch convinced Holiday that there was something inexplicable involved in the mystery. He was not alone in his sensitivity to the loch's uncanny atmosphere. Tim Dinsdale confessed that when he first saw Loch Ness he felt himself helpless, in the grip of strange forces:

It was as though I was standing in the field of an immense electro-magnet which took control of me, drawing me irresistibly forwards.[1]

Dinsdale felt that there were parts of the loch which were soaked in evil vibrations, hangovers from ancient massacres and dark rites. They were a nuisance because they led to trouble in operating camera equipment. Dinsdale preferred to move to another part of the loch and forget about them.

Holiday felt that the occult was at the heart of the Loch Ness mystery. In *The Great Orm of Loch Ness* he hinted that he had established psychic contact with the beast in 1962. Some years later he had the good fortune to see a large mustard-yellow monster at the surface for over an hour, but the light was too bad to bother filming it. In his next book, *The Dragon and the Disc* (1973) he confessed for the first time that in reporting the mustard-yellow monster he had written 'It

1 *Project Water Horse*, p. 60.

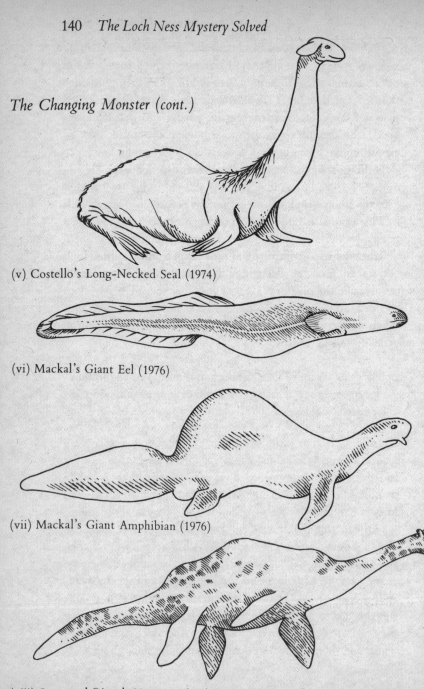

The Changing Monster (cont.)

(v) Costello's Long-Necked Seal (1974)

(vi) Mackal's Giant Eel (1976)

(vii) Mackal's Giant Amphibian (1976)

(viii) Scott and Rines's *Nessiteras rhombopteryx* (1980)

might have been a boat.' Engagingly, he explained that the monster somehow exerted a mysterious influence which made people want to deny seeing it. The monster, Holiday asserted, was related to UFOs, apparitions, and dwarf visitors from outer space. He therefore asked the Reverend Donald Omand, 'exorcist extraordinary', to rid the loch of its evil spirits. Dr Omand was sympathetic to the project, explaining,

> The many honest folk who have beheld Nessie have been mistaken. What they saw was not something which was actually taking place at that precise moment. They possessed the same mysterious receptiveness I inherited from my mother. The gigantic creature which they were so privileged to see was no longer in the land of the living. It was something seen out of time. The so-termed Loch Ness monster is not physical but psychical.[1]

Dr Omand exorcised Loch Ness on 2 June 1973, and later repeated the exorcism for the benefit of television. It was, he explained, 'a very fascinating challenge. It is the size that worries me. Up until now I have not exorcised anything larger than a circus big-top.'[2] Afterwards he travelled to Sweden and exorcised monster-haunted Lake Storsjon. Admirers of the Reverend Omand reported that the incidence of marital breakdown in the area had 'dramatically decreased' after his visit. The Loch Ness monster, however, seems still as much alive as ever.

Like Roy Mackal, F. W. Holiday eventually lost interest in the Loch Ness mystery. In 1977 he transferred his attention to Welsh humanoids and subsequently produced *The Dyfed Enigma*, a spine-chilling collection of sightings of beings from outer space.

1 Marc Alexander, *To Anger the Devil: An Account of the work of exorcist extraordinary the Reverend Dr Donald Omand* (Sudbury: Neville Spearman, 1978), pp. 79–80.
2 *Ibid.*, p. 80.

Not everyone gave up on the monster so easily. In the early sixties Tim Dinsdale experimented with devices which would complement the photographic quest. The most dramatic of these was a dart which could be fired at a nearby monster in order to obtain a tissue sample. Experiments with a bow and arrow in the garden of his suburban home in Reading were not successful. Dinsdale did not enjoy having to go round to his neighbour and ask for his arrow back. He joined the local archery club, but almost shot himself. After that bows and arrows were abandoned.

In 1961 Dinsdale had cautioned, 'Keep off the water at all costs. A boat makes a poor platform from which to film – and the Monster does not like them, and is very rarely seen from a boat.' But watching the loch from a stationary position at the shoreline is boring, lonely work. In the end Dinsdale ignored his own stern advice, began messing about in boats, and was duly rewarded with two brief sightings, the first in August 1970, the other in September 1971. Unfortunately the sightings were over before Dinsdale had the chance to use his camera.

Others took to the water to try baiting, acoustic noise, transmitters designed to influence mammals, hydrophones and other forms of acoustic device. In the late sixties the famous yellow submarine *Viperfish* arrived at the loch, as well as the Vickers submarine *Pisces*, Wing Commander Wallis's gyrocopter, and an amphibious Volkswagen. These aroused great press interest but were of negligible value in proving the existence of monsters.

As frustration mounted a new alternative presented itself. *Look for monsters elsewhere*. In 1968 the Bureau organised an expedition to the west coast of Ireland in an attempt to trap a monster in one of the region's tiny loughs. There had been numerous sightings and it was an exciting new development. Mackal grimly recounts how 'I unpacked my harpoon gear, checked my supply of .38 calibre ammunition, and joined David, Dick, and Howard for our trek to the lake.'[1] The

1 *The Monsters of Loch Ness*, p. 41.

expedition was a complete failure, and Roy, David, Dick and Howard trekked away again, ammunition intact. Other Irish expeditions also ended in failure. What was more Dr David Piggins, an authority on fish and fish-populations in Western Ireland, stated that no evidence for a large unknown fish predator in these Irish loughs had ever been brought to his notice. Another cherished monster myth – that the beast lived off salmon – began to crumble.

By 1969 morale was at a low ebb at Loch Ness.

Investigation members had begun to sense a feeling of stalemate. The report of the McDonnell-Simpson sighting at Morar exploded into this somewhat overcast scene with the force of a hurricane, scattering doubts and lifting morale to new heights.[1]

McDonell and Simpson were two long-distance lorry drivers who claimed that they had been sailing on Loch Morar when 'a thing' had surfaced behind their boat and collided with it. Simpson fired a shot at the mystery beast and it went away, leaving them shaken by the experience. That, at least, was what Simpson told his uncle, who (to the men's fury) told the press. Returning from their next long-distance trips they discovered to their embarrassment that they were famous.

David Scott of L.N.I. went over to the West coast and interviewed the two men.

When I spoke to the witnesses a fortnight after the incident, both appeared embarrassed and unwilling to speak. It took some time to draw them out, occasionally one would contradict the other on a point of detail.[2]

Scott felt that the men were telling the truth. Both agreed that the creature was 25 – 30 feet long with three low humps, about eighteen inches out of the water at the highest point. McDonnell later changed his mind and said he thought they

1 *The Search for Morag*, p. 47.
2 *Project Water Horse*, p. 108.

were undulations rather than humps. Sketches of the 'thing' appeared in the *Sunday Post*, 24 August 1969, bearing little resemblance to the orthodox picture of the Loch Ness monster. Sceptics wondered what two lorry-drivers out fishing were doing with a rifle in the first place.

The episode inspired the setting up of the Loch Morar Survey, which arrived at the loch with a team of student biologists and keen young monster-watchers (including the authors of this book) the following year. The Survey spent a total of three summers at the loch, then abandoned the investigation. No film at all had been shot.

Elizabeth Montgomery-Campbell, a freelance journalist who had helped organise the Survey, subsequently wrote a book about the whole affair, entitled *The Search for Morag* (1972). The investigation had proved something of a disappointment, sightings had been brief and inconclusive, and the evidence of a monster 'tradition' at Loch Morar was sketchy. Nor had anyone ever managed to snap Morag the monster. An anonymous fellow-reporter did however claim to have come across a poem about the monster in 'a Victorian collection of old Scottish lays'.

> Morag, harbinger of death,
> Giant swimmer in deep-green Morar,
> The loch that has no bottom ...
> There it is that Morag the monster lives.

Though this episode smacks of a leg-pull (no-one ever managed to track down either the poem or the volume) Mrs Montgomery-Campbell proudly quoted this doubtful example of Scottish lyricism as the epigraph to her book.

Meanwhile, back at Loch Ness, the great monster hunt continued.

iii

> They sought it with thimbles, they sought it with care;
> They pursued it with forks and hope;
> They threatened its life with a railway-share;
> They charmed it with smiles and soap.

But the Barrister, weary of proving in vain
    That the Beaver's lace-making was wrong,
Fell asleep, and in dreams saw the creature quite plain
    That his fancy had dwelt on so long.

      Lewis Carroll, *The Hunting of the Snark* (1876)

I, William Seward, captain of this lushed up
hashhead subway, will quell the Loch Ness
monster with rotenone ...

      William Burroughs, *The Naked Lunch* (1959)

Surface surveillance of the loch seemed to be getting nowhere. At this juncture the investigation took a dramatic new turn. It was decided to extend the search underwater. Apart from the use of submarines the new projects included searching the bottom for remains, and the use of sonar and underwater cameras.

Dredging the bed of the loch for animal remains seemed a good idea. The *Pisces* submarine spent a total of 250 hours underwater in Loch Ness and observed the wreck of an old wooden boat near Temple Pier, as well as ancient weapons in the silt of Urquhart Bay. They had, it seemed, probably been dumped there after the 1745 uprising and the defeat of Bonnie Prince Charlie. These were exciting discoveries, for if the remains of an old boat and weapons could still be seen on the loch floor then surely if the monster was either a reptile or a mammal skeleton remains ought to be visibly present. But still nothing was found.[1]

1 This aspect of the great monster hunt is still continuing up to the present day. Since 1974 the Loch Ness and Morar Project has been engaged in a sustained search for organic remains. Despite the use of divers, cables ¾ mile in length, and dredging trials to a depth of 1000 feet the Project's efforts have met with no success. As the Project's leader, Adrian Shine, acknowledges, 'This method, if pursued methodically, must prove decisive in the end – one way or the other. If there have been large live animals in Loch Ness for the past 6000 years, then there are large dead animals there now.'

146 *The Loch Ness Mystery Solved*

Sonar and underwater photography, by comparison, produced spectacular results which revived the flagging faith of the monster-hunters. Attempting to find evidence of underwater activity by large unknown animals in Loch Ness had been extensively tried by the Cambridge University expeditions of 1960 and 1962. A Report on these investigations by Dr Peter Baker stated flatly that 'on neither occasion was any evidence obtained for the presence of a large creature in the loch.'[1] Dr Baker went on to consider the perplexing results of the expedition searches. The Cambridge team had used a fleet of boats drawn up in a line, and then sailed from one end of the loch to the other and back again, setting up a 'sonic curtain'. The negative results suggested that if there was a monster in the loch it must be a very poor reflector of ultra-sound. In other words it would have to be a creature which lacked bones, lungs or air-sacs. Alternatively the monster might escape detection by living on or in the mud at the bottom of the loch. Baker suggested the use of very high intensities of ultra-sound to make life intolerable for the animals and drive them to the surface. This was eventually tried in 1969 by a Plessey research team which flooded the loch with acoustic reverberations on a frequency of 10 kHz. In the event, no monsters surfaced.

What purports to be the first underwater recording of a monster was obtained in December 1954 by a Peterhead trawler. Its echo-sounder recorded what appeared to be a large underwater object which kept pace with the trawler for half a mile, before disappearing. The problem was if the chart did show a monster then why didn't other trawlers passing up and down the narrow loch obtain similar recordings? 'On the face of it, it does seem a little peculiar,' mused Tim Dinsdale in the first edition of *Loch Ness Monster*. After all, several hundred trawlers sail the length of the loch every year, and they leave their echo-sounding equipment on all the time as a matter of course. The answer, Dinsdale decided, was 'probably a simple one'. The monster did not

1 The Report is reproduced as an Appendix in *The Great Orm of Loch Ness*.

seem to like noises or vibrations and since it could swim at speeds in excess of 30 m.p.h. it would have no problem keeping out of the way of shipping. Quite why the monster had chosen to accompany the trawler in 1954 Dinsdale did not explain. In later editions of his book Dinsdale deleted this episode.

F. W. Holiday agreed with Dinsdale that searching for the monster underwater was a waste of time. The only thing that would really convince sceptics would be close-up motion film. Those who disbelieved in the beast, he bluntly asserted, were 'not likely to be brought to sanity by a bit of shading on a graph.'

There the matter rested until 1968, when a team from the Department of Electronic and Electrical Engineering of the University of Birmingham arrived to carry out trials of a new type of sonar equipment. In April 1968 some target tests were carried out from R.V. *Clupea*. One of these tests involved lowering a target to the bed of the loch, pointing the transducer array vertically downwards and observing the display. When the target was raised a group of objects appeared and rose with it. Further trials were carried out in August, using sonar fixed on Temple Pier and directed straight across the loch. In this experiment a fortnight's continuous twenty-four-hour-a-day probe produced one unusual recording lasting thirteen minutes. In it, a large object appeared to rise from the loch floor at a vertical velocity of about a hundred feet a minute, then descend to the floor, then rise again. While this was going on another mystery object appeared in the beam travelling at the astonishing speed of fifteen knots on the horizontal plane and with a rate of dive of about four hundred and fifty feet a minute. The size and speed of the objects seemed to rule out the possibility of their being fish. Professor D. G. Tucker and Hugh Braithwaite, the men in charge of the Birmingham team, promptly published their extraordinary results in *New Scientist* magazine (19 December 1968).

The monster-hunters were jubilant. At long last there was scientific proof of monsters in Loch Ness! Their delight deepened when an editorial in Nature magazine condemned the Birmingham results and announced that the sonar equipment had been tested by the Fisheries Laboratory at Lowestoft, where it had been found to be 'prone to ambiguities'. Nature was wrong. The sonar equipment had never been to Lowestoft. Once again the scientific establishment seemed to be making a fool of itself, reinforcing the intuition of the monster-hunters that they, the amateurs, were right, and had been all along.

Their jubilation was perhaps premature. If the Birmingham team had picked up evidence of monsters in the loch then the behaviour patterns seemed very peculiar. A cross-section of Loch Ness had been kept under sonar surveillance for 20,160 minutes continuously. During almost the entire period no large unknown objects were logged. Then, suddenly, in a single thirteen-minute episode, one 'monster' rose from the loch floor, while another dived into view from near the surface. This indicated that the odds in favour of obtaining a sonar 'sighting' were even worse than those for surface surveillance. The idea that a herd of twenty-four giant animals were swimming about in the depths of Loch Ness began to look dubious.

Tucker and Braithwaite had rushed into print with the dramatic announcement that it was both a 'temptation' and a 'possibility' that they had observed 'the fabulous Loch Ness monsters ... for the first time in their underwater activities.' At the same time they tried to take back with the other hand what they had just delivered, remarking that their data were 'quite inadequate to decide the matter'. A lot more investigation would be required at Loch Ness 'with more refined equipment' before definite conclusions could be reached.

A year later, in September 1969, the Birmingham team returned to Loch Ness for a more comprehensive exercise. On this occasion their continuous sonar probe disclosed no unusual underwater activity at all. Their efforts were reinforced by a joint L.N.I./Independent Television News investigation which involved exhaustive sonar trawls up and down the entire length of Loch Ness. The journalist Vincent Mulchrone observed the great sonar hunt and concluded that the monster was a myth:

> Look at the facts. For two weeks now Loch Ness has been combed up and down as never before by sonar beams which can spot not only a diver but even the rope he is using. In Loch Ness they found – nothing. Because – it seems to me a reasonable deduction – there is nothing there.

> (*Daily Mail*, 27 September 1969)

The Birmingham team decided that further 'very extensive fieldwork' would be necessary, though in general their sonar system seemed very satisfactory. They did however add the proviso that the main lesson learnt from their research at Loch Ness was '*the fundamental difficulty of making accurate assessments and comparisons of accuracy in such an unpredictable environment*'[1] (our italics).

The following year the Birmingham team paid a fourth and last visit to Loch Ness. Again their intensive sonar probe drew a complete blank.

The conclusion seemed inescapable. When the Birmingham team first visited the loch to test their equipment they tracked 'monsters.' When they returned for more comprehensive tests they did not see monsters. Books about the mystery hailed the 1968 results as conclusive scientific proof of monsters. What their authors appeared not to realise was that in a little-known research paper published in 1970 Professor Tucker radically modified some of his earlier interpretations of the 1968 experiment. In this paper he again emphasised the great problems involved in interpreting sonar data. For example, referring to the 'large group of objects' seen rising from the bed of the loch in April 1968 he commented: 'These objects persisted after the removal of

1 *University of Birmingham, Research and Publications*, No. 40 (1968/69), p. 49.

the target, and extended downwards for nearly 100 metres. *Their nature might falsely be explained in terms of animal life. Probably they were gas bubbles released when the target disturbed the bottom*[1] (our italics).

Professor Tucker went on to explain that in deep water such as Loch Ness thermal conditions may distort the sonar display at medium and long ranges (i.e. beyond a distance of approximately two hundred yards). The Birmingham probe scanned a cross-section of the loch almost exactly *three thousand* yards in length. Thermal gradients made interpretation of the display 'difficult' at medium and long ranges. Also 'Display observations indicate that thermal conditions change from hour to hour, and it is known also that thermal profiles are not constant over an enclosed volume of fresh water. This makes ray analysis from thermal or velocity measurements almost impossible.'

In other words the 1968 'monster' recording was now subject to a number of technical reservations. Tucker still stood by the horizontal velocities recorded then (though even in 1968 he and Braithwaite had written that the accuracy of their figure for the horizontal velocity of Object C was 'low'). But as far as the vertical movements were concerned they were now 'not so certain'. In other words, the mystery object which appeared in the frame and dived at 450 feet a minute might not have been doing any such thing.

After 1970 the Birmingham team did not return to Loch Ness. In a newsletter issued to L.N.I. volunteers David James explained that underwater research was perhaps not so important after all:

> While sonar is fascinating, it is an imprecise tool when it comes to giving one dimensions of a living creature and there are good grounds for believing that a full profile photograph, which simply must fall into someone's lap sooner or later, remains by far and away the most effective means of solving our problem.

1 D. G. Tucker and D. J. Creasey, 'Some Sonar Observations in Loch Ness.' *Proceedings of the Challenger Society*, Vol. IV (1970), pp. 91–92.

The work of the Birmingham team had shown up some of the ambiguities and problems involved in using sonar to solve the mystery.[1] In later years, as a variety of American investigators arrived at the loch, a new danger arose: the partisan interpretation of complex technical data by operators with a passionate commitment to the beast's existence.

In the early summer of 1970 David James received a letter from a 'Dr Robert H. Rines, President of the Academy of Applied Science, Belmont, Mass.' enquiring about the Bureau's attempts to lay bait for the monster. The letter went on to say that the Academy was planning experimental research at the loch using sexual as well as food attractants.

This sounded, at the very least, interesting. A team of zoologists and technicians from an impressive-sounding academic institution would certainly assist in giving the monster credibility, as well as helping to solve the mystery. The Bureau responded in friendly fashion.

Later it transpired that the Academy, despite its impressive name, was not an academic institution but largely the creation of its wealthy 'President', Dr Rines. Dr Rines, it turned out, was not a scientist but a lawyer. He specialised in patents. He titled himself 'Dr' on the strength of a degree he was given by National Chiao Tung University of Taiwan. A Rines associate explained that the degree was awarded after submission of a paper on 'how to start high-technology companies in developing countries.'[2] It also emerged that Rines's 'Academy' consisted largely of businessmen, including such figures as the President of 'Chu Associates', the President of 'Prototech Inc', the President of 'Megapulse Inc' and the President of 'Astrodynamics'. Among the Academy's published aims was to debate 'Current Tax Proposals –

[1] Since this book was first published new sonar findings have been put forward by the Ness and Morar Project, described at length by project leader Adrian Shine in *New Scientist*, 17 February 1983. These results are discussed in the Postscript to this Star paperback edition.

[2] See Jon Swan, 'A Question of Degree', *New Scientist* (26 August 1982), p. 578.

Stimulus or Barrier to Invention' and the 'Problems of Rekindling the Innovative Fire of Employed Inventors and Others Through Appropriate Attitudes, Policies and Incentives.'

In September 1970 an Academy team of three began research at Loch Ness. The team consisted of Rines, Dr Martin Klein (who ran a sonar equipment business) and Ike Blonder, 'President of the Blonder-Tongue Laboratories.' Their use of sex lures soon attracted the attention of the popular press. 'Rines claimed that shy though the monster might be, it was quite a sexy brute. A mock monster made of plastic buoys and covered in salmon oil had been run off with one day and never been seen again.'[1] The kind of cor-what-a-whopper! coverage this elicited was, to say the least, predictable.

Meanwhile Rines's associate Dr Klein had fixed up one of his firm's high-definition side-scan sonars near Temple Pier, close to where the Birmingham team had operated from. Almost immediately after installing his equipment Klein began to register the presence of monsters. In the space of just one hour he three times picked up a large object passing through the sonar beam. His success rate, when compared with the long barren labours of the Birmingham researchers, was truly phenomenal.

Over the next two days Tim Dinsdale obligingly ferried Klein and Rines to the western end of the loch. More large mysterious blips appeared on Klein's sonar screen. What was more his equipment picked up evidence of undercuts along the precipitous sides of the loch. Were the old legends of fabulous underwater caverns perhaps true after all? Unfortunately there was no time in which to pursue these exciting new developments; on the third day Klein had to depart because of other commitments. Dinsdale shook him firmly by the hand and thanked him for 'making history'. Certainly no-one else could claim such spectacular results after just a few days at the loch.

1 Peter Costello, *In Search of Lake Monsters*, p. 120.

Soon afterwards Rines went down to London to give a national press conference. There he made the dramatic announcement that the monster was 'albino white, about 35 feet long and probably blind due to living in the murky gloom 200 feet down.'[1]

Klein subsequently produced his own report in which he claimed he had made three important discoveries at Loch Ness. These were (i) 'There are large moving objects in the Loch', (ii) 'There is abundant fish life in the Loch which could support a large creature', (iii) 'There are large ridges in the steep walls of the Loch which could conceivably harbour large creatures.'

This third 'discovery' was a new and controversial one. It later turned out that it stemmed from an overenthusiastic reading of the data. Side-scan sonar can easily present the appearance of caves on a chart when no caves actually exist. Klein's conclusions were contradicted by the work of other sonar operators at the loch. Sonar expert Robert Love was hired by L.N.I. to conduct sweeps of the loch, and after far more comprehensive exercises than Klein's stated categorically that no indications of caverns or overhanging ledges had appeared on any of his recordings.[2] Of course if there were caves then it ought to have been possible, as Klein himself admitted, to use a narrow conical beam sonar to explore the caves. This, it seems, was never done.

In 1971 Rines arrived back at the loch with an underwater camera and stroboscopic flash attachment. The equipment was successfully tried out, and the following year the Academy published a glossy brochure, *Underwater Search at Loch Ness*, which showed the results of these experiments, under the heading 'Proof That We Can Obtain Rare Photographs'. The brochure included a conjectural photograph of a 'flipper' which had appeared in front of the lens when the camera unit had mysteriously vanished one night, only to re-appear some hours later floating in the middle of

1 Costello, *Op. Cit.*, p. 120.
2 See the Loch Ness Investigation Report (1969), p. 3.

the loch. Tim Dinsdale believed poachers were probably responsible for moving the rig. There was also a photograph of what appeared to be a log on the loch's bed, teasingly identified by the Academy as a possible monster carcass.

Rines returned to Scotland in 1972 to begin new experiments with a linked sonar and camera unit which, upon registering the presence of a large moving object, would trigger the strobe-camera, photographing every fifty-five seconds. Almost immediately Rines achieved a spectacular success. On 8 August, between 1.45 a.m. and 2 a.m., a large echo appeared on the Raytheon oscilloscope, setting off the underwater camera. The mystery object was only about 100–150 feet away, in the Temple Pier area. When processed three frames of film revealed the presence of indistinct, murky objects. Rines asked a friend at the N.A.S.A. Jet Propulsion Laboratories to computer-enhance the photographs. One photograph failed to respond to enhancement, but the other two revealed what appeared to be a large flipper attached to a portion of an animal's body (*Plate* 9). Members of the Academy interpreted the 'flipper' as being up to 4 feet wide and 8 feet long, though in the absence of any controls this estimate seemed to be speculative.

Although computer-enhancement is an acceptable method of removing 'clutter' and improving a photographic image it remains unclear how far the process contributed to the clarity and focus of the image. In a 'Confidential Newsletter' rushed out to its members at the end of October 1972 the Bureau reported that the underwater photograph showed 'a triangular appendage appearing to contain five digits'. The five digits mysteriously vanished from the print of the photograph released to the world's press, raising doubts about the way in which the image was being interfered with.

To believers the two 'flipper' photographs were conclusive proof of the monster's existence. On the face of it the possibility that the object photographed was part of a known species of fish seemed unlikely. A hoax could be ruled out. That only seemed to leave the monster.

Or did it?

There were a number of curious features to the affair which suggested that a hoax by someone either within the investigation, or outside it, was, if seemingly improbable, by no means impossible. The episode took place at night close inshore in the relatively shallow water of the Temple Pier area – an area much frequented by frogmen, and frequently used in diving experiments. No-one actually *saw* a monster in the vicinity that night, though L.N.I. members were present, armed with a searchlight. Of the 2000 frames on the film only three showed anything at all. By an amazing chance a full 'flipper' appeared in two of these.

The timing of this great success was fortuitous for the Loch Ness Investigation. By August 1972 morale was at a low ebb. There had been no new photographic developments since the movie film of a wake shot five years earlier. The dramatic 1968 sonar results had not been repeated. Gyrocopters, submarines and baiting had all failed, as had expeditions to other monster-haunted waters. Sponsors were beginning to pull out and money was becoming a problem. To cap it all the local council had refused the Bureau permission to continue using the Achnahannet site. Then, out of the blue, to redeem ten years of seemingly fruitless and wasted effort, came the incredible 'flipper' photographs. Suddenly hopes once again began to soar, and lingering doubts extinguished. There *was* a monster there after all ...

There is a pattern here which has happened many times before in the Loch Ness story. In 1934, after the monster had lost credibility as a result of a clumsy and quickly exposed hoax, and just as sightings dwindled, the Surgeon's photograph exploded on the scene to renew the faith of believers. In the fifties, when interest in the monster lay dormant, there sudenly appeared the amazing Lachlan Stuart photograph. Further publicity about the beast produced the Cockrell and MacNab photographs. Ironically, the last still photograph of the monster before Rines's 'flipper' was Peter O'Connor's, now widely regarded as dubious even by believers. The O'Connor photograph and Rines's 'flipper' photograph have much in common. Both were taken by flashlight, both were taken at close range, and both show the monster in startling detail. But there is no evidence *from the photographs themselves* that they were taken at Loch Ness. Yet, though both photographs possess a kind of grainy authenticity they add curiously little to our knowledge of the monster.

The idea that any of the Loch Ness investigators would indulge in hoaxes is invariably regarded by believers as a preposterous and unthinkable idea. This is perhaps to take too rosy a view of human nature. Loch Ness has attracted more than its fair share of hoaxers and charlatans in the last fifty years, and the fraternity of believers have been quick to forget embarrassing episodes such as the Bureau's admiration for Frank Searle. Monster 'experts' have also not always been over-scrupulous with the evidence in seeking to convert the uninitiated to the idea that something funny lives in Loch Ness.[1]

At this juncture it is worth recalling the greatest hoax of twentieth-century British science. This was the so-called 'Piltdown man'. The Piltdown skull (named after the place in Sussex where it was excavated) was believed to be millions of years old, the oldest human skull ever found. It was discovered by a team which included a solicitor, a public analyst, a theologian, an anthropologist and a dentition expert from the British Museum, and a prominent anatomist.

1 In 1969 the *Sunday Express* published a photograph taken by Mrs Jessie Tait showing what was obviously a boat's wake. In the 1969 L.N.I. Annual Report David James protested that the newspaper had gone ahead and printed the photograph of this 'known and recorded wake against our most urgent advice.' The Report even published Mrs Tait's photograph, emphasizing that it was a good example of 'The commonest source of error, bow waves from a vessel which has already passed out of sight.' Soon afterwards L.N.I. member Nicholas Witchell published *Loch Ness and the Monster — A Handbook for Tourists*. There on the cover and inside the brochure was the Tait photograph, with a caption hinting it portrayed the monster. Later David James himself obligingly wrote an introduction to William Owen's tourist brochure *Scotland's Loch Ness Monster*, which also presents the Tait photograph as evidence for a large unknown animal in the loch.

At least one of these worthy figures was a hoaxer, though at the time a host of experts testified that the skull was genuine. The Piltdown site was established as a National Monument, and a stone was erected which can still be seen there today. Tourists poured there by the coachload, the nearby Lamb Inn quickly changed its name to 'The Piltdown Man' and the locals did a roaring trade selling picture postcards entitled 'Searching for the Piltdown Man'. Over the years some five-hundred scholarly articles were written. Then, decades later, in 1953, it was discovered that the skull was a hoax, put together from bits and pieces of bone from a variety of skulls, and nowhere near as old as had previously been believed.

The Piltdown skull was unveiled before a densely packed audience at Burlington House in December 1912, creating a sensation. Anyone with a sceptical mind might well have found an echo of this event in the hullabaloo which surrounded the announcement in 1975 that the Academy had obtained more underwater photographs of the Loch Ness monster.

These new photographs were reputed to be so spectacular that they provided the final proof – proof that not even the most hardened cynic could quarrel with. The news was leaked to the press, where it immediately made the front-page headlines:

LOCH NESS MONSTER FOUND
Is it a beast from 70 million years?

The Loch Ness monster has been found. New evidence which proves the existence of the beast is being examined by a group of the world's top zoologists.

They are to meet in Edinburgh next month to classify the new creature and consider measures to protect the species, which may well be a relic from prehistoric times.

Only a small group of the world's most eminent specialists have been informed of the nature of the new evidence, which is being kept a closely-guarded secret.

But it can be revealed that underwater close-up

photographs have been taken of a large unknown animal, the like of which has not been known since a marine dinosaur known as the plesiosaur is supposed to have become extinct, 70 million years ago.

Details of the discovery, which ends nearly 50 years of international controversy and confirms Scottish legends stretching back thousands of years, are to be revealed at a symposium in Edinburgh next month.[1]

The Symposium was to be held in Edinburgh on 9 and 10 December, under the auspices of the Royal Society, with joint sponsorship by the University of Edinburgh and Heriot-Watt University. Monster-hunters began boasting that the meeting was proof that their cause had, at long last, acquired academic respectability. The great goal of converting scientists to the beast's existence seemed about to come to fruition. Excitedly Tim Dinsdale told the *Observer*: 'It's like the calm of a battle field before the crunch. A few star shells have gone up, showing where everybody is. Soon, the gunfire will start.'

It did, but not quite in the way Dinsdale had envisaged. On 1 December the Royal Society, irritated by all the advance publicity which had ruined the plan for a press release *after* the photographs had been examined and discussed, issued a chilly statement cancelling the Symposium:

Recent wide publicity, from prospective participants on both sides of the Atlantic, at variance with this understanding has forced the Royal Society of Edinburgh and the Associated Universities to the regretful conclusion that no useful or impartial discussion can take place at this time, and under these circumstances.

The monster fraternity had tried to jump the gun and pre-empt the verdict on the mysterious new evidence. The Royal Society's reaction was a crushing disappointment. Putting a

1 *Yorkshire Post*, 22 November 1975.

brave face on the matter David James and his L.N.I. colleagues hired a room at the Palace of Westminster and arranged a press conference. At the last moment their thunder was stolen by Rines and Peter Scott who held their own press conference a few hours earlier. Rines and Scott announced that the monster's official scientific name was henceforth *Nessiteras Rhombopteryx*. A wit quickly pointed out that this could be an anagram of 'Monster hoax by Sir Peter S.' The entire episode ended on a note of anticlimax, and Rines's credibility was not helped by a *Sunday Times* 'Insight' team investigation which reported his efforts to profit from the pictures. According to their report Rines had attempted to sell the photographs for more than $100,000 to the *National Geographic* magazine. The offer was declined. Rines then tried to sell them to *Time*, but this magazine also declined to buy them.

The photographs finally appeared in all their smudgy glory across the pages of the British tabloids. After all the publicity ('the greatest thing that has happened this century' one Academy spokesman modestly remarked) the pictures were disappointing. One purported to show the monster's head, neck and forward flippers. Another was identified as a close-up of the creature's hideous face, complete with snarling open mouth and horns (*Plate* 10).

According to Rines, a sonar contact in June 1975 had triggered a unit of two cameras. The main rig turned out not to have photographed anything, but the back-up camera (significantly, the same one that took the 1972 'flipper' snaps) captured an object which resembled the front portion of a monster. Some eight hours later this camera took two more photographs, one allegedly of the monster's head, the other of its stomach. Sceptics quickly pointed out that the pictures showed only outlines, not features. Why, they asked, did Rines's camera take crisp sharp photographs of salmon and eels but only vague fuzzy pictures of monsters? Why hadn't Rines used a control in the photographs to establish comparative size and focus? Brian Peterson, Harvard Professor of vertebrate palaeontology, acidly commented that whatever was in Rines's photographs 'could only be taken seriously if someone put a net over it.' Another zoologist told the *Sunday Times*, 'The effect of computer enhancement may be to make into a definite outline what is in fact a vague one.' Sceptics also wondered why Rines had not sent the original film for enhancement but only a copy – a copy, moreover, in which he had (according to the *Sunday Times*) adjusted the contrast.

The publicity surrounding Rines's new underwater photographs was greatly swelled by the paperback publication of Nicholas Witchell's *Loch Ness Story* (1975). In August, before the Penguin edition had yet gone to the printers, Witchell received a dramatic trans-Atlantic telephone call:

> Bob Rines came on the line to announce news that meant the search for the 'Monster' of Loch Ness was finally over. 'Nick,' his voice came clearly and steadily over the thousands of miles, 'we've got it, we've hit the jackpot. We have detailed close-up colour photographs of the head, neck and body of one of the animals.'

Time would show this to be a preposterous claim, but Witchell immediately flew to Boston, where Rines treated him to a private showing. Thrilled, Witchell despatched an urgent cable back to England: *Amazing picture of horrific head*, it began, *Greta Finlay was correct*. Witchell subsequently returned home and wrote a dramatic postscript to his forthcoming paperback, announcing that he had seen with his own eyes 'the final, conclusive evidence'. He provided a somewhat colourful and over-imaginative description of the as-then unpublished pictures, and solemnly stated that by the end of the year (1975) the Loch Ness mystery would finally be over:

> By then the material will have been examined by a team of experts led by Dr John Sheals, Keeper of Zoology at the British Museum, whose responsibility it will be to ratify the discovery of the animals.

Unfortunately for Witchell, Dr Sheals did no such thing. On behalf of the team of five Museum scientists Dr Sheals issued a statement asserting that, in their opinion,

> The photographs do not constitute acceptable evidence of the existence of a large living animal. All the photographs appear to show different objects and there is no reason to associate them with any previous photographs. The indistinctness of the images is such that a whole variety of speculative interpretations seems equally plausible.

Ironically, the truth of this last point was illustrated by Witchell's own writing. In the first Penguin edition he had excitedly described parasites hanging from the monster's belly and the possibility that the creature's 'anal fold' was visible. In the second edition these features of the monster vanish and Witchell speaks more cautiously of 'a covering of what appeared to be lumps or growths.'

In a television documentary about the monster broadcast in June 1976 Dr Sheals continued his criticisms of Rines's pictures:

> I don't believe these photographs prove a thing. There's no evidence whatsoever to support the view that the objects in the photographs are large living animals. The earlier 'flipper' photograph is of course quite intriguing. But there's the problem of scale. I feel Dr Rines has insufficient evidence to make his assertion that this object is 6–8 feet in length. Now if it was smaller – and some photographic experts have said that it could be very much smaller – then obviously one would be very inclined to think in terms of fish fins, although there are of course other possibilities. It seems to me that in this situation some control runs might be useful. That is to say, it would be useful if the investigators photographed the fins of familiar fishes in turbid water with a strobe light and then subjected the results to the computer enhancement process. This might help to solve the mystery.

The naturalist David Attenborough also suggested that the 1972 'flipper' might in fact simply be the fin of a small fish photographed at an unusual angle. Although at the time the flipper photograph seemed to lend credibility to the popular plesiosaur theory it has since been recognised that the flipper's structure does not show an efficient design for swimming. The problem is a somewhat academic one anyway, since Rines has not been forthcoming with evidence of control runs. As so often before in the Loch Ness story the situation ended inconclusively. Since then Rines has had the 1975 pictures computer enhanced – but has chosen not to release them. This is, to say the least, curious.

Nicholas Witchell's description of these underwater photographs as 'the final, conclusive evidence' was, then, merely hyperbole. Adrian Shine, who has considerable experience of diving in Loch Ness, believes that Rines's camera photographed debris lying on the bed of the loch. As our own photographs demonstrate it is not hard to discover decayed timber on the loch's shore which bears remarkable similarities with Rines's 'head' picture (*Plates* 11 (a) and (b)). After the extraordinary publicity which this episode garnered it is amusing to think that the source of all the fuss may simply have been, literally, a load of old rubbish.

In 1976 Penguin Books published a revised edition of *The Loch Ness Story*. Witchell, in a more chastened mood now, rewrote his conclusion and denounced British scientists for their scepticism and indifference:

> Although the most recent episode in this strange saga ended in disappointment the final note must be one of great hope. The veil around the animals has now been lifted and the coming months are bound to produce more and greater efforts at Loch Ness. The final answers will soon be found – with or without the help and blessing of the British scientific Establishment.

The sense of *déjà vu* about this passage is overwhelming. Year after year the monsters-hunters promise the final proof – and year after year the evidence continues to elude their grasp.

Amid all the controversy surrounding the 1975 under-water photographs one simple thing was forgotten. In terms of providing evidence for monsters they were *a regression*. The great monster-hunt began in 1962 with the stated aim of producing unambiguous close-up movie film of a large unknown animal. The attempt failed. No convincing motion film has ever been obtained of a 'monster' in Loch Ness. The Rines underwater photographs merely return us to all the problems, doubts and ambiguities which surround still photography.

Since the mid-seventies the Loch Ness and Morar Project has also operated underwater cameras at both lochs, besides maintaining observation from a submersible chamber. These exercises have been without success. As the Project leader Adrian Shine frankly admits, 'The unpalatable truth is that fixed underwater cameras – television or still – may remain on station for months without picking up a target.'

Meanwhile small groups of adventurers continue to haunt Loch Ness and Loch Morar, often bearing back familiar tales of woe:

I estimate that from the moment I saw the object to the time it vanished beneath the waters of the loch, about 15 to 17 seconds had elapsed ... There were no photographs. Evans did not have any film in his 35mm Nikon motordrive camera with 500mm lens, and he was in the act of changing films in his 16mm Bolex cine camera when the creature surfaced.[1]

1 Sydney Wignall, *In Search of Spanish Treasure* (David & Charles, 1982), p. 233. In an Epilogue Wignall puts forward the original idea that motionless monsters at the surface may well be females giving birth. He suggests that one way to solve the mystery would be to land a Microlite seaplane beside a stationary monster and then dive in with a watertight camera for 'an eye-ball to eye-ball confrontation.' Although this scheme turned out to be 'impractical' Mr Wignall nevertheless returned from Loch Morar in 1981 triumphantly in possession of film of 'a large, purply-coloured object' which received wide publicity in the media. The object, alas, betrayed no signs of motion and seemed to bring a solution to the monster mystery no closer.

The author reports that he gave a 'wan smile' – as might the reader.

The optimism and excitement which characterised the beginning of the great monster-hunt back in 1962 has now largely dwindled away. Two decades later, and sobered by an unending series of defeats, the monster fraternity have begun to change tack. In his book *The Monsters of Loch Ness* Roy Mackal dismisses continued photographic surveillance of the loch's surface as being of little value. As far as he is concerned we already know all there is to know about the monsters; all that is required now is a live specimen. But almost all of Mackal's analysis is founded on eye-witness sightings. What people can see must, if really there, be possible to photograph.

Similarly, in *The Mysterious Monsters of Loch Ness*, Anthony Harmsworth includes a picture of one of the L.N.I.'s powerful 35mm cine-cameras and blandly states, 'Once popular it has now been generally accepted that these long lens cameras have outlived their usefulness in the investigation.'

This may well be the new orthodoxy of the monster faithful, but it is nevertheless an evasion, a papering over of the stark fact of failure. These are the arguments of the defeated. They serve only to highlight the inescapable reality that after half a century no-one has been able to provide convincing photographic evidence of a family of large unknown animals in Loch Ness. Rather than speculate on the possible evolution of the plesiosaur, we need to look elsewhere for a solution to the enigma.

9   The Beast At The Surface

It is argued that, on the basis of a single experience, a number of verbal statements are justified. The character of such statements is investigated, and it is contended that they must always be confined to matters belonging to the biography of the observer; they can be such as 'I see a canoid patch of colour', but not such as 'there is a dog.' Statements of this latter kind always involve, in their justification, some element of inference.

Bertrand Russell, *An Inquiry into Meaning and Truth* (1940)

I'm a reliable witness, you're a reliable witness, practically all God's children are reliable witnesses in their own estimation – which makes it funny how such different ideas of the same affair get about.

John Wyndham, *The Kraken Wakes* (1953)

The case for the Loch Ness monster rests overwhelmingly on eye-witness evidence, and this is just where the difficulty lies. No-one has been able to film what eye-witnesses claim they see. This paradox lies at the heart of the Loch Ness mystery.

The dangers in placing too much reliance on the unsupported claims of individuals are highlighted by the way in which some classic monster sightings have altered with time. Mr and Mrs Spicer saw an animal which crossed the road in front of them in a matter of seconds. At first Mr Spicer said it was between six and eight feet long. A year later the Spicers were telling people that their creature was twenty-five to thirty feet in length.

The way in which sightings, like wine, improve with the years is graphically illustrated by the Greta Finlay episode. On 20 August 1952 Mrs Finlay and her little boy walked round their caravan and were shocked by the sight of a 'monster' directly opposite them, just a few yards from the shore. Harry Finlay afterwards did a sketch of their monster, which in its shape and proportions greatly resembled a deer. The drawing was reproduced in *More Than a Legend*. Four years later Harry obligingly redrew his 'monster' for Tim Dinsdale. The new sketch was altogether more impressive and duly appeared in *Loch Ness Monster* (see illustration).

Inconsistencies of this sort abound in the literature of the Loch Ness mystery. The case for the beast's existence is scarcely helped by the rather unscrupulous approach which believers adopt. The sightings record is riddled with inconsistencies and contradictions from which the faithful diplomatically avert their eyes. The case of Alex Campbell provides a striking example both of a witness changing his mind and of the gullibility of the believers, who prefer to leave certain uncomfortable questions unasked.

Just as some stories get better over the years, others vanish altogether. Loch Ness Investigation chief, David James, gave a dramatic account of a monster which showed 'six to eight feet' of back 'about 200 yards away' (*Observer*, 17 May 1964), but now says he has never seen the beast. Nicholas Witchell reported sighting a 'dark pole-like object about three feet in height' at Loch Ness in August 1972,[1] but subsequently wrote in the paperback edition of *The Loch Ness Story*, 'I have never seen the animals of Loch Ness, despite having spent many months at the loch and many tens of thousands of hours watching for a surface appearance.'

Individual interpretations of the size and speed of objects or

1 'Sightings 1972.' Unpublished L.N.I. leaflet.

Figure 5

The monster that grew bigger

(i) Greta Finlay's monster in *More Than a Legend* (1957). Could it have been a roe-deer? (see *Plate* 16.)

(ii) Greta Finlay's monster redrawn in Dinsdale's *Loch Ness Monster* (1961 edition).
Drawings by Harry Finlay

disturbances which are only momentarily glimpsed are often unreliable, especially if the witness has a strong belief in monsters. For example, in 1971 one of the authors of this book and a colleague on the Morar Survey saw a small wake moving parallel to their Zodiac inflatable boat as they moved out into Loch Morar one night. The experience was slightly unusual, but nothing that could not have been produced by a fish. Nevertheless both witnesses had a strong commitment to the Survey's goals, and both were aware of the depressing paucity of evidence to have emerged from the Survey's surveillance of the loch. It was against this background that the sighting report was filled in on behalf of both witnesses. The wake's speed was given as 'approximately twelve knots'. In retrospect it was an absurdly subjective estimate. The incident happened so quickly that an accurate assessment of speed was impossible. Both witnesses recognised the inconclusive nature of their experience and were reluctant to ascribe it to the presence of a monster. The 'sighting' nevertheless found its way into *The Search for Morag* where it appears as quite convincing evidence for Morag the monster. This kind of thing probably occurs more often than is usually admitted.

In *The Case for the Sea-Serpent* (1930) Rupert Gould observed, 'It is quite true that if you are eagerly on the look-out for something, and expect to see it, you are very likely to be misled by anything bearing even a faint resemblance to the thing which you expect to see.' This factor, which Gould called 'expectant attention', is of much greater significance than has generally been recognised. In many ways Tim Dinsdale's experience at Loch Ness was typical. Monster-hunters who arrive at the loch for the first time do tend immediately to see the beast. Having proved to their own satisfaction that it exists they then devote weeks, months or even years to a barren quest for another sighting.

When Tim Dinsdale brought his family to the loch for the first time they, too, had a sighting. Again the experience was archetypal. In *Project Water Horse* Dinsdale describes how his family spent their first night at the loch telling stories about the monster. His two youngest children showed 'signs of nervousness, the Monster looming large in their imagination.' Dinsdale himself was convinced that they might encounter the beast in Urquhart Bay, where they were spending the night on board a catamaran. His family survived the experience, but the very next morning saw the monster. Driving along the north shore road they came in sight of Inchnacardoch Bay. 'What's that?' someone shouted. Dinsdale saw nothing because he was concentrating on driving. The bay was in view only for a split second before being hidden behind a clump of trees and bushes. Dinsdale braked and ran back. There was nothing there.

> I questioned the witnesses closely. They had all seen something big, moving away, and leaving a wake. My wife thought it might have been a rowing boat with the pointed bow creating the impression of a hump, but the two girls and Angus said it *was* a hump. Ian Smith had naturally concluded it was a boat, because of its size, but Simon who had exceptional eyesight said it was the Monster.[1]

In other words, the adults thought they had seen a boat, and the children thought they had seen Nessie.[2] Dinsdale's daughter drew a sketch, touchingly entitled 'Alexandra – 13 yrs. Sketch of Large Hump.'

The whole episode was absurdly inconclusive, but Dinsdale nevertheless managed to extract monstrous significance from it. 'Whatever it may have been it could not have been a boat, because in 20–30 seconds it could not have simply disappeared.' But once again Dinsdale was almost certainly guilty of exaggeration. If he was driving at 40–50 m.p.h. (a reasonable speed for that stretch of road) it would surely have taken him at least two minutes to realise what was happening, brake, bring the car safely to a halt, get out, and run back up the road to where the loch could be seen. By that time a boat might

1 Tim Dinsdale, *Project Water Horse*, p. 65.
2 'I eschewed the evidence of children – they may be accurate observers, but the tendency to "go one better" is always present.' Rupert Gould, *The Loch Ness Monster and Others*, p. 13.

easily have passed out of sight and hearing. Dinsdale implies he had a panoramic view over the loch at this point; it was actually highly restricted.

The belief that the eye is a foolproof and objective instrument which gives us accurate pictures of 'reality' (a belief implicit in the old adage 'seeing is believing') is wide of the mark. The eye is an imperfect optical system. Light waves not only have to pass through the lens and liquids of the eyeball, none of which is a perfect transmitter of light, but also have to penetrate the network of blood vessels and cells that lie on the inside of the eye before reaching the photoreceptors where light is converted into nervous impulses.

There is a good example of the way in which the eye can fool an observer described in *The Leviathans*:

> A young L.N.I. cameraman had shot film from high up on the northern shore, which had been ruined by the sunglaze. The photographer, whose iris had contracted to compensate visually, could see a hump ploughing through the water, but in the film one could barely see the wake.

This has all the appearance of being a classic example of 'expectant attention' occurring in conjunction with visual deception. No hump appeared on the film because there was no hump there in the first place, not because of any sunglaze.

Our ability to perceive the size of objects is not innate, it is learned. Things normally appear to look smaller the further away they are because our retinal image of objects varies according to distance. We are able to recognise the size of familiar objects from memory of past experience. They acquire 'size constancy'.

Professor Richard Gregory, a leading figure in perception research and the man in charge of teaching neuropsychology at Bristol University, has commented (*Sunday Times*, 2 November 1980):

Our visual system is always having to stretch beyond the few clues supplied to it. The nerve channels cannot handle much information anyway so a whole area of our 'seeing' has to do with guessing well, or laying bets.

When we follow the same rules in a strange environment, out in the country, for example, then we are liable to be tricked by our own over-confidence. So I would say that this sighting of strange creatures often has a lot to do with mis-perception.

If we are travelling on a motorway early in the morning and there is only one vehicle ahead, we know by its geometric features whether it is a car or a lorry. Because we 'remember' the size of lorries we are able to estimate the vehicle's distance from us. But if we were travelling a straight road across a flat featureless desert and suddenly saw a camel without ever having previous knowledge of these animals then our ability to perceive accurately its size would be very limited. If the camel was well away from the road we would have no objective frame of reference at all.

A large expanse of empty flat calm water is a similar kind of visual desert. The only frame of reference is subjective. It is precisely in this kind of visually impoverished environment that the eye can play strange tricks, including falsely perceiving movement where none exists, over-estimating size or misinterpreting commonplace objects.

It is surprising just how many classic sightings of the Loch Ness monster have been abrupt, unexpected and short-lived. Tim Dinsdale's 1971 head and neck sighting is interesting in this respect, since he describes how he 'spotted' the mystery object 'out of the corner of [his] eye.' Later, on television, he explained how the whole experience was over in a moment: 'Very quick! Seconds! But it was real. And it had a startling effect on me.' So startling, in fact, that in a state of great excitement Dinsdale immediately crashed his boat on to a spit of shingle.

An even more revealing sighting was described by monster-photographer 'Doc' Shiels's wife, Christine:

It was at the edge of my vision, and when I tried to focus on the image it simply and suddenly wasn't there. After two or three frustrating attempts to get a clear picture of the thing by staring straight at it, failing each time, I decided to allow it to be coy, to stay 'in the corner of my eye' so to speak. This worked. For several seconds I saw a large, dark, long-necked hump-backed beast moving slowly through the water, then sinking beneath the surface.[1]

Believers, reluctant to ascribe monster-sightings to misperception, invariably point to the witnesses' absolute conviction that they have seen a huge unknown animal. But here, too, recent research has shown that an eye-witness's confidence about the evidence he or she gives is no guide to its accuracy.

In 1980 Clive Hollin, a psychology graduate working for the Home Office, reported on some experiments which he had carried out into eye-witness behaviour. A group of people were invited to watch a simulated crime such as a mugging take place and then report on what they thought they had seen. The results were surprising. Witnesses who exuded self-confidence about their testimony were just as likely to be wrong as those who expressed hesitation and uncertainty. Hollin's research, described in *The Guardian*, 27 October 1980, has since received support from the findings of other experimental psychologists. Dr Michael Gruneberg, senior lecturer in psychology at the University of Wales, has recently drawn some conclusions from this work which seem of crucial relevance to the Loch Ness enigma:

In the area of eyewitness research, finding after finding is casting serious doubts about the adequacy of a legal system which relies heavily on eyewitness testimony.

It is not merely a question of a witness making the occasional mistake. Research is showing again and again under numerous conditions practically every individual is capable of gross inaccuracies.

1 Letter to the *Falmouth Packet*, 9 July 1976. Quoted in Janet and Colin Bord, *Alien Animals* (London: Granada, 1980).

Research on eyewitnessing has shown that accuracy is often limited and is affected by the kind of question asked.

What is important is that eyewitness testimony on its own, without any real substantive supporting evidence, must be treated with the greatest of caution.[1]

The situation Gruneberg describes is exactly the one which obtains at Loch Ness. Over the years a quantity of eye-witness testimony has been accumulated *without any real substantive supporting evidence*.

It is often said that the Loch Ness eye-witness evidence is all very much the same, and points in the direction of the popular plesiosaur-shaped image which the monster has taken on in the literature about the mystery. Nothing could be further from the truth.

Witnesses actually say very different things about the monster, leading to the conclusion that the monsters are present in the loch in a variety of shapes, colours and sizes, or that some of the witnesses are mistaken. To Nicholas Witchell 'It is the very discrepancy in the points of detail which give weight and substance to the reliability and integrity of the reports.' Zoologists have difficulty in responding to that kind of zany logic with much sympathy.

In practice the monster fraternity are highly selective in their dealings with the accumulated evidence of fifty years. Some eye-witness reports do not fit the consensus image of the monster and in consequence are discarded. Others which reinforce the orthodox view are respected as classic sightings. Witnesses who claim that they have seen something in the loch resembling an upturned boat will find themselves taken seriously; those who report seeing crocodiles, giant frogs or tortoises will not. Commander Meiklem, who saw the monster's black knobby back, is remembered; Miss Nellie Smith, who only hours earlier saw the monster waving its legs in the air, is not. Roy Mackal discards 90% of the eye-witness sightings, but if 90% is to go, then why not 100%? Who is to say that those who see

1 Michael Gruneberg, 'The blind eyewitness', *The Guardian*, 1 March 1982.

plesiosaurs in the loch are any less deluded than those who see crocodiles?

The most important question-mark which hangs over eye-witnesses of the Loch Ness monster is whether or not they were familiar with the loch and the explicable objects which periodically appear on its surface. Why is it that time and time again the monster-watchers stationed by their powerful cameras see nothing, only to learn that a tourist two miles up the road has just had a spectacular sighting of the beast? The usual explanation is 'bad luck' (though F. W. Holiday eventually decided that the only explanation for this baffling situation lay in the realms of the occult). In practice there is a rather simpler explanation, which is that inexperienced or over-enthusiastic observers at Loch Ness mistake for 'monsters' what are either inanimate objects or known natural phenomena.

ii

'The soil in your neighbourhood is particularly black and rich. Consequently it provides the moles with particularly rich nourishment, and so they grow to an unusual size.'
'But not to such a size as that!' exclaimed the teacher, and he measured off two yards on the wall, somewhat exaggerating the length of the mole in his exasperation.

Franz Kafka, *The Giant Mole* (1931)

A monster is no more than a combination of parts of real beings, and the possibilities of permutation border on the infinite.

Jorge Luis Borges with Margarita Guerrero, *The Book of Imaginary Beings* (1954)

It is now impossible for anyone to visit Loch Ness without associating its waters with a mythical monster. And, as we suggested earlier, 'monster' is a word which carries powerful associations. It is therefore not surprising that those who are unfamiliar with the loch and with the objects and wake-effects which appear on its surface are sometimes misled into seeing 'monsters'.

The expectations generated by the word 'monster' are inseparable from many sighting reports. An example of this can be seen in the famous Lowrie sighting. According to the Lowrie family they were travelling down Loch Ness in their motorized yacht when they found themselves being pursued by a playful monster which swam around them. The fact that the whole episode goes against the orthodox behaviour of the beast, which is normally reckoned to be extremely shy and nervous of motor vessels, has not prevented its appearance as a classic of monster lore. The Lowrie family kept a log of the incident, which is very revealing. Brian Lowrie enquired, 'What is this monster supposed to look like? There is something coming up astern.' Everyone on board then observed 'a curious form' coming up astern, '*looking like a couple of ducks*, occasionally submerging, and a neck-like protrusion breaking surface. *The Monster – nothing less*.' (Our italics). But though identified as 'The Monster' the phenomenon was obviously quite small if it merely resembled two ducks, no matter how large the wake may have appeared in flat calm surface conditions. The object causting the disturbance was nevertheless immediately translated into a Monster with a capital 'M'.

Time and time again at Loch Ness the concept of a monster is superimposed onto experiences which clearly provide no substantive basis for the presence of (in the strict dictionary definition) an 'animal or thing of huge size'. Ironically the monster mystery was built upon the experience of Mrs Mackay who in April 1933 saw what 'At first she thought … must be a couple of wild ducks fighting.'

Commander Gould's trump card was that the monster moved at such fantastic speeds and created such a commotion in the water that it could not possibly be anything else but a huge aquatic animal. These two aspects of the monster's behaviour have proved impossible to verify, and neither was observed or filmed during the great monster watch of 1962–72. As the Cambridge expedition discovered the only large wake-effects visible on Loch Ness were those caused by trawlers. The high-speed monsters seemed harder to explain away, and Constance Whyte revealed in *More Than a Legend* that witnesses were still reporting sighting monsters travelling at speeds of up to 50 m.p.h. Such sightings were often made by motorists and seemed difficult to explain. It is now generally recognised that such witnesses were mistaken, and that birds can easily account for fast-moving humped 'monsters'. William Owen recounts how once,

> while travelling to Inverness at a point where the road is perhaps seventy feet above the loch I saw what appeared to be three undulating humps. I watched fascinated as they travelled through the water at about the same speed as I was travelling along the road. It was wintertime and the sky was grey and the waters of the loch were dark. I was almost convinced that I was watching a large animal until the first hump appeared to rise up from the water, split into three parts and become three dark-backed geese which had been flying in single file close to one another and close to the surface. From above and against the dark and broken water they had appeared as one.[1]

If the geese had simply continued flying close to the water and been lost to sight behind the trees it might have been a very different story: another classic sighting would have entered the records.

The monster fraternity, acknowledging that some witnesses may be genuinely mistaken about what they think they see, would argue that there are still too many, in total, for them all to be wrong. In *The Loch Ness Story* Nicholas Witchell asserts that there are '4000 witnesses, numerous photographs, films and sonar recordings to prove that there is substance to the story of "Nessie". As we have shown, the evidence on film and sonar is inconclusive and unconvincing. But what about the 4000 eye-witnesses? It is difficult to know

---

1 William Owen, *Scotland's Loch Ness Monster* (Jarrolds, 1980), p. 13.

how Witchell arrived at this figure, though he is by no means the only writer to bandy it about. There is no single published source giving that many eye-witness statements, and if all the published sources from 1934 to the present day are collated there are in fact less than four hundred actual sightings recorded.[1] Many of these sightings are dubious and insufficient evidence is provided to establish the context of the experience (weather conditions, position of the observer etc.). A large number of the most dramatic and least ambiguous sightings in *The Loch Ness Story* date from the seminal years 1933 and 1934, and derive from Rupert Gould's analysis of the mystery. The case for the Loch Ness monster rests heavily on Gould's book, and on the subsequent derisory figure of less then ten sightings (on average) a year.

We have seen how Gould decided in favour of the beast's existence after only two days at the loch, and how his book rests on the central assumption that there was only one monster, which was not indigenous to Loch Ness but which had recently swum up the River Ness. Though Gould was prepared to consider the negative evidence his presentation of alternative explanations was an ingenuous exercise in false logic, and one which most later authors have adopted. Only by comparing the explanations *individually* against the eye-witness testimony *en masse* was he able to assert so confidently that they failed 'without exception to cover the whole of the evidence'. Gould capped his argument with the conclusion that the monster's speed and turbulence provided 'insuperable' objections to explanations based on tree trunks, otters or other natural phenomena. Ironically, later students of the mystery have abandoned all Gould's conclusions about the monster but kept his eye-witness sightings. No-one now seriously believes that Loch Ness is inhabited by a solitary giant newt which became trapped in the loch in the early 1930s and which periodically swims along the surface at

1 The list of 251 monster sightings at the end of Roy Mackal's *The Monsters of Loch Ness* has been compiled carelessly; some sightings are listed on more than one occasion (e.g. 18, 19 and 20 which are all the same sighting).

immense speed creating huge foaming commotions. *But the evidence which led Gould to these curious conclusions is still regarded as gospel.*

The most interesting item of negative evidence which Gould put forward in considering the possibility that the monster involved 'misapprehension' of inanimate objects, natural phenomena, or some known but unrecognised living creature was Alex Campbell's monster sighting. Campbell saw a thirty-foot long monster in mirage conditions which, when the mist thinned, resolved itself into a group of cormorants. Campbell himself emphasized the peculiar effects which heat-haze could cause:

> But the most important thing was, that owing to the uncertain light the bodies of the birds were magnified out of all proportion to their proper size. This mirage-like effect I have often seen on Loch Ness ... it only occurs under certain conditions and if the Loch is calm. Then it gives every object – from, say, a gull or a bottle to an empty barrel – a very grotesque appearance provided that such objects are far enough away from the observer.

Campbell's reference to barrels is extremely relevant to sightings from 1933, since as Gould admitted 'as a result of extensive road-repairs around the Loch shores, floating tar-barrels are far from uncommon, at present, in its waters.'

When he surveyed the evidence Gould played down the importance of mirage effects. In fact 1933 was the hottest summer on record at Loch Ness. Many of the eye-witness statements publicised by Gould were submitted to him weeks or even months after they had occurred, and are vague about weather conditions. But at least 28 of Gould's classic sightings occurred in warm, sunny conditions when the loch was 'calm', 'dead calm', 'like glass', in the months May to October.

J. H. Orton wrote in to the *Times* (6 January 1934) to offer an explanation of the mystery:

The experiences of a naturalist on the Morecambe Bay sands off Cark may be of interest in relation to observations of a Loch Ness monster. It is well known that objects seen at distance on these wet sands three or four miles off shore are highly deceptive, especially in sunny weather. I have myself been so completely deceived as to imagine a common seagull resting on the sand a mile or more away to be a man.

On 14 October 1933 I saw in the distance what appeared to be a peculiar stranded boat. When we reached the object it was a fish-box about 2′ by 1′ by 1′ deep. The sun was on our right, very hot and dry, so that the sands were heating up and drying off rapidly after a long forenoon exposure. Anyone might incorrectly interpret in good faith a relatively small object seen at a distance under these conditions as some kind of curious monster.

The mirage theory is usually given short shrift by students of the monster, who regard the phenomenon as so rare as to be not worth discussing. When the Royal Geographical Society came to make a Bathymetrical Survey of Loch Ness in 1903–4 they did not think so. They even produced an Appendix to their main Report, entitled 'Mirages on Loch Ness.' Of course in 1904 the monster had not yet been invented. Their Appendix begins: 'A kind of mirage is among the most familiar phenomena on Loch Ness, especially in winter and spring. It is best seen in the morning.' *Best seen in the morning*. Exactly the conclusion that the pioneer monster investigators reached about the best chances for a sighting of the beast!

Even more remarkably, the vast majority of sightings occur on very hot, windless days when the loch is mirror calm. In the 1966 L.N.I. Annual Report David James excitedly announced,

During the course of last winter I had taken 90 reports of the best sightings over the course of the last 35 years and looked up the relevant Synoptic Charts at the London

Weather Centre, and 87 of these proved to have been under mirror calm conditions.

For years the monster fraternity have argued about whether the correlation between monster sightings and hot sunny weather with flat calm surface conditions indicates a behavioural preference on the monster's part or is because the beast is easier to spot under such conditions. A third possibility – that such conditions make it much easier to be fooled by commonplace objects – finds further support in the Royal Geographical Society's Report. It noted that 'The most constant feature of the Loch Ness mirages is seen at promontories some miles distant.' Objects known to be beyond the horizon were brought into view – particularly boats. These mirage images appeared 'very large'.

The Report gave examples of mirage effects involving steamers. Clearly a vessel emitting smoke from a funnel could not be mistaken by even the clumsiest observer for a giant unknown animal. Small dark fishing boats or canoes would be a different matter. It may not be entirely a coincidence that the birth of the Loch Ness monster coincided with the disappearance of large smoky steamers from its waters and the arrival of the *Scot II* pleasure boat in 1932. *Scot II* was a motor vessel with peculiar ice-breaker bows, and the Loch Ness Investigation soon learned in the nineteen-sixties to discount any sightings which occurred within half an hour of the boat's twice daily passage up and down the eastern end of the loch.

Mirage phenomena, the Report went on, were most noticeable at extreme distances from the observer. But sometimes they could be observed at lesser distances – especially if the observer was near the water-level. The Report gave a typical example of a mirage effect at Loch Ness: 'The promontory at Dores appears as a conspicuous island in the middle of the loch.' This example is an extraordinary one, since it helps to explain what some people have seen when they report sighting a huge black object in the middle of the loch. Mirage effects also help to explain the monster's ability to vanish in a second, leaving no trace at all of a ripple, wake or other water disturbance.

More support for the theory that the Loch Ness monster may be a mirage-related phenomenon came in 1979 with the publication in *Science* of an important scholarly article on 'Atmospheric Refraction and Lake Monsters' by Professor W. H. Lehn of the University of Manitoba (*Plate* 12). Professor Lehn has observed and photographed numerous mirages on Lakes Manitoba and Winnipeg (one of which, at least, has a monster tradition). Once, while swimming in Lake Manitoba on a hot day, he even saw a 'monster' himself: 'Experience dictated that the observation be attributed to atmospheric refraction, but very little help from the imagination would have been required to interpret the shape as a long black serpent.'

Lehn points out that very many eye-witness sightings of monsters occur during atmospheric conditions that are ideal for generating distorted images. Loch Ness, like many other monster lochs, is situated in a cold temperate region of the Northern Hemisphere. The surface water temperature of such lakes is usually significantly below that of the air above it for the first half of the year. This guarantees a temperature inversion near the water surface, with the result that when the surface is calm conditions become perfect for developing a strong shallow conduction inversion capable of transmitting stable but distorted images to the human eye. This type of atmospheric refraction has the effect of magnifying and distorting familiar animals and objects so as to render them unrecognisable. The likelihood of this kind of phenomenon occuring is greatly enhanced if the elevation of the eye-witness is close to the level of the lake surface – as in the case of a witness on the shore, or in a boat.

The behaviour of the monsters which so many eye-witnesses report is, Lehn argues, consistent with the observation of refractive effects. Under mirage conditions inanimate objects can appear mobile and may grow, shrink, move about, and appear and disappear without a sound or ripple. 'It may well be,' Lehn concludes, 'that many sightings of monsters can be explained as the sighting of a distorted and hence unrecognized image of a familiar creature or phenomenon.'

Mirages of this sort are not restricted to inland lakes but may also occur at sea. In an article in *Nature* (January 1981) Professor Lehn and Professor I. Shroeder argue that the legendary Norse merman was also an optical phenomenon. They point out how a warm air mass moving slowly over cooler surface air on very warm sunny days can produce weird optical effects, strong enough to make quite ordinary objects unrecognisable, even at fairly short range. They show how familiar ocean animals like the killer whale and the walrus can appear distended into shapes which greatly resemble the classic pole-shaped 'head and neck' of the Loch Ness monster. Even rocks are capable of producing this dramatic illusion, as their photograph so vividly demonstrates (*Plate* 12).

Of course, there are no killer whales or walruses in Loch Ness, but there are numerous objects at the loch which may magnify into 'monsters'. Floating tar barrels and tree trunks (*Plate* 13). now seem obvious and likely contenders in explaining the origin of the 'upturned boat' single-hump aspect of the monster.

There are a n umber of curious and remarkable features to the earliest sightings of the Loch Ness monster back in 1933–34. One is the length of time the monster showed itself at the surface. The experience of most later monster watchers has been of brief, momentary sightings. In 1933 people reported monster sightings which lasted up to forty minutes; Nessie has never repeated such behaviour for the hungry cameras of later investigators. But two of the better-known monster photographs – Cockrell's and Searle's 1973 two-humped monster – show what are unmistakably parts of floating tree trunks.[1]

1 Robert P. Craig's 'Loch Ness: the monster unveiled' (*New Scientist*, 5 August 1982, pp. 354–7) introduced a variation on Maurice Burton's rotting vegetation theory by arguing that sightings of the monster could be explained by gas-propelled waterlogged pine trees. Craig claims that

Other minor phenomena which may sometimes give rise to bogus monster sightings are shadows and windslicks, which may resemble large black moving objects when seen from a distance. The proprietor of the Foyers Hotel told Gould that a monster sighted by a tourist 'was most undoubtedly produced by a sudden flaw of wind striking the loch.'

Probably the most common phenomenon in Loch Ness resulting in spurious monster sightings is the V-wake produced by a boat. There are numerous lay-bys along the lochside which permit motorists to pull in and look *across* the loch, but which provide only restricted views in either a south-westerly or north-easterly direction. It can take up to 20 minutes for a wake to reach the shore, by which time the boat creating it has long passed out of sight. In flat calm conditions the wake created by a trawler can be considerable, creating the impression of a huge shiny sinuous humped creature moving along just below the surface.

It is important to remember that Rupert Gould, one of the earliest and most influential propagandists of the Loch Ness monster, made no effort to look for the creature himself. It was precisely because he did no field research at the loch that Gould failed to appreciate just how common a phenomenon strange wake-effects actually were. Gould claimed that 'The presence of the vessel herself would, I imagine, very soon undeceive the most casual observer.' In fact on a calm sunny day standing waves can commonly be witnessed at Loch

there are only three monster lochs (Ness, Morar and Tay) and contrasts them with Loch Lomond, which has no monster tradition. The clue, he suggests, is that Loch Lomond, though similar in its physical features, lacks pine trees around its shores. However, the foundations of Craig's theory are flawed by some quite basic errors. Scotland contains not three but dozens of 'Lochs na Beiste' including Oich, Canisp, Assynt, Lochy, Shiel, Quoich and, ironically, Loch Lomond. It is simply not true that Loch Ness and Loch Morar are 'surrounded by Scots pine'. The theory is equally as implausible as Burton's (see Ch. 2) and only 'explains' a fraction of the evidence. No single phenomenon can possibly account for the totality of fifty years of widely differing eye-witness reports from Loch Ness.

Ness, and it is easy enough for the vessel which produced them to be twenty minutes away up the loch, out of sight. Most, if not all of Gould's multi-humped monsters and 'washes from nowhere' would appear to have been caused by boats. This is not to say that boats alone are necessarily the sole cause of 'monster' washes. Inverness resident W. R. Cumming has described how he was once fooled at Loch Ness:

> I saw a heavy wash or wake such as a motor-boat might produce, and I thought: 'Now when I get round that rocky promontory I'll possibly see the Monster.' But when I rounded the bend I saw a couple of swans. On the smooth water the waves appeared out of all proportion to their source.[1]

A correspondent to the *Edinburgh Evening Dispatch* (27 November 1933) offered a further explanation for turbulent 'monsters':

> The Loch Ness 'Monster' is simply a rise of fish, which I have often seen and recognised as such in the course of a considerable residence in the Ness district. The fish are shoals of the salmon species ... they cavort and frivol on the surface in sea-serpent-like undulating lines.

Gould, ignorant of Captain MacDonald's similar retort to Alex Campbell's first monster news item in May 1933, brusquely dismissed the suggestion as 'A simple explanation – the product, apparently, of a simple mind.' The simplicity of mind was actually Gould's; the Commander seems to have known as little about fish behaviour as he did about palaeontology or human psychology. Fish *can* cause curious disturbances at the surface which might easily be misinterpreted as evidence for a 'monster' by an inexperienced onlooker. In *Raven Seek Thy Brother* Gavin Maxwell gives an

1 Quoted in Burton, *The Elusive Monster*, p. 105.

interesting description of mackerel '"rushing" at the surface' near Glenelg Bay: *'The effect to the onlooker is that of an intermittent moving flurry of white spray.'* (Our italics.)

Loch Ness contains massive numbers of salmon, trout, eels, sticklebacks, char and pike. In theory none of them could cause immense commotions in the water. The largest salmon ever caught in Britain was five and a half feet long, and there is unlikely to be any species of eel in Loch Ness other than *anguilla anguilla*, which is not known to exceed five feet in length. It is highly unlikely that the larger marine species of eel would survive very long in the fresh water of Loch Ness.

Charles St John fished Loch Ness and was surprised by the strength and power of its trout:

> The strength and activity of the large loch trout is immense, and he will run out your whole reel-line if allowed to do so ... I have little doubt that the immense depths of Loch Ness hold trout as large, if not larger, than are to be found in any other loch in Scotland.

Unusually large fish are not unknown in British waters. There is for example the Regalecus fish, found off the north-east coast. It reaches lengths of 20 feet and more, though its thickness does not exceed four inches. Fishermen call it the Oar-fish. When it wriggles through the water with the dorsal fin on its head sticking up in the air it resembles the classic image of the sea-serpent.

Elsewhere in the world some fish grow to immense sizes. There are sturgeon in the Volga River and the Black and Caspian seas which grow up to lengths of 28 feet. Such monsters are not alien to British rivers. There is, for instance, the extraordinary story of the sturgeon which Alec Allen caught in the Rowy Towy at Nantguredig near Carmarthen, on 28 July 1933. It weighed 388 pounds, was nine feet two inches long, and had a girth of 59 inches. Allen noticed 'enormous waves' in the river, and by a fluke managed to hook the huge creature. His catch produced an interesting example of 'hysterical reaction': a sightseer who glimpsed the enormous bulk of the fish ran off shouting in terror. Allen managed to trap the fish in shallow water, then waded in and beat it to death with a rock. His record-breaking catch was ignored by the national press and became only a small news item in the local paper.

There is an interesting twist to this story of a giant sturgeon, which brings to mind the role of river gods in pagan cultures. Allen seemed a quiet, unimaginative man to his friends, and he rarely talked about his great catch. But when he died suddenly in 1972 his will was found to contain a passage requesting that he be cremated and that his ashes be scattered in the river at the spot where he had caught the monster fish. It seemed to be a way of returning to nature what he had once taken.

There is no evidence that Loch Ness contains similarly large sturgeon, though it seems far from impossible. In 1661 a giant sturgeon 12 feet long was reportedly caught at Kirkhill, near Inverness.

Before leaving the subject of fish and monsters mention should be made of a popular way of poaching fish in the Highlands, which may well be responsible for causing some of the apparently inexplicable V-wakes seen on the loch. A short line and hook is attached by the poacher to a bottle, which is then floated in the loch with a bait attached to it. The fish, on taking the bait, rushes about dragging the float with it, causing what from a distance may appear to be a mysterious wake.

It now seems clear that fish activity and boats' wakes account for many sightings of sinuous six-humped monsters and mysterious turbulences. But equally it is clear that some witnesses have genuinely seen a living animal at the loch's surface. One of several likely candidates for such sightings is the common otter, *Lutra lutra* (*Plates* 15(a) – (f)).

As an explanation the idea is not a new one. When Sir Walter Scott first heard of a Scottish monster he was unimpressed. Writing to Lady Compton in 1815, he commented, 'A monster long reported to inhabit Cauld-shields Loch, a small sheet of water in this neighbourhood, has of late been visible to sundry persons. If it were not that an otter swimming seems a very large creature I would hardly know what to think of it.' Cauldshields Loch is a tiny shallow lake on Cauldshields Hill, to the south of Scott's house at Abbotsford, in the border region of lowland Scotland. Some local people disagreed with Scott's commonsense interpretation; however, little more seems to have been heard of this particular 'monster'.

There is also the case, reported in *The Field* (3 February 1934) of the Loch Arkaig monster. A party of English tourists encountered a large unknown animal which came to the surface amid much turbulence while they were crossing the loch in a steam pinnace. The tourists were convinced they had seen a monster but as Sir Herbert Maxwell afterwards discovered when he interrogated the party's stalker, the man quietly explained that what they had seen was an otter. He had heard the English gentlemen excitedly discussing their monster but had not felt it proper that a servant speak out and correct them.

The suggestion that otters might account for sightings of the monster usually evokes great indignation and derision among believers. But as our researches have shown, local people who actually knew the Loch Ness environment were themselves among the first to offer this explanation when sightings of a 'monster' were first mooted in 1930 and 1933. And as Gould himself discovered, otters were seen on Loch Ness in 1933 and erroneously attributed to the monster. On 15 December the *Daily Mail* ran a report about a monster sighting which the witness, a local gamekeeper, afterwards retracted: 'I told the press-man that I saw some black object going slowly along but could not tell what it was. But I understand since then that otters have been seen there, and it certainly looked like three or four otters together, going in a bunch.'

In his Guide to the Loch Ness Monster Exhibition at Drumnadrochit, Anthony Harmsworth reproduces a photograph of a small cuddly-looking otter, and states, 'Otters are quite tiny animals and, being mammals, spend most of their time at or near the surface. Most mammals are curious and friendly so these various factors almost certainly rule out that

Nessie could be mammalian' (*The Mysterious Monsters of Loch Ness*, p. 21). This suggests that Harmsworth knows very little about wild otters. The otter has always been a rare and elusive creature; indeed, 'So seldom was the otter seen on land or swimming at the surface of river or lake that, centuries ago, people thought it was a large fish.'[1]

In twentieth-century Britain the otter has become an exceptionally rare creature, largely owing to shooting, industrial pollution and otter hunts. Otters are not densely distributed and are far more likely to be found in Scotland than in England. They are very shy animals and wary of man, due to centuries of persecution. Even experienced naturalists count themselves lucky if they see an otter in the wild.

Otters are semi-aquatic and widely distributed throughout the Highlands and Islands. They are found along the coast as well as around coastal waters. It is a general rule in zoology that animals in highland regions tend to be larger than their lowland counterparts of the same species, so it is reasonable to assume that otters in northern Scotland will be larger than average. Corbet and Southern's *Hand-book of British Mammals*, the standard work of reference, gives the maximum recorded length as 180 cm – about 6 feet. This is exceptional, however, and most otters are in the region of 3½ to 4½ feet in length.

Otters have long bodies, short legs, a long tail, and a head not much wider than the neck. Their pelage is a variable shade of brown, though it would usually appear dark in water, with paler underparts. Although semi-nomadic, sometimes wandering up to fifteen miles in a single night, otters respect each other's territorial claims.

Although otters are now more familiar than they were in the 1930s, due to the success of Gavin Maxwell's trilogy, television documentaries, and the efforts of conservation bodies like the Otter Trust in Norfolk, not everyone is interested in natural history. Otters may well appear to be

1 Liz Laidler, *Otters in Britain* (Newton Abbot: David & Charles, 1982), p. 8.

harmless little creatures in photographs. But in reality very few people have ever seen an otter or could identify one if they did. In *Ring of Bright Water* Gavin Maxwell records the extraordinary 'variety of guesses as to what kind of animal this might be' when he led his pet otter Mij through the streets of London. These guesses included 'seal', 'walrus', 'hippo', 'beaver', 'newt' and

> even, with heaven knows what dim recollections of schoolroom science and a bewildering latinized world of sub-human creatures – a 'brontosaur'; Mij was anything but an otter.

Leaving aside the obvious disparity in scale, one in fact only has to compare the profile of a brontosaurus with that of an otter to see that there is more of a resemblance between the two than Maxwell appeared to realise (at any rate, certainly more than between a newt or a hippopotamus and an otter) (*Plate* 15(e)). The comparison of the skeleton of an otter with that of the fossil remains of a plesiosaur is also illuminating. It now seems overwhelmingly obvious that the two classic 'land sightings' from the 1933–34 period were of otters. Mr Spicer's description of the six to eight feet long 'dragon or pre-historic animal' which rushed across the road in front of him provides only a marginally exaggerated description of an otter. Spicer's choice of metaphor is fascinating in the light of Gavin Maxwell's description of his first glimpse of Mij: 'The creature that emerged ... did not at that moment resemble anything so much as a very small medievally-conceived dragon.'[1]

Arthur Grant's description of the creature which bounded across the road in the middle of the night is consistent with the appearance of an otter, but for the exaggeration of size. His sketch of the beast, reproduced in Oudemans's *The Loch Ness Animal*, bears a remarkable resemblance to an otter. Some versions of the episode also appear to refer to what

1 Gavin Maxwell, *Ring of Bright Water* (London: Pan, 1963), p. 84.

sounds very much like an otter slide and tracks. The fact that Grant was a veterinary student does not necessarily signify that he knew anything about wild animals. A vet's income is derived mainly from ministering to domestic pets or farm animals. Even today zoo-vets are specialists, and in 1933 there were no zoos in the Highlands.

Otters in the water are equally as likely to be mistaken for monsters by the inexperienced (*Plates* 15(a) – (f)). Otters possess many of the characteristics attributed to the monster. They are exceptionally elusive; they are most likely to be seen at dawn; they possess a curious ability to squeeze and contort their bodies as if they were boneless. When an otter is fishing 'The body curves into a question mark on the surface and all you see is a dark hump as rudder follows body through the arc.'[1] Moreover, 'Submerged, otters can maintain an almost vertical position by treading water with their hind paws, a stance which allows the head and neck to be raised out of the water.'[2] When in this position otters possess the ability to sink with barely a ripple. They can swim underwater at speeds of up to 9 m.p.h.; they can remain submerged for up to six minutes; they can travel up to ¼ mile underwater.

Charles St John described his own encounters with otters in the nineteenth-century Highlands:

There have come in my way, during my rambles through the Highlands, many a fair and beauteous loch, placed like a bright jewel in the midst of the rugged mountains, far out of reach of steam and coach, accessible only to the walking traveller, or at most to a highland pony, where the only living creature to be seen is the silent otter playing its fantastic gambols in the quiet of the evening.

In solitary and undisturbed situations I have sometimes fallen in with the otter during the day. In a loch far on the hills, I have seen one raise itself half out of the water, take

1 Laidler, *Op. Cit.*, p. 18.
2 *Ibid.*, pp. 18–19.

a steady look at me, and then sink gradually and quietly below the surface, appearing again at some distance, but next time showing only part of its head.

A pair of otters, or perhaps an adult with two or three well grown young, swimming in line astern – as they often do – could easily create an impression of a multi-humped animal on a mirror calm surface. If a single otter (or any animal at the loch's surface, including a bird) were perceived as being of exaggerated size, the error would also be projected on to the animal's wake. And any wake can give an illusory impression of one or more solid humps behind the structural one caused by the animal or bird's back. The back of an otter is not seen as a continuous line in the water but creates the impression of a hump.

The *Daily Mail* (27 October 1933) carried a vivid account by the Director of the Scottish Marine Biological Association describing just such a 'monster' which he had witnessed in the Clyde three years earlier:

I watched this 'creature' for an hour through field glasses. The reptilian head was a dog otter, the first hump on the surface the mother, and the second hump and the lashing tail were baby otters.

The dog otter, swimming with its head erect, had seen me and given a warning. The mother and the babies dived, and I was just in time to see the dog otter's head and the backs of the others. They stretched over 18 feet of water.

There remains a tiny handful of reports of 'horned' monsters, of which the most famous is Greta Finlay's. Such sightings clearly cannot be attributed to otters. The solution, almost certainly, is that the witnesses saw deer.

Deer are abundant around the wooded shores of Loch Ness, though they are rarely seen, being secretive and shy in their habits. At least three species occur – the Red, Sika and Roe. They are good swimmers and though they do not make a habit of it very occasionally an individual may swim across the loch. In his *Short Sketches of the Wild Sports and Natural History of the Highlands* (1846) Charles St John commented, 'For some unknown reason, as they do it without any apparent cause, the roe sometimes take it into their heads to swim across wide pieces of water. I have seen one swim Loch Ness.'

When Peter Costello visited Loch Ness in the summer of 1967 he learned that a few days before his arrival the monster had been seen near Aldourie Castle (precisely where Greta Finlay saw her monster). A photograph of the beast, when enlarged, revealed it to be a deer. Costello was surprised and unimpressed by the indifference of L.N.I. personnel. In his book *In Search of Lake Monsters* he tells how he found the incident 'unsettling, especially as the expedition members seemed to attach little importance to the incident or the photograph. Nor has anyone, so far as I know, referred to this incident in print. So much for scientific rigour.'

Photographs of roe deer swimming are rare – rarer even than photographs of the Loch Ness monster (*Plates* 16(a) and (b)). The creatures are shy and outside most people's experience. At the close of the last century the deer expert J. G. Millais complained that 'No British animal has received less attention at the hands of the naturalist than the roe. In what are called standard works he is dismissed with a few lines ...' In his classic study *British Deer and their Horns* (1897), Millais noted the way in which 'Roe swim very deep in the water, in fact, deeper than any other British quadruped, *yet the head is held clear and high, and the animal gives one the impression of being quite at home in the water.*' (Our italics.) Interestingly enough, Millais mentioned two places connected with Loch Ness in his discussion of roe deer – Dochfour (not far from where Mrs Finlay saw her monster), and Foyers, where a pied variety of roe was to be found.

In a 1976 television interview Alex Campbell acknowledged that although roe did occasionally swim in Loch Ness they would be easily identifiable because of their antlers. This would seem to indicate that Campbell is a poor naturalist. Only stags have antlers, and they shed them annually, growing new ones each autumn. Roe deer do not have true antlers but short two-pronged horns. They look least like the traditional image of deer, and their dark faces might well appear sinister and diabolic to the inexperienced and the nervous.

Deer, when swimming, present a curious aspect. Because of the inverted curve of their spines they present a gap between the neck and the rump. This results in the impression of a long neck followed by a hump. Leaving aside the inconsistencies of size in Mrs Finlay's 'monster' there can be little doubt that what she and her son saw in August 1952 was a roe deer. They were even camping in a secluded, wooded part of Loch Ness where one would expect to encounter deer.

But deer obviously cannot explain the handful of reports of a long thin neck breaking the surface of Loch Ness – an image fixed for all time by the Surgeon's photograph. Ten years of intense surveillance showed that Dinsdale's belief that the head and neck of the monster appeared in almost half of all sightings was unfounded. But reports of the monster's head and neck persist, and it is the image of the monster which has probably most captured the imagination of the public and monster-enthusiasts alike. To believers the head and neck sightings are the most difficult to explain away, and obviously cannot be attributed to floating tree trunks, boats' wakes, otters or deer.

The neck may bend, or the head turn from side to side in an alert watchful manner. It has *real* motion, and is almost certainly animal. Alex Campbell gives the clue to this. His sighting of a 'monster' in September 1933 is worth quoting in detail because it sounds so convincing:

At about half-past nine in the morning, I was watching this end of the Loch [i.e. the area around the mouth of the Caledonian Canal at Fort Augustus]. The light was very uncertain, there being a fairly thick haze on the water, and along with this the sun was shining directly in my eye through the mist, making the visibility very bad. I had not

Figure 6

Alex Campbell's 'monster'

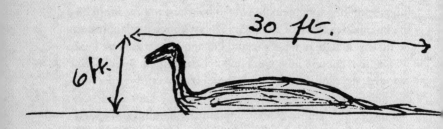

(i) Drawn by Campbell himself. Note the bird-like profile.

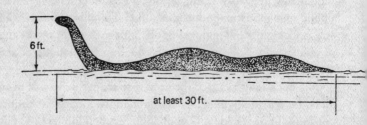

(ii) Another version of the same sighting from the revised edition of Tim Dinsdale's *Loch Ness Monster* (1972)

been watching for more than a minute before I noticed a strange object on the surface about six hundred yards from where I stood. It seemed to be about 30 feet long, and what I took to be the head was fully 5 feet above the surface of the Loch. The creature, if such it was, *and at the time I felt certain of it*, seemed to be watching two drifters passing out of the Canal and into Loch Ness; and, *whether it was due to imagination or not, I could have sworn that it kept turning its head and also its body very quickly*, in much the same way as a cormorant does on rising to the surface. I saw this for fully a minute, then the object vanished as if it had sunk out of sight.

Last Friday I was watching the Loch at the same place and about the same time of day. The weather was almost identical – practically calm and the sun shining through a hazy kind of mist. In a short time something very like what I have described came into my line of vision and at roughly the same distance from where I stood.

But the light was improving all the time, and in a matter of seconds I discovered that what I took to be the Monster was nothing more than a few cormorants, and what seemed to be the head was a cormorant standing in the water and flapping its wings, as they often do. *The other cormorants, which were strung out in a line behind the leading bird, looked in the poor light and at first glance just like the body or humps of the Monster, as it has been described by various witnesses.*

But the most important thing was, that owing to the uncertain light *the bodies of the birds were magnified out of all proportion to their proper size*. This mirage only occurs under certain conditions and if the Loch is calm. Then it gives every object – from, say, a gull or a bottle to an empty barrel – a very grotesque appearance provided that such objects are far enough away from the observer.[1]

Campbell's account is not only fascinating in terms of his

---

1 Our italics. Quoted in Gould, *The Loch Ness Monster and Others*, pp. 110–12.

own later role as high priest of the mysteries, but because it helps to explain how the Loch Ness monster was so convincingly established as a phenomenon in 1933. That summer was, as we have said, the hottest on record. Many of the early sightings occurred off Fort Augustus in the vicinity of the two rivers which flow into Loch Ness there. Most sightings were by local residents, some of them neighbours of Campbell. Fort Augustus was then a tiny community of less than a thousand inhabitants, and monster fever had clearly afflicted a sizeable slice of its population.

Campbell's testimony is also crucially important because the behaviour of birds has rarely, if ever, been discussed in the context of the Loch Ness mystery. Compared to estuaries and inland waterways in other areas of Britain, the deep-water Scottish lochs do not attract abundant numbers of water birds. Ducks, geese and swans do occur, but in small numbers and are usually transitory. This is because their diet comprises mainly water-weed, which can only flourish in relatively shallow water, and so is precluded by the deep, steeply-shelving shoreline of Loch Ness. Geese only flock in large numbers in the vicinity of water meadows, where they 'graze' on grass. If they occurred in large numbers on Loch Ness they would be familiar objects, providing easy markers against which to estimate the size of other objects in the water. As it is they are rarely seen at the loch. Black-headed gulls are occasionally seen in some numbers at Loch Ness, but being light in colour and very vocal are easily recognisable. At 16 inches in length they are also quite small.

Birds which are exceptions to the above, and which find Loch Ness an acceptable feeding area, are the fish-eating 'diving ducks', particularly the Red-Breasted Merganser (*Mergus serrator*) and the Goosander (*Mergus merganser*). Other birds sometimes found at the loch are the true divers (*Colymbidae*) and the Grebes (*Podicipitidae*).

Of the three species of divers found in British waters the Great Northern is the largest at 31 inches in length. It is only a winter visitor and almost exclusively a sea-bird. The Red-Throated and Black-Throated species prefer to nest by isolated mountain tarns and lochans. The Great Crested Grebe is the largest of its tribe at 21 inches and occurs in small numbers on Loch Ness.[1] (*Plate* 17.)

That such birds account for some of the monster 'head and neck' sightings seems obvious. For example, in *More Than a Legend* Mrs Whyte includes a sighting of a monster which resembled 'a large duck' with a head and neck about 2 feet above the water. Its colour was black, with a white breast. The monster was seen from a crowded bus in August 1950, one passenger commenting, 'I never believed the Monster story, but now must believe the evidence of my own eyes.'

Merganser, divers and grebes are not especially gregarious species, unlike many other water birds such as ducks and geese. Moreover they are usually seen singly or in pairs, unless accompanied by their young. They are all rather shy and do not occur in sufficiently large numbers at Loch Ness for anyone other than bird-watching enthusiasts to be particularly aware of them. In other words (and this is important) they are not familiar objects at Loch Ness.

In *Project Water Horse* Tim Dinsdale describes sighting the antics of young grebe on the loch, though as a committed believer the significance of the birds' behaviour did not occur to him:

> They cover great distances each day, thinking nothing of swimming across the bay and back, a distance of a mile and a half at least. They can also *run* on the water. Honestly, exactly that, and very quickly too, for perhaps a hundred yards at a stretch. They are still too young to fly, and I have tried to film them in slow motion doing this, leaving V-wakes like a small flotilla of speed boats. They absolutely pelt along, then dive as a final resort.

1 The dark ear-tufts of the Great Crested Grebe can, as one of our photographs demonstrates, create the impression of a horned animal. The description of a monster given by one of Sir Edward Mountain's watchers, Mr P. Grant, sounds suspiciously like a grebe: two small stumps on the head, eyes like slits, a dark brownish body which appeared to be lighter underneath, 'and where neck and body met appeared considerable swelling which resembled a fowl with a full crop.'

In appearance birds of these three species are all moderately long-necked, of darkish plumage above, and have streamlined but short-tailed bodies. They use their webbed feet to propel themselves both on and under the water. The legs of the divers, in particular, are placed so far back that they cannot walk properly, and they can often be discerned to the rear of the bird when it is in motion on water. They all have narrow pointed bills (including the Merganser and Goosander).

Rupert Gould includes an interesting anecdote about these birds:

> Mr Milne has described to me an incident which he witnessed in the middle of August 1933. He was watching the Loch in company with a number of visitors, and he noticed four merganser taking off from the water one after the other, causing considerable commotion. The spectacle was at once hailed by the crowd with exclamations of 'Look, there's the Monster!'[1]

Of all the water birds found at Loch Ness undoubtedly the most dramatic and sinister in appearance is the cormorant (*Phalacrocorax carbo*) (*Plate* 18). Though predominantly a sea-bird, most associated with rocky coasts where it may often be seen in small scattered groups, it does occasionally occur on inland waters. These are usually solitary appearances.

The cormorant is a large bird, 3 feet long, almost entirely black in colour, and the serpentine appearance of its neck is accentuated by the upward tilt of its long tapering bill. When swimming a cormorant holds its neck erect, and in silhouette on water it does indeed resemble a plesiosaur.

The name 'cormorant' derives from the Latin *Corvus marinus* or sea-raven, and the raven has always been regarded as a bird of sinister reputation. Milton saw the cormorant as a sinister, primeval creature, and in Book Two of *Paradise Lost* compares Satan to a cormorant, 'devising death'. The

1 Gould, *The Loch Ness Monster and Others*, p. 193.

cormorant also appears as a sinister, satanic emissary in Mantegna's painting *The Agony in the Garden*. Divers also have a sinister appearance which 'conveys a sense of the prehistoric.'[2] They have long been associated with death and the supernatural. In Charlotte Brontë's *Jane Eyre* the heroine paints a stormy sea in which a cormorant, 'dark and large,' perches on a half-submerged mast above a drowned body. Divers were long believed to accompany the souls of the dead in the Faeroes; in Norway their cries presaged a death.

All the above species have certain behavioural characteristics in common. They are all fish-predators and therefore diving birds, frequently submerging for two or three minutes at a time (occasionally even longer). They have been known to submerge to depths of over a hundred feet. They are torpedo-shaped powerful swimmers under water, and so can travel some distance before re-emerging. When fishing they usually dive head first, but when alarmed, cormorants and divers can sink vertically until only their necks or even just the tips of their bills show. When swimming on the surface they frequently turn their heads from side to side. These are all typical characteristics of the 'monster'.

The Red-Breasted Merganser has a fascinating courtship display. In his classic study *Birds of the British Isles*, David Bannerman describes how 'The drakes in their eagerness often rush through the water with slightly opened wings, making the water foam about them ... they seem to rise in the water with wings close to the side until they almost seem to stand on tip-toe.'

Mirage-effects or no mirage-effects, a large black bird like a cormorant surfacing vertically out of a tranquil mirror-calm loch surface would be sufficiently startling to anyone not familiar with the species to trigger an immediate

2 See Francesca Greenoak, *All the Birds of the Air* (1981). In her account of the shag, a bird very similar in shape to the cormorant, Ms. Greenoak refers to R. M. Lockley 'who watched shags on his island home of Skokholm, [and who] remarked on how like reptiles the birds sometimes seemed.'

association with the monster tradition. In people of a suggestible nature (and most of us are) the bird could easily assume an awe-inspiring and sinister appearance. Since we can only perceive what we *know*, the absence of any object for comparison, combined with the preconception of the 'monster' being large, will result in a grossly exaggerated estimate of size. This is the inevitable by-product of an eye-witness's dependence on a purely subjective frame of reference.

If the bird then sinks, or dives, re-surfacing perhaps minutes later, outside the observer's angle of vision, the dramatic effect will be complete. That person will be absolutely convinced he or she has seen a monster. The eerie nature of such an unexpected encounter will leave the witness feeling confused, perhaps shocked. In the few minutes following the event misconceptions coloured by emotions will harden and set. The result may be a sighting anecdote which seems indisputable, and which may become all the more persuasive after sympathetic interrogation and promptings by monster enthusiasts.

Support for our interpretations is lent by the sightings record itself. Dr Jan Olaf-Willums, formerly of M.I.T., has described the results of a statistical analysis of 258 sightings made between 1961 and 1970. 83% of sightings were made in calm surface conditions. Only 35% of these reports referred to a movement in the object witnessed; a staggering 82% of witnesses reported a height above the water of *less than four feet*.

This would seem to indicate that the monster is of relatively small proportions, though wakes may create the impression of humps and abnormal length. Moreover if a variety of natural phenomena are responsible for such sightings then one would expect major discrepancies between the kinds of monster seen. This is in fact exactly what has happened at Loch Ness; indeed, it was because of this that zoologists in 1933 soon tired of the mystery. What they did not realize at the time was either the extent of the public's craving for monsters, or the unique combination of factors at Loch Ness which would ensure the continuation of the enigma for another fifty years.

10 A Necessary Monster

By heaven, he echoes me
As if there were some monster in his thought

> Shakespeare, *Othello* (1604)

monster: imaginary animal compounded of incongruous
elements

> *The Concise Oxford Dictionary of Current English* (1911)

Mankind has been fascinated by water since the beginnings of time. In primitive societies water was associated with the world of spirits, and many rivers and lakes had their gods.

Water comprised another, separate world: its surface mirrored the known world of *terra firma*, but its depths were dark, impenetrable, mysterious. It is probably this pagan tradition which lies behind the old Highland belief in water-horses and water-bulls.

When Charles St John travelled through Scotland in the nineteenth century he heard about two sorts of water monster, one the traditional water-bull, the other 'some strange mermaid-like monster having the appearance of a monstrous fish with long hair.' However, though well acquainted with Loch Ness, St John never associated it with monster lore, nor, as an accomplished naturalist familiar with the behaviour of otters, did he take the legends seriously.

In the last half century water has lost much of its traditional romance and mystery. In the age of skin-diving, submarines, sonar and underwater photography, the marvels of underwater life have become the common currency of television documentaries. Loch Ness, with its black peat-filled depths and inaccessible shores, provides a suitable terrain for the last great modern myth.

The Loch Ness monster has a family tree which stretches back well beyond 1933. Monsters gripped the public imagination in the nineteenth century just as much as they do today. The concept of prehistoric monsters entered popular consciousness with the discovery of various fossils, including, in 1823, the first plesiosaur remains. The extent of the public's fascination was demonstrated by the short, lucrative career of 'Dr' Albert C. Koch. Koch was a man who devoted much time, labour and money to the collection of genuine fossil remains. He then reassembled them, in defiance of anatomy and palaeontology, into fantastic 'monsters' designed for public consumption. In 1842 and 1843 he exhibited the 'Missouri Leviathan', an enormous skeleton built from bones excavated in that State. The 'Leviathan' was actually a fraudulent construction, ingeniously put together from the remains of mastodons and elephants. After the exhibition was over the 'monster' was purchased by the British Museum, and promptly reduced to its constituent parts.

In 1845 Koch had an even greater success with a gigantic fossil 'sea-serpent'. He achieved this by obtaining the vertebrae and other sections of two specimens of Zeuglodon (an extinct marine cetacean of great size) and re-arranging them to make up a serpent creature 114 feet long, complete with bogus paddles. This masterpiece of synthesis Koch dryly christened 'Hydrarchos Sillimani', in honour – so he said – of Professor Silliman, the American naturalist. Since Silliman believed that the survival of plesiosaurs provided a convincing explanation for sea-serpent sightings this leg-pull was perhaps no more than he deserved. The 'sea-serpent' was exhibited with great success in New York and Boston, and was finally sold to a museum in Berlin. Afterwards Koch was exposed as a hoaxer, but by then he was a rich man.

Prehistoric monsters had by that time so captured the popular imagination that six years later a large collection of lifesized reinforced concrete dinosaurs were exhibited at the Great Exhibition held at Crystal Palace in 1851. They can still be seen there today. Perhaps Charles Dickens went to look at them since *Bleak House*, the novel which he began in London in November of that year, opens with a comic vision of

> As much mud in the streets, as if the waters had but newly retired from the face of the earth, and it would not be wonderful to meet a Megalosaurus, forty feet long or so, waddling like an elephantine lizard up Holborn Hill.

The idea that prehistoric monsters might not actually have vanished forever from the earth was one which became increasingly attractive to the Victorian mind. For one thing, it provided a pleasing stick with which to beat Darwin, and his uncomfortable doctrine of evolution. But even thirty years before Darwin it had been suggested by Charles Lyell, in his *Principles of Geology*, that the entire fossil record represented but a brief moment in time, part of a great circle wheeling back to the day when 'the huge iguanodon might reappear in the woods, and the ichthyosaur in the sea.'

The currency and force of this public longing for monsters was vividly demonstrated by the long-running saga of the Stronsa carcass. In 1808 the rotting remains of a large marine animal were discovered lying on a beach in a remote island in the Orkneys. The affair became something of a zoological *cause célèbre* as loyal Scots naturalists hotly defended the reality and uniqueness of their monster against Sassenach scepticism. In his book *The Case for the Sea-Serpent* Rupert Gould ruefully observed:

> There can be little doubt that this creature was, actually, an enormous basking-shark, partly decomposed; but the original reports are so curious, and the accepted explanation so much at variance with them, that the case deserves more than a cursory mention, if only as an

instance of how misleading it is possible for honest testimony to be.

It should be explained that the carcass was never examined by any person of education, and that the evidence relating to it, although given on oath, is that of the local fishermen and crofters. Similarly, the only extant drawing of it was made by an amateur who had not seen the creature, from an exceedingly rough sketch supplied by one of the witnesses and amended according to his verbal description of it. Yet, on reading the depositions, one might be pardoned for thinking that the creature was, most undoubtedly, a modern plesiosaurus.

In 1822 an Edinburgh naturalist wrote that the existence of the sea-serpent, 'a monster fifty-five feet long', was 'placed beyond a doubt' by the Stronsa carcass. As late as 1854 the monster was being defended by Scottish zoologists, though their arguments were, in Gould's words, 'largely founded upon false assumptions, or upon sheer ineptitude.' Once specimens of the monster's bones were submitted for analysis anatomists confirmed that the remains belonged to a cartilaginous fish, and were from the vertebrae of the basking shark, *Selache maxima*.

The man perhaps most responsible for legitimising the popular craving for real-life water monsters was the amateur naturalist Philip Gosse. In his highly successful and revealingly-titled *The Romance of Natural History* (1860) Gosse put forward the idea that plesiosaurs were still alive and explained contemporary sea-serpent sightings. Significantly this book was published just one year after Darwin's *Origin of Species*. Gosse had earlier made a complete fool of himself with *Omphalos*, a book which attempted to stave off the theory of evolution with the doctrine of a single, sudden act of creation. His argument that God had created fossils in order to fool geologists was greeted with derision, and Gosse henceforth joined the ranks of all those other anti-rationalists, 'supplying a sugar-and-water panacea for those who could not escape from the trend of evidence, and who yet clung to revelation.'

In the seventeenth century many scientists had argued that the extinction of any species would be inconsistent with God's goodness and perfection. Gosse's suggestion that plesiosaurs might still be alive can be seen as an amateur's attempt to surreptitiously revive this line of argument. If plesiosaurs *were* still alive then perhaps so were other extinct animals, and Darwin's theory of evolution was, after all, wrong. In a sense, then, Philip Gosse is the true father of the Loch Ness monster – which is immensely ironic in the light of the portrait of Gosse's humourless, authoritarian, dogma-obsessed personality drawn by his son Edmund in his famous autobiography, *Father and Son* (1907).

Each year a handful of individuals visit Loch Ness and have the good fortune to see a 'monster', very often without even intentionally looking for one. They are probably unaware of just how much their behaviour mirrors that of their Victorian ancestors. The Victorians were very much aware of sea-serpent sightings, and discussions of this mysterious and elusive creature were common in the English press between the 1840s and 1880s. What was more the Victorian middle-classes enjoyed spotting 'sea-serpents' with great frequency at coastal resorts all round Britain. (This is surely what the mysterious Miss Woodruff was *really* doing on the end of the Cobb at Lyme in John Fowles's *The French Lieutenant's Woman*: she was watching for a sea-serpent, and only invented her lieutenant so as not to appear foolish in the eyes of her Darwinian admirer, the 'serious' Mr Smithson.)

An instructive example of Victorian sea-serpent enthusiasm is provided by the case of Mr Henry Lee. This young gentleman was strolling along Brighton beach on the morning of 16 February 1857 when he experienced a sight so extraordinary that he afterwards felt obliged to communicate it immediately to the *Brighton Gazette*:

I was walking along the beach below the terrace at Kemp Town at about twenty minutes past eight. As I approached the bathing machines which stand there some boys who were playing about called out 'A sea-snake! A sea-snake!' Supposing that they had probably found an eel upon the beach, I walked on, and took no notice, but as their continued exclamations evinced considerable excitement, I was induced to look in the direction to which they pointed. Coming from the westward, and about a quarter of a mile from the shore, I saw what I at first thought was a very long galley, very low in the water; but as it came towards and passed in front of us I saw it was that which the boys had pronounced it to be – a veritable sea monster. It was swimming on the surface, at the rate of from twenty-five to thirty miles an hour, and had exactly the appearance represented in one of the illustrated newspapers a few months since. I should say that about forty or fifty feet of it was visible, and I counted seven dorsal fins, if such they were, standing up from its back. It continued in view for six or seven minutes ... There was no possibility of mistake. The sun was shining brilliantly, the sea was smooth, and the creature was, as I have before said, not more than a quarter of a mile from the beach.

Mr Lee might well have gone to his grave still clinging to the conviction that he had witnessed the legendary sea-serpent. However, unlike most other eye-witnesses Mr Lee went on in later life to obtain an education in marine biology. In 1873 Henry Lee, F.L.S., F.G.S., F.Z.S. published *The Octopus*, and some years later *Sea Monsters Unmasked*, in which he sheepishly recalled his Brighton sea-serpent:

The above description, written twenty-seven years ago, conveys clearly enough the impression made upon my mind at the time, but it is characterised by an unwise impetuosity of assertion, and an unwarranted assurance of infallibility. I hope that with greater experience, I should write with less positiveness and more caution now. For, by the irony of fate, I who was so indignant by anticipation at the very thought of a suggestion of inaccuracy, or of the reasonableness of explanation, have had to condemn my own observation as erroneous, and to perceive that others, with equal sincerity of intention, may have been similarly mistaken. 'No possibility of mistake' forsooth! I now know that the erect dorsal fins that I saw belonged to 'long-nosed porpoises' or dolphins, and, by their shape and height, am able to recognise their owners as having been of the species *Delphinus delphis*. My sea-serpent was composed of seven of these cetaceans swimming in line, and, as is their wont, maintaining their relative positions so accurately that all the fins appeared to belong to one animal.[1]

Sea Monsters Unmasked (1884) was an earnest attempt to demolish the case for the Kraken and the sea-serpent, attributing such sightings to the squid. The book includes a detailed demolition of the famous *Daedalus* sea-serpent sighting of 1848 – a 'sighting' which is still quoted as a classic today. Lee also took up the gauntlet thrown down by Gosse in *The Romance of Natural History*. Gosse had listed ten characteristics of sea-serpent sightings, including a length of sixty feet, appendages on the head resembling a mane, and the appearance of swimming at the surface with 'the head and neck projected and elevated above the surface'. 'To which of the recognized classes of created beings can this huge rover of the ocean be referred?' Gosse had thundered, confident of stunning his critics into silence – to which Lee retorted, 'I reply: "To the *Cephalopoda*." There is not one of [Gosse's ten] judiciously summarized characteristics that is not supplied by the great calamary, and its ascertained habits and peculiar mode of locomotion.'

Perhaps Lee's book had some effect. The public interest in sea-serpents waned considerably towards the end of the century. Nevertheless the line of descent from the great sea-serpent enigma down to the Loch Ness monster is not hard to

1 Henry Lee, *Sea Monsters Unmasked* (London: William Clowes, 1884), pp. 428–9.

trace, helped on its way by such romantic real-life adventures as the Gobi Desert expeditions of the 1920s, which brought back the first dinosaur eggs. Tennyson's much-anthologised poem 'The Kraken' gives acute expression to that haunting sense of the marvellous which mythical deep-water beasts can inspire, while the idea that prehistoric monsters might actually be alive and well and living in remote corners of the world was given popular fictional expression in Arthur Conan Doyle's *The Lost World*.

The birth of the movies soon saw films taking over the territory of the fantastic and bizarre which had previously been the province of science fiction. The 1924 version of *The Lost World* set the fashion for trick-photography and ingenious mechanical monsters. It is probably no coincidence that the Loch Ness monster was discovered at the very moment that *King Kong*, the masterpiece of the genre, was released across Scotland in 1933. Indeed, when Rupert Gould came to interview that all-important star witness Mr Spicer, Gould casually referred to the diplodocus-like dinosaur in *King Kong*. Spicer breezily admitted that he, too, had seen the film, and that his monster had 'much resembled' the one Gould had mentioned. Significantly the rediscovery of the Loch Ness monster in the nineteen-fifties coincided with a flood of monster movies, including *The Creature from the Black Lagoon, The Phantom from 10,000 Leagues, Monster from the Ocean Floor*, and *The Beast from 20,000 Fathoms*.

This, then, is the real 'tradition' which lies behind the Loch Ness monster, as opposed to the bogus sightings tradition examined in Chapter Three. What is fascinating about the monster is how its initial credibility depended on a unique conjunction of factors. The announcement of a monster in 1930 flopped; the announcement of a monster in 1933 proved a dazzling success. It is relevant to ask why. The immediate answer seems to be that in 1930 the weather was poor and no-one who lived around Loch Ness seemed ever to have heard of, let alone seen the monster. But in 1933, just as the story was once again about to die, a London tourist who happened to be in the area at the time the subject was being first aired in the local press, had a frightening experience with an otter on a lonely road. This tourist, Mr Spicer, subsequently wrote a melodramatic letter to the *Courier*, which treated his 'sighting' as a major news item. This in turn inspired a tiny handful of other sightings by impressionable teenage girls, passing tourists, and local eccentrics like Commander Meiklem. Ironically some of the more recent studies of the monster have begun to express reservations about land sightings by witnesses like Spicer. What they appear not to realise is just how much the whole legend of a monster depended on the timely appearance of Spicer's letter in the local press.

James Froude, the Devon historian, remarked some years ago: 'Once possess people with a belief and never fear, they will find facts enough to confirm it.' In the summer of 1933 the Loch Ness environment was peculiarly favourable to monsters (something which is borne out by the sightings statistics over fifty years). It was, significantly, one of the hottest summers of this century. Conditions for mirages and distortions due to heat-haze at Loch Ness were perfect. Moreover its waters were actually full of bobbing black tar-barrels, thrown in by workmen doing road repairs along the entire north side of the loch. In these circumstances the growing 'reality' of the monster is not entirely surprising, egged on as it was by Alex Campbell's anonymous promotion in the local press and afterwards assisted by such partisans of the sea-serpent as Philip Stalker and Rupert Gould and leg-pullers like Hugh Gray and Dr Wilson.

Ironically only a few years earlier Kafka had written a short story with considerable bearing on the Loch Ness mystery. 'The Giant Mole' is about another kind of legendary 'monster' and the human weaknesses which lie behind the promotion of mysterious giant animals. The dark joke in Kafka's story – perhaps there never really was a giant mole in the first place, but the mystery once created won't ever go away – finds an echo in the Loch Ness saga. Yet by the nineteen-fifties the story seemed to be over, and Compton Mackenzie wrote a surprisingly astute comic novel, *The Rival Monster* (1952), which gently poked fun at what by then seemed to be a long-dead topic. But Mackenzie had reckoned without Constance Whyte and Tim Dinsdale, who, despite the half-hearted scepticism of Maurice Burton, succeeded in setting monster-mania back on the road again in the nineteen-sixties.[1]

And so the Loch Ness mystery was given a new lease of life, and the monster myth has survived to the present day. But the paradox remains. Still no-one has been able to produce a convincing piece of movie film of the creature which witnesses have claimed to see. Oudemans's massive volume on the sea-serpent opened with the stirring words:

> Voyagers and sportsmen conversant with photography are requested to take the instantaneous photograph of the animal: this alone will convince zoologists, while all other reports and pencil drawings will be received with a shrug of the shoulders.

That photograph was never taken. Likewise after fifty years of highly publicised effort the Loch Ness investigations have got nowhere, and conclusive proof of the beast's existence is as far off as ever.

In a sober assessment of the zoological difficulties which a 'monster' raises, Adrian Shine has commented:

1 Since this book was completed Maurice Burton has once again stepped into the arena with three short articles in *New Scientist* (24 June – 8 July 1982), which reiterate his belief that sightings of the monster can be attributed to gas-propelled rotting vegetation, boats' wakes, tree trunks, otters and birds. For reasons given earlier the first of Burton's explanations is patently absurd, while the others provide a part – but only a part – of the answer. In these articles Burton gives a rather misleading account of *The Elusive Monster*, and he now seems as anxious as his detractors are to bowdlerise the conclusions he reached in that book. He obscures the fact that the major thrust of *The Elusive Monster* was to distinguish between two kinds of 'monster'. Burton actually hinged his book around the 'land sightings', which he was convinced were genuine, and devoted most of his energy to debunking sightings of the monster in the water. Ironically the land sightings were almost certainly inspired by the very animal which Burton now points to as a source of surface sightings: the common otter. We have already suggested in Chapter Seven the reason why Burton was so anxious to discredit surface sightings. As Shakespeare put it: 'the heresies that men do leave/Are hated most of those they did deceive.'

The presence of an adapted marine fish-predator within the loch is not, in itself, particularly remarkable. What is remarkable is that it seems to be an unknown animal. Furthermore, some of its 'characteristics' raise difficulties no matter what class of animal is considered. ...[1]

As Shine frankly admits there are sound reasons why the monster cannot be a plesiosaur, or an amphibian, or a reptile, or a mammal: 'The least unlikely solution would be a fish ... Unfortunately, most sighting reports do not seem to describe a fish.'[2]

Perplexed by the scientific question marks which the monster mystery provokes, Shine finally concludes: 'If we have any faith in human nature, then the sheer volume of testimony from Loch Ness justifies the search.'[3] It is at this point that Shines's argument breaks down, for as we have shown the monster myth had its origin in some very dubious 'testimony' indeed, and the volume of eye-witness sightings over half a century is considerably smaller than anyone has previously realised. Moreover, recent research into the psychology of perception has cast grave doubts on the reliability of individual eye-witness evidence.

The procedures adopted by most writers on the monster, carefully selecting the 'evidence' to fit a pet theory about the beast's true identity, are circular and self-verifying. The eye-witness evidence and the photographs are so varied that they could fit a dozen different types of 'monster'. In reality they fit none. In truth, no single imaginary 'monster' could possibly account for the muddled and contradictory 'evidence' which has piled up at Loch Ness.

To psychologists the human fascination with monsters is

1 Adrian Shine, 'A Very Strange Fish?', *The Unexplained* (1980), No 13, p. 244.
2 *Ibid.*, p. 245.
3 Adrian Shine, 'To Catch a Monster', *The Unexplained*, No 14, p. 268.

not hard to explain. People *like* believing in monsters; they make the world a more colourful and exciting place. As children we all live in a fantasy world and invent all kinds of imaginary beings. To take an arbitrary example: in the 1860s the sisters Madelene and Louisa Pasley wrote and illustrated a secret diary in which they represented themselves as adults, caught up in a strange world of gigantic creatures. Boat trips on nearby Lake Windermere were threatened by pterodactyl-sized attackers, and the sisters heroically captured monstrous caterpillars. Education puts an end to such fantasies, teaching us to believe only in that which can be proven to exist. Most of us are able to give up our imaginary creatures, but a few individuals cannot. In retrospect what is striking about the Loch Ness story is the extent to which it has depended on a tiny handful of enthusiasts and star witnesses. Figures like Mr Spicer, Greta Finlay and Torquil Macleod have achieved an importance in monster lore which seems out of all proportion to the merits of their 'evidence'.

Psychologists would argue that some people do indeed 'see' monsters, but that the monsters are not actually creatures of flesh and blood but a projection of internal anxieties. This is borne out by the accounts of those who have suffered from depressive illness. For example in a painful, moving autobiographical narrative about the experience of mental breakdown, Tony Lewis wrote:

> Most of us have fantasies. But my imagination went haywire ...
> As a child I was given some colour photographs of marauding, charging Great White bull sharks. Those forgotten pictures now suddenly impinged themselves on my mind. Terror seized me at the sight of any expanse of water – a pond, a river or even an open window at night, which would offer to my over-sensitive mind the medium of murky water from which the hideous snout of the beast might emerge. That was the end of my swimming.

(*Guardian*, 3 May 1982)

Such experiences are, thankfully, perhaps rare. It does nevertheless seem significant that there should be such a strong correlation between sightings and mirror-calm conditions at Loch Ness. When the loch is a *mirror* it reflects, perhaps, images from the unconscious. Certainly the Loch Ness myth fuses some very potent psychological motifs: a serpent-like monster or dragon from another age, which both repels and attracts; an abyss of unknown depth; and a magic lake of impenetrable darkness. As Borges remarked, 'There is something in the dragon's image that appeals to the human imagination. It is, so to speak, a necessary monster.'[1]

Monster-hunters can never quite bring themselves to admit what their jumbled motives are in devoting their time to the pursuit of a mythical beast. When pressed on the subject they usually talk in highminded tones about the great need for 'conservation' of these wonderful and rare animals. Nicholas Witchell has solemnly urged that it is the 'vital responsibility' of Her Majesty's Government 'to warn that any interference with the animals will not be tolerated.' There is something slightly absurd and comical about such tender concern, in view of the monster's astonishingly elusive nature.

Psychology is not something the believers care to know much about. It is the great monster hunt that matters, the agonisingly suspenseful wait for the next dramatic sighting, the next blurred snapshot. Paradoxically, far from doing anything to conserve their 'monster' the believers have merely attracted worldwide attention to it, and encouraged a crass, vulgar commercialism to invade the loch's shores.

In their fascinating but little-known sociological study of the monster Roger Grimshaw and Paul Lester conclude that,

The quest after the monster might appear to the militant

1 *The Book of Imaginary Beings*, p. 17. There is a persuasive Freudian 'reading' of the monster in a mimeographed broadsheet *The Meaning of the Loch Ness Monster* (1976), by Roger Grimshaw and Paul Lester, issued by Birmingham University's Centre for Contemporary Cultural Studies.

sceptic a burlesque of previous culturally accredited monuments of human heroism, exploration and discovery. It, in fact, reflects to a degree at least the contraction of the frontier of earthly explorational mysteries. At the same time it goes some way towards satisfying an individualistic thirst for exploration, adventure and detection. It is worth noting also the obvious affinities which exist between our monster entrepreneurs and that other archetype of western individualism and investigative enterprise – the private detective.[1]

The analogy is an apt one, since monster hunters do tend to be solitary individuals, chasing after the solution to a mystery in the face of a hostile world. Often they have had no formal education, and they revel in their amateur status. One day they know that they, the outsiders, will be proved right. They look forward with anticipation to the great day when the professional zoologists will be humbled.

The force which drives the monster-hunters on seems to involve much more than the simple pleasures of amateur detection. The Loch Ness mystery has now taken on some of the overtones of a fringe religion, with witnesses and faithful believers. Tim Dinsdale has often talked of his 'crusade' against scepticism and 'battle' against indifference. The favourite metaphors employed by the monster fraternity are religious and military ones. The main 'enemy' is establishment science – the zoologists of the museums and universities and other government-funded institutions.

In reality this conspiratorial scientific establishment is largely a fiction of the monster-hunters' own devising. Since believers themselves cannot agree about whether their monster is reptile, mammal, vertebrate or invertebrate, and without any hard data to go on, it is difficult to know what scientists are expected to *do*. John Napier, M.R.C.S., I.R.C.P., D.Sc., Visiting Professor of Primate Biology at Birkbeck College, London, has tartly observed:

1 *Op. Cit.*, p. 24.

It has become a boring cliché of the monster establishment that scientists are afraid that the frailties of their own doctrines would be exposed should they so much as admit the existence of unknown animals or unknown forces.

On the contrary, I have found that nothing intrigues a scientist more than monster tales. Most of my colleagues in Britain and the United States delight in speculating on possible theories, and often come up with ingenious solutions that seem to owe more to science-fiction than to the principles and methodology of science. This is the stuff of which coffee-breaks are made, and I can assure the monster establishment that their suspicions are quite without foundation. If there is a conspiracy of silence it derives at best from scientific caution, and at worst from sheer ignorance of the issues, but certainly not from a desire to hush up the truth.[1]

Scientists can scarcely be accused of ignorance of the issues at Loch Ness. Many of them seem in fact to have had a good idea of what was going on, right from the beginning.

Believers never tire of quoting the case of the coelacanth, an archaic fish discovered to be still alive off the coast of South Africa. The implication of its discovery, they hint, is that scientists can be wrong and that creatures supposedly extinct for 70 million years can still survive. But the case against living plesiosaurs rests on the fossil record. Scientists are unlikely to deny the survival of a species out of mere prejudice, not least because many species still extant such as crocodiles and turtles are known to have been contemporary with the dinosaurs. Monster-hunters also shut their eyes to one rather obvious fact about the discovery of the coelacanth. The first coelacanth was caught in 1938 and, although decomposed, was instantly recognized as such. A second specimen was captured in 1952 and a short-lived mystery was over. The relatively short period of time which

1 John Napier, *Bigfoot* (London: Jonathan Cape, 1972), p. 14.

elapsed between a coelacanth being first observed in the ocean, and a number of others being trapped and identified (seventy, at the latest count) is in marked contrast to the long-drawn-out Loch Ness saga, in which a hypothetical species of giant-sized animal has eluded even credible photographic 'capture' in a relatively tiny area of water.

The failure of believers to come up with any convincing evidence for the monster has been spectacular, but the faithful do not lose their faith so easily. Onward they march, disciples of the beast, armed to the teeth with movie cameras and sonar scanners. The monster has attracted the attention of reputable individuals like Maurice Burton and Sir Peter Scott, but equally it is a mystery which has absorbed the interest of self-taught amateur enthusiasts. 'My consuming interest in the problem of the Loch Ness Orm or monster began in 1933 when I was twelve years old,' breezily confessed F. W. Holiday. And in his book *The Dragon and the Disc* Holiday pressed the mystery to an appropriately adolescent conclusion – that in the enigma of Loch Ness lay the clue to the riddle of the universe, and the overthrow of Darwin, Einstein and the science of the European enlightenment with its narrow-minded insistence on empirical evidence, measurement and controls.

That other fervent champion of the monster, Nicholas Witchell, concludes his study of the mystery on a note of world-weary wisdom:

> To be perfectly honest, the question of the physical characteristics and peculiarities of the creatures, whatever they may be, does not excite me very much. I am not a scientist and have no more than a perfunctory interest in zoology and natural history.

That, scientists might well retort, is just the problem. Throughout its fifty-year existence the Loch Ness saga has been a matter for enthusiastic amateurs, cheerfully ignorant of zoology, natural history, human psychology or even the history and ecology of Loch Ness itself. The kind of rigour and questioning attitude which any academic discipline properly encourages is alien to the monster hunters. They are people who *know*, and anything which contradicts their faith is to be brushed aside. So convinced of the monster's existence are they that the believers have never even bothered to scrutinise the dubious origins of the mystery, or the bogus sightings 'tradition' erected around it. Nor do they seem aware that an immense creature fifty or sixty feet long which swims at high speed in pursuit of fish would be remarkable in other ways than just its elusiveness or monstrous appearance. The bigger and more active that animals are the more energy they burn up and the more food they require. As Paul Colinvaux points out in his book *Why Big Fierce Animals Are Rare*:

> We can now understand why there are not fiercer dragons on the earth than there are; it is because the energy supply will not stretch to the support of super-dragons. Great white sharks or killer whales in the sea, and lions and tigers on the land, are apparently the most formidable animals the contemporary earth can support. Even these are very thinly spread. [They] represent the largest predators that the laws of physics allow the contemporary earth to support.

The Loch Ness monster can easily be associated with the popular image of prehistoric monsters as huge fast-moving predators. But as Colinvaux shows, the idea of prehistoric reptiles which was formulated in the nineteenth-century and which is reproduced today in innumerable 'lost world' adventure movies is simply wrong. *Tyrannosaurus rex* was not a ferocious brute keen to engage in battle with the nearest herd of brontosauri. It did not stand upright, nor did it hop. Instead it spent much of its time resting on its belly, periodically waddling sluggishly off in search of carrion. '*Tyrannosaurus rex*, as popularly portrayed, is a myth,' Colinvaux concludes, 'But it is probably safe to say that it will be as durable as any other myth in our culture.' One might say the same about the Loch Ness monster.

Loch Ness monster addicts are, apart from being incurable optimists, incurable romantics. A 'sighting' is to them something almost akin to a miracle, an occurrence so rare that it is like (to quote one witness) 'the time of revelation' – something which exerts an often benign, strangely spiritual influence upon the observer. The effect has also been noted on those who have seen flying-saucers. Not for nothing is Loch Ness a place of pilgrimage, and the monster a creature whose very existence depends upon the word of 'witnesses'.

Many people cannot accept that seeing *isn't* always believing.[1] To doubt your own cognitive faculties is to disturb your own sense of yourself. The individual's sense of personal security can be put at risk and shaken by this recognition. The urge to prove that all these people who have seen monsters were right stems, in part, from fear and insecurity.

It is precisely these religious overtones which begin to remove the mystery from the realm of natural history. To enter the Loch Ness Monster Exhibition at Drumnadrochit is to enter a temple filled with sacred objects and writings. The Exhibition Handbook is written with the same missionary zeal found in the pamphlets of fringe religious sects:

WHAT CAN YOU DO?

Tell people what you have seen in the Exhibition, talk to people about the evidence, use this guide to help explain to people why the loch cannot be drained, why the submarines were unsuccessful, and why most newspapers use a light-hearted approach to sightings. Explain how the hoaxes over the years have all but destroyed the credibility of even monks.

Overwhelming public opinion, together with more detailed research at the loch, will eventually awaken the interest of the scientist establishment and full-scale expeditions will be staged.

1 Alas, the truth of this was demonstrated by the Smirnoff vodka advert. At Loch Ness things are never what they seem. The beautiful girl being towed on water-skis by the monster was, it turns out, born a man. See Chris Hutchins, 'Uncovered – the truth about Tula the sexy cover girl.' *Sunday Mirror*, 27 September 1981.

When that time arrives, the whole world will suddenly realise that there is a very exciting new species to be studied, filmed and conserved. Whether it will be a remnant of the era of the dinosaurs, or a totally new genus, everyone in the world will one day acknowledge the animal with the common name of LOCH NESS MONSTER, as the EIGHTH WONDER OF THE WORLD!!!

How can you disbelieve the word of so many? ask the believers, a puzzled, pleading look in their eyes. To which the answer must be: because the psychology of 'sightings' is known to us from studies of visionary experience. To experience conversion is, as the psychologist William James pointed out in his classic study *The Varieties of Religious Experience* (1902), to be regenerated, to gain reassurance. James pointed out how at moments of emotional crisis individuals are peculiarly vulnerable to suggestion.

I might multiply cases almost indefinitely, but these will suffice to show you how real, definite and memorable an event sudden conversion may be to him who has an experience. Throughout the height of it he undoubtedly seems to himself a passive spectator or undergoer of an astounding process performed upon him from above.

He quoted John Wesley, who wrote that in London alone he had found six hundred and fifty two individuals 'who were exceeding clear in their experience, and whose testimony I could see no reason to doubt.' In James's opinion such experiences were, literally, all in the mind, and were greatly fuelled by mental or physical exhaustion.

In the previous chapter we listed a number of phenomena which people probably mistake for 'monsters'. But there will always be other monsters which cannot be explained in terms of the mis-perception of familiar objects. Probably Maurice Burton's greatest mistake in *The Elusive Monster* was to take every eye-witness sighting literally, with the result that he was forced into absurd and unconvincing explanations involving deer which collapsed from sudden heart-attacks and highly-accomplished gas-filled logs. Loch Ness has attracted all manner of people who claim to have had strange experiences there. Some of them are as inexplicable in terms of a large unknown animal as they are in terms of known natural phenomena. For centuries people have been seeing monsters in a variety of countries. In *Strange Creatures from Time and Space* (1975) John Keel gives a blood-curdling list of twentieth-century sightings of plesiosaurs, pterodactyls, bird men, 'luminous dwarfs', and all manner of weird and wonderful phenomena. Explanations drawn from natural history can only satisfactorily explain a fraction of such sightings.

This does not mean that the world is crammed with unknown animals awaiting zoological discovery and identification. Nor can the problem be dissociated from the astonishing fifty-year saga of the Loch Ness mystery. 'The follies of mankind are innumerable, and time adds hourly to the heap', wrote that old misanthrope, Jonathan Swift. T. S. Eliot was a little kinder. 'Human kind,' he acknowledged, 'cannot bear very much reality.' But the real mystery of the Loch Ness monster and other such creatures around the world is why they should periodically seize the wider public imagination and continue to be given credence, even when much of the evidence can be shown to be suspect.

The great appeal of the Loch Ness mystery is perhaps the way in which it offers everyone the chance to become an amateur sleuth, pore over the evidence, visit the dark mysterious waters, and concoct a new theory about what it is which has baffled the world for so long. The Reverend Omand may have exorcised Loch Ness, but the enigma is surely not yet over. There will be more dramatic snapshots, more amazing eye-witness testimony, maybe even a snatch of movie film of something dark and ambiguous, churning away into the far distance. After fifty years one conclusion about the mystery can reasonably be drawn. There is no scientific evidence whatsoever of monsters in Loch Ness, and a handful of individuals will go on seeing them there.

a h'uile latha a chi's nach fhaic
('to every day you see and every day you don't see')

Postscript

The fiftieth anniversary of the discovery of the Loch Ness monster passed with a number of new developments, some of which confirmed the theories put forward in this book. The *Daily Mail* tracked down the couple credited with the sighting which set Nessie-mania rolling back in 1933. Now in their eighties, Mr and Mrs Mackay confirmed that Alex Campbell's historic *Courier* news item was inaccurate and that only one of them had seen the monster. Moreover the sighting had taken place in March and not, as traditionally reported, April. This was a fascinating revelation since the sighting took place from the north shore road which had always been there, and was unconnected with the later roadworks long believed to have been a factor in Nessie's 1933 début. The theory that Alex Campbell was responsible for the abortive 1930 monster reports in the local press is strengthened by Mrs Mackay's subsequent interview for BBC radio, in which she recalled that Campbell had visited her to ask if he could publicise the sighting in the *Courier* 'to find out if somebody else had seen it'. Sadly, Alex Campbell died soon after this book was first published. He was 81 and had been ill for some time.

The 1983 monster-hunting season got off to an early and dramatic start on 16th February when the ITV 'News at Ten' announced that what appeared to be two very large animals moving at great depth had been recorded on sonar by scientists at Loch Ness. This news report turned out to be a preview of Adrian Shine's article 'The Biology of Loch Ness', published the next day in *New Scientist*. Shine revealed that a 1500-hour sonar search during 1982 had resulted in 40 significant contacts, of extraordinary strength, depth and movement. 'If there are large creatures in Loch Ness,' he wrote, 'then they would appear on sonar just as we have recorded them.' Excitingly, ITV reported that the next stage of the investigation would involve identifying the target by moving special cameras on to it the next time it appeared. Shine and his team were confident of solving the mystery 'within a couple of years'.

Viewers might reasonably have drawn the conclusion that Nessie was at last, after fifty years, scientifically credible. A close reading of Shine's *New Scientist* article, however, reveals some serious drawbacks to his findings. Nowhere is the *size* of the target identified, an omission which considerably weakens his dramatic conclusion that the data is 'consistent with the presence of large animals'. The Ness and Morar Project had, it turned out, been calibrating their sonar against a gas-filled sphere 24cm in diameter. As a control this is inadequate, since Shine fails to provide any clue as to how large a fish would have to be to return an echo of similar strength. By making various assumptions it is possible to estimate that Shine's results might well have been obtained from freshwater fish lying somewhere within a range of sizes from 12 Kg (about 100cm long) to 85 Kg (about 200cm long). Shine skirts around this crucial question and fails to relate signal strength to any objective scale of monstrosity (by, say, lowering cod carcasses with artificial swim bladders into the loch to achieve a true calibration). The dull truth is that it is well within the bounds of possibility that salmon, pike or even (though this is unlikely) sturgeon provided the allegedly mysterious targets picked up by the Ness and Morar Project's sonar. Ironically, Shine's results – a contact in the deep midwaters on average once every 37½ hours – completely contradicts Roy Mackal's conclusion that sonar reveals the monsters to be bottom and side-dwellers which move into the midwaters 'almost as infrequently as they are observed at or near the surface.' If Nessie appeared at the surface once every 37½ hours the photographic evidence would be abundant and there would be no mystery.

Sonar is an inexact technique, though the hardware may appear awesomely complex to the layman. It is easy to overlook the fact that what appears on a sonar chart may be a ghost echo with no material existence at all. In May, for example, the Norwegian navy abortively hunted a mystery submarine in Hardanger Fjord, after which a spokesman explained that the sonar signals which had been picked up 'were probably false, and this could be due to disturbances like the mix of salt and fresh water, temperature differences, and motor boats moving'. The fallibility of sonar has been further underlined by the discovery that the remarkable and much-publicised 1969 *Pisces* submarine sonar depth reading indicating that Loch Ness was over 1000 feet deep was false.

The monster's fiftieth anniversary attracted a number of newcomers to the loch. Much publicity surrounded wildlife photographer Eric Beckjord's announcement that he planned to hunt Nessie using a video recorder and light-intensifying camera. Beckjord subsequently had the good fortune to sight the monster within hours of his arrival, and he quickly came up with film not just of Nessie but also of three baby monsters. The bookmakers William Hill promptly reduced the odds of the creature's existence being proved within a year from 100–1 to 33–1. It seems clear that the murky waters of Loch Ness will continue to yield this kind of evidence of monsters both at the surface and in its depths for many years to come.

Bibliography

1 *Books about the monster*

R. T. Gould, *The Loch Ness Monster and Others*. London: Geoffrey Bles, 1934.

Constance Whyte, *More Than a Legend: The Story of the Loch Ness Monster*. London: Hamish Hamilton, 1957.

Tim Dinsdale, *Loch Ness Monster*. London: Routledge & Kegan Paul, 1961. Second Edition, 1972; Third Edition, 1976; 1982.

Maurice Burton, *The Elusive Monster: An Analysis of the Evidence from Loch Ness*. London: Rupert Hart-Davis, 1961.

F. W. Holiday, *The Great Orm of Loch Ness*. London: Faber, 1968.

Nicholas Witchell, *The Loch Ness Story*. Lavenham: Terence Dalton, 1974; Revised Edition, Penguin Books, 1975; Second Edition, 1976; Corgi Edition, 1982.

Tim Dinsdale, *Project Water Horse: The True Story of the Monster Quest at Loch Ness*. London: Routledge & Kegan Paul, 1975.

Roy P. Mackal, *The Monsters of Loch Ness*. London: Macdonald and Janes, 1976; Futura, 1976.

2 *Booklets and articles*

W. T. Calman, 'The Evidence for Monsters.' *The Spectator*, 22 December 1933, pp. 925–6.

Sir Edward Mountain, 'Solving the Mystery of Loch Ness.' *The Field*, 22 September 1934, pp. 668–9.

A. C. Oudemans, *The Loch Ness Animal*. Leyden: E. J. Brill, 1934.

R. L. Cassie, *The Monsters of Achanalt*. 2 Vols. Aberdeen: D. Wyllie & Son, 1935–36.

J. A. Carruth, *Loch Ness and its Monster*. Fort Augustus: Abbey Press, 1950.

Maurice Burton, 'The Loch Ness Monster.' *Illustrated London News*, 20 February 1960, p. 316.

A. M. Campbell, 'No, Dr Burton!' *The Scots Magazine* (May 1962), pp. 95–100.

David James, *Loch Ness Investigation*. Inverness: *Courier*, 1968.

Gavin Maxwell, 'I Saw the Secret of the Loch.' *TV Times*, 31 July 1969, p. 5.

Nicholas Witchell, *Loch Ness and the Monster*. Inverness: J. Arthur Dixon, 1971; Revised Edition, 1976.

Martin Klein, R. H. Rines, T. Dinsdale, L. S. Foster, *Underwater*

Search at Loch Ness. Belmont, Mass.: Academy of Applied Science, 1972.

Nicholas Witchell, 'The New Side to the Loch Ness Monster.' *Mayfair*, Vol. 8, No. 6 (1973), pp. 16–18, 38, 87.

Tim Dinsdale, *The Story of the Loch Ness Monster*. London: Universal-Tandem, 1973.

Dan Greenburg, 'Japanese Come to Catch Loch Ness Monster: A Penetrating Account of a Big-Game Hunt That Never Quite Got Beneath the Surface.' *Oui* (May 1974), pp. 51–2, 82, 112, 114–6, 118–22.

Roger Grimshaw and Paul Lester, *The Meaning of the Loch Ness Monster*. University of Birmingham: Centre for Contemporary Cultural Studies, 1976.

Frank Searle, *Nessie: Seven Years in Search of the Monster*. London: Hodder and Stoughton, 1976.

Tim Dinsdale, *The Facts About Loch Ness and the Monster*. London: Johnston & Bacon, 1977.

Rosemary Border, *Loch Ness Monster*. London: Macdonald, 1979.

W. H. Lehn, 'Atmospheric Refraction and Lake Monsters.' *Science*, 13 July 1979, pp. 183–5.

William Owen, *Scotland's Loch Ness Monster*. Norwich: Jarrold, 1980.

Anthony G. Harmsworth, *The Mysterious Monsters of Loch Ness*. St Ives: Photo Precision, 1980.

—, *The Loch Ness Monster Exhibition Souvenir Handbook*. Drumnadrochit: Harmsworth, 1980.

Adrian Shine, 'A Very Strange Fish?' *The Unexplained*, Vol 2, No 13 (1980), pp. 241–5.

—, 'To Catch a Monster ...' *The Unexplained*, Vol 2, No 14 (1980), pp. 264–8.

W. H. Lehn and I. Schroeder, 'The Norse Merman as an Optical Phenomenon.' *Nature*, 29 January 1981, pp. 362–6.

Maurice Burton, 'A Ring of Bright Water?' *New Scientist*, 24 June 1982, p. 872.

—, 'A Fast Moving, Agile Beastie.' *New Scientist*, 1 July 1982, pp. 41–2.

—, 'A Flurry of Foam and Spray.' *New Scientist*, 8 July 1982, pp. 112–3.

Robert P. Craig, 'Loch Ness: the Monster Unveiled.' *New Scientist*, 5 August 1982, pp. 354–57.

3 *Other Material*

Janet and Colin Bord, *Alien Animals*. London: Granada, 1980.

Jorge Luis Borges with Margarita Guerrero, *The Book of Imaginary Beings*. New York: Avon, 1970.

A. D. Cameron, *The Caledonian Canal*. Lavenham: Terence Dalton, 1972.

Daniel Cohen, *A Modern Look at Monsters*. New York: Tower, 1970.

Paul Colinvaux, *Why Big Fierce Animals Are Rare*. London: Allen & Unwin, 1980.

G. B. Corbet and H. N. Southern, *The Hand-book of British Mammals*. London: Blackwell, 1976.

Peter Costello, *In Search of Lake Monsters*. London: Garnstone Press, 1974; Panther, 1975.

Tim Dinsdale, *The Leviathans*. London: Routledge & Kegan Paul, 1966; Revised Edition, Futura, 1976.

Richard Franck, *Northern Memoirs*. Edinburgh: Constable, 1821.

R. T. Gould, *The Case for the Sea-Serpent*. London: Allan, 1930.

Stephen Jay Gould, *Ever Since Darwin: Reflections in Natural History*. Harmondsworth: Penguin Books, 1980.

Francesca Greenoak, *All the Birds of the Air: The Names, Lore and Literature of British Birds*. London: Deutsch, 1979; Revised Edition, Penguin Books, 1981.

F. W. Holiday, *The Dragon and the Disc: An Investigation of the Totally Fantastic*. New York: Norton, 1973.

William James, *The Varieties of Religious Experience*. London: Collins, 1960.

John A. Keel, *Strange Creatures from Time and Space*. London: Sphere, 1976.

Liz Laidler, *Otters in Britain*. Newton Abbot: David & Charles, 1982.

Henry Lee, *Sea Monsters Unmasked*. London: William Clowes, 1884.

Compton Mackenzie, *The Rival Monster*. London: Chatto & Windus, 1952.

Gavin Maxwell, *Ring of Bright Water*. London: Longmans, 1960.

—, *Raven Seek Thy Brother*. London: Longmans, 1968.

Ronald Millar, *The Piltdown Men*. London: Gollancz, 1972.

Elizabeth Montgomery-Campbell, *The Search for Morag*. London: Tom Stacey, 1972.

H. V. Morton, *In Search of Scotland*. London: Methuen, 1929.

A. C. Oudemans, *The Great Sea-Serpent: An Historical and Critical Treatise*. Leyden: E. J. Brill, 1892.

Randall Jones Pugh and F. W. Holiday, *The Dyfed Enigma*. London: Faber, 1979.

L. T. C. Rolt, *Thomas Telford*. London: Longmans, 1958.

W. Douglas Simpson, *Urquhart Castle*. Edinburgh: H.M.S.O., 1976.

T. C. Smout, *A History of the Scottish People 1560–1830*. London: Collins, 1969.

Robert Southey, *Journals of a Tour in Scotland in 1819*. London: John Murray, 1929.

Charles St John, *Short Sketches of the Wild Sports and Natural History of the Highlands*. London: Longmans, 1846.

Peter Tremayne, *The Curse of Loch Ness*. London: Sphere, 1979.

Sydney Wignall, *In Search of Spanish Treasure*. Newton Abbot: David & Charles, 1982.

Index